The Healing Family

by Stephanie Matthews Simonton
GETTING WELL AGAIN (*with* O. *Carl Simonton, M.D.,*

by Robert L. Shook
SURVIVORS: Living with Cancer

The Healing Family

The Simonton Approach for
Families Facing Illness

by Stephanie Matthews Simonton
with Robert L. Shook

Bantam Books
Toronto • New York • London • Sydney

THE HEALING FAMILY

A Bantam Book / March 1984

All rights reserved.
Copyright © 1984 by Stephanie Matthews Simonton.

Book design by Renée Gelman.

This book may not be reproduced in whole or in part, by
mimeograph or any other means, without permission.
For information address: Bantam Books, Inc.

Library of Congress Cataloging in Publication Data

Simonton, Stephanie.
The healing family.

Bibliography: p. 236
Includes index.
1. Cancer—Treatment.   2. Cancer—Prevention.
3. Cancer—Psychological aspects.   4. Cancer patients—
Family relationships.   I. Shook, Robert L., 1938-
II. Title. [DNLM: 1. Neoplasms—Therapy. 2. Neoplasms—
Psychology. 3. Family. 4. Home nursing—Psychology.
QZ 266 S611h]
RC270.8.S56   1984   616.99'40651   83-19762
ISBN 0-553-05050-8

Published simultaneously in the United States and Canada

PRINTED IN THE UNITED STATES OF AMERICA

FG   0   9   8   7   6   5   4   3   2   1

To Jerry, Rebecca and Jennifer,
my new family whose love I cherish.

Contents

Acknowledgments

I am grateful to my patients and their families who opened their hearts and experiences to me. Their courage in the face of uncertainty and possible death was the inspiration for this book. In particular, I would like to thank those who allowed me to share their stories in these pages.

Bob Shook's tireless enthusiasm, organization, and writing gifts helped bring this book from concept to reality. I am especially thankful to Bobbie Shook for bringing us together.

My gratitude also to Grace Bechtold, my editor, at Bantam Books.

I am indebted to my friend and colleague, Mark Voeller, Ph.D. from whom I learned a great deal about family dynamics. Robert Beavers, M.D. and the Southwest Family Institute of Dallas, Texas provided an invaluable opportunity to study family systems theory.

I appreciate the many years of association and collaboration with Carl Simonton, M.D., with whom I've shared many visions.

With special gratitude to Steven Reeder, M.D. and Larry Dossey, M.D., two of the finest healers I have had the privilege of knowing.

The Healing Family

Introduction

Whil hen someone you love receives a diagnosis of cancer, it can have the impact of an emotional hydrogen bomb. While you want to focus on helping your loved one, you may also want to try to deal with the effects of this trauma on other family members and on yourself. This illness could be a catastrophe—the worst blow ever to strike your family. And, although you would do anything you could to help the others in your family, you may also feel overcome by confusion and helplessness. Even when the prognosis is good, far too many people somehow believe cancer is synonymous with death. A typical reaction when a wife and mother is found to have cancer is, "Oh no, she may die." What is too often forgotten is the other possibility: "She may not die."

I believe that hope is an essential ingredient in healing. In the ten years since I founded the Cancer Counseling and Research Center in Dallas, I have worked directly with thousands of cancer patients and their families. Time and again I have seen evidence that hopefulness plays an important role in recovery. At the Center, we believe there are specific techniques someone with cancer can use to enhance the possibility of his recovery (these are detailed in *Getting Well Again*, a book I coauthored with O. Carl Simonton, M.D.).

In this book, I will emphasize how *you*, a family member,

can support the patient, make a significant contribution in helping him recover, and maintain hope while knowing the outcome is uncertain. So often family members, even those with the best intentions, give the wrong *kind* of support, which sometimes hurts more than it helps. This book is about what you can do to create the positive, healthy environment I call *the healing family.*

Too often we associate healing only with medical treatment; a patient may say, "It's the doctor's job to heal me." I do not in any way want to minimize the role of the physician and other health care professionals. I believe every person with cancer should seek the best medical treatment available, and in fact a chapter of this book is devoted to choosing and working with a physician. However, I also believe that healing is more than just physiological and that the patient can take part in his own recovery. The family can offer a vital supportive environment in this effort.

Today's understanding of cancer supports the theory that healing can be deeply influenced by psychological and emotional factors. We are coming to realize that the possible contributory factors to cancer include genetic predisposition, exposure to carcinogens, and response to stress. We also realize that a combination of these and other factors may exist and that it is not always possible to arrive at a cut-and-dried explanation of the cause of any individual's cancer. For this reason, treatment should have as many aspects to it as possible and deal with both physiological and psychological factors.

In my work, I have concentrated on teaching people with cancer to cope more effectively with stress and to encourage them to use visual imagery to enchance their belief that their bodies can be healed. Each patient, however, lives in an emotional environment that may be either a positive force for healing or a negative force. In this book I will focus on how the cancer patient's family members can work together to create an open, honest, supportive environment that encourages the patient's efforts to become well.

While I am convinced, as are many others, that stress frequently contributes to the development of cancer, it is never possible to precisely pinpoint the role stress has played in a patient's illness. There is no doubt, however, that it plays a role in breaking down resistance to many kinds of illness. This is not only common wisdom but is also the subject of a great deal of study. Research indicates that if a person doesn't eat well, doesn't sleep enough, works too hard, gets a divorce, and is trying to deal with a son who has a drug problem, that person is more likely to become ill—at the very least, come down with a bad cold!

On this premise, I believe a person with cancer may want to ask the question, "Did stress, and my response to stress, have anything to do with lowering my resistance to disease?" This includes examining his life for several years before the diagnosis, looking both at traumatic events (such as the death of a parent or a major career change) and at his general lifestyle. If his life during that time has undergone a great deal of change—and change is a major stress—it may be that his emotional coping mechanisms have not been adequate. While this self-examination can be painful, it is also very positive; for when we find that our responses to stress have been unhealthy, we are in a position to change for the better. None of us can avoid change and stress, but we can learn to deal with stress in ways that help us remain healthy.

Stress management is very important in that it leads to a better quality of life for the patient, and we know that the will to live is related to how well the individual's life is going—how satisfying life has been and what the future seems to hold. Through our work, we have seen thousands of patients' health improve as their lives became more meaningful and their healing mechanisms were no longer impaired by depression and hopelessness.

As a person with cancer learns to fight his illness and to manage stress better, the family plays an important role by either supporting or resisting the change that occurs. You, as a member of the patient's most intimate support system, are a vital factor in his recovery; you can be a buffer against undue stress, and in many ways you can encourage the patient in his effort to manage stress and make a smooth transition toward necessary changes. This book is about how the diagnosis of cancer changes the life within a family, and how you as a family member can change positively to provide a healing environment for the patient.

This may seem like an awesome undertaking, but remember that becoming a healing family does not mean becoming a perfect family. No individual and no family is perfect. Fortunately, combating cancer does not require perfection. It does require commitment and teamwork, so that family members pull together to create the best possible outcome for the patient. This means becoming a source for confrontation, feedback, encouragement, and appreciation for the patient; it means freely giving love, support, and empathy.

While this entails effort and flexibility, I have worked with many families who have found that when they supported the patient's focus on change, they themselves reaped unexpected benefits. Often family problems that have been buried and unresolved will surface during this time, and as the disease is treated, so are these other problems. Because the family is working together as a unit—perhaps for the first time—it has an opportunity to look at itself and reorganize in ways that make every member's life better. Dr. Carl Menninger, founder of the Menninger Clinic in Topeka, Kansas, has noted that some patients who have had psychological breakdowns come out of their disease "weller than well." In the same way, a family that deals directly and in healthy ways with the trauma of a cancer diagnosis can learn and grow—although this in no way implies that dealing with cancer is painless or easy.

One important element of dealing with a cancer diagnosis is allowing yourself and the person with cancer to experience and express feelings and reactions. Suppressed feelings frequently increase emotional depression that can retard healing. Developing open communication within the family not only helps the patient but also helps family members come to terms with the complex feelings they are likely to have in response to this illness. Not only can each individual grow from the experience but also the family itself can function far better as a team to create a healing environment.

Because I am asking you to take an optimistic stance as a family member, without being able to offer any guarantees as to the outcome of the disease, I feel I must also try to help you be prepared for not getting the results you hope for. Some people find the thought of disappointment so painful that they do not let themselves hope for the patient's recovery. And yet, this risk is one we must take if we are to love people at all. In many ways, love opens us up to being affected by others, disappointed, hurt, or deeply grieved. The only way to avoid the risk is to become an emotional hermit, living in isolation— and none of us can survive that. But it is possible to cope with pain and disappointment. *The Healing Family* was written on the premise that the best way to deal with a diagnosis of cancer is to work toward health in every way and to affirm life and hope. Realistically, however, the patient may not get well. For this reason, I have included a chapter that deals with that possibility and how a family can face a recurrence of the disease or death.

I think it's important to note that the word "cancer" is used for more than one hundred different kinds of disease. Adding to the complexity is the fact that cancer has such a wide array of symptoms that the prognosis may vary for individual patients with the same form of cancer. Yet, in spite of these wide variations, all patients who are seriously ill have certain basic needs in common. *The Healing Family* focuses on the needs of the patient and how his family can be supportive in a time of crisis.

While on one level this book is a guide for a family that seeks to help the cancer patient become well again, my goals are not limited to the patient's recovery or to lengthening the patient's life span. Instead, this book focuses on what the patient and family can do to improve the quality of each member's life. A family that is committed to this kind of love and support is what I consider to truly be a healing family.

Chapter 1

The Simonton Approach—
A Positive Approach

T he method of treating cancer patients that is now known as the Simonton approach had its beginnings in 1968. At that time, I was working in Portland, Oregon, in the field of motivation, with special emphasis on helping executives set and affirm goals. My friend, Carl Simonton, was finishing his residency in radiation therapy at the University of Oregon Medical School.

I was always interested to hear about Carl's research with patients who had Hodgkin's disease. While this disease now has an excellent prognosis when detected in the early stages, at that time the survival rate was significantly less. Carl was working with a very promising experiment in giving these patients radiation treatments twice a day, but he was constantly frustrated by the fact that many of them would agree to the program and then refuse to show up. He, like the other physicians, knew that this attitude was not confined to patients with Hodgkin's disease; lung cancer patients would refuse to stop smoking; liver patients would keep drinking.

While these seemed to be psychological problems, many physicians of that time were suspicious of the effectiveness of psychiatry, and it was not common practice to apply its theories to the treatment of physical diseases. Carl, however, was very interested in my work with motivation and with teaching people how to reach their potential. It was natural for him to discuss an uncooperative patient with me and ask, "What would *you* do to motivate this patient?"

The answer to that was not obvious, needless to say, but the question was intriguing. I felt sure of one thing: when you change your thinking, you change the whole system inside you. In working with motivation, I operated on this belief, and tried to teach people that only their internal limitations kept them from being almost anything they wanted to be.

Carl and I became more and more intrigued by the possibilities. We began to look at the motivations of some of his patients and at their attitudes toward their cancer. We found some whose prognosis was good, who could be expected to live for many more years with proper treatment, but who displayed apathy, depression, and hopelessness. They contrasted sharply with other patients who had been told their cancer was terminal but who had far more positive, hopeful attitudes. Some of these "terminal" patients defied all the statistics. Sent home after minimal treatment, with the expectation that they would die within a few months, some returned year after year for their semiannual examinations in good health and living full, active lives. Immediately these people interested me since in the field of motivation we always study the successful to find out what they do. It was intriguing to observe cancer patients who had spontaneous remissions. (Full recovery from a life-threatening disease with no apparent medical explanation is called spontaneous remission.) We began asking these people, "You're doing much better than we anticipated. What do you think accounts for that?"

Their answers were illuminating. "I can't die yet, not until my children grow up. They still need me." "I've got a business to run, and it won't make it if I'm not around." Whatever the exact answer, these patients had something in common—a strong will to live because they had something that to them was worth living for.

The Will to Live

When we began really looking at the histories of people with cancer, we found more evidence that the will to live was important. During this time, a woman who lived near my hometown in Idaho was sent to the medical school for treatment. She was diagnosed with cancer of the kidney that had metastasized. The surgeon was not able to remove her tumor, and it was not responsive to any known treatment. (We later realized that she was also a classic case of precancer stress; two years before her diagnosis her husband had died, and she had been left with a large farm to run and had become quite depressed.)

Interestingly enough, the surgeon had been rather vague with her about her prognosis, and she somehow went home under the impression that he had removed all her cancer. Although her family knew better, they sheltered her from the truth.

Once home, she fell in love with the foreman she had hired to run her ranch, a man younger than she, and they got married. As long as the marriage lasted, she had no symptoms of cancer. But when the man left her after five years, her cancer metastasized and she died.

The Placebo Effect

In addition to cases such as this, Carl and I looked at other bits and pieces of knowledge about healing. One of these was the well-known placebo effect. A placebo is an inactive medication, such as a sugar pill, that a doctor may prescribe for a chronic complainer. Naturally, the doctor doesn't tell the patient that the "medicine" is useless and quite often the patient comes back to report that the symptoms are reduced or even gone altogether—even when the ailment is one for which there is no cure. In these cases, it seems that *the patient's belief and positive expectations restore good health.*

The placebo effect, which has been known to doctors for many centuries, is well documented. In one study, arthritic patients were divided into two groups. The first group was given sugar pills instead of their regular painkiller. The second group received their usual painkiller. In both groups, the same percentage of patients reported that their pain was reduced. The researchers then added another factor; those in the placebo group who had no reduction of pain were given an injection of sterile water. Interestingly enough, 64 percent of those people reported relief from their pain as a result of the shot. Evidently, these people had greater confidence in injections than in pills. It was their *belief* that eased their pain. In the same way, treatments of the past were often effective when we now know that they should not have been. The medieval practice of bleeding a sick patient is a good example. Since everyone believed it would work, it sometimes did.

Some statistics suggest that approximately 30 percent of all positive response to medication is really due to the placebo effect—the conviction that it will help. This by no means says that human beings are foolish; instead, it points out the vital factor of belief. And that is why I feel deeply concerned when a patient comes to me who has been brutally discouraged by his prognosis. Sometimes, in the effort to be realistic and not hold out false hope, doctors destroy *all* hope in patients. Yet, "hopeless" patients, such as the woman I knew with kidney cancer, can survive, driven by their will to live.

Spontaneous Remission

Another medical phenomenon that fascinated me when Carl and I began to study healing was spontaneous remission. We saw this happen again and again with patients who ought to have died.

Carl might say to me, "Old Mr. Jones was back today. He should have died years ago, and by God, he's better!"

"Why? Why is he better?"

"Who knows? Some people just get better."

From my vantage point outside the medical profession, I was very interested in this. Carl assured me that spontaneous remission had been studied every which way—physically—with very little understanding of it. I began to wonder if there were any psychological explanations for this phenomenon.

I had come from a background in business. In that field, unusually successful people are studied and found to have

specific mental and emotional qualities and behaviors that lead
to their success. So we began to talk to the unusual survivors to
see whether they possessed psychological resources that other
cancer patients might benefit from adopting.

I need to interject here that today, as fourteen years ago, we still
know very little about real health. There has been a great deal
of study of disease processes, but almost nothing is known
about people who never have a major illness and die quietly in
their sleep when they're in their eighties or nineties. We don't
know what they eat, what kind of families they come from,
how much they exercise, or anything else about them that
might correlate with their good health. It remains my belief that
we can learn about health not just by studying people with
disease but also by studying those who are well.

Our questioning of old Mr. Jones and others who had unusual responses led to the conclusion that these people felt an
enormous commitment to some goal, a purpose in their lives
that invested them with a tremendous fight to live. When their
physicians told them they might die of their illness, these people
would often respond with something like, "The hell I will!"

Biofeedback and the Surveillance Theory

While we were exploring the motivation of these patients, we
were also looking into two interesting new areas of research at
that time: biofeedback and the surveillance theory. In both
these areas, evidence was coming forth that the mind could
greatly influence the body.

Biofeedback concretely illustrates the power of the mind. In
biofeedback training, an individual is hooked up to a device
that feeds back information on his physiological processes.
What is monitored depends on the person's needs. A patient
with tachycardia, an irregular heartbeat, might be hooked up to
an oscilloscope, which will give a constant visual readout of the
heartbeat. The patient watches the monitor while attempting to
relax. He might do this by visualizing some slow, rhythmic
movement, such as a little girl going back and forth on a swing.
When he succeeds in slowing his heart down through his thinking,
he is rewarded immediately by seeing that fact on the visual

display. The biofeedback instrument itself does nothing except tell him what he is accomplishing.

Remarkable things have been demonstrated through biofeedback with both humans and animals. Laboratory rats have been taught to increase the flow of blood to one ear by dilating the vessels and to decrease the flow to the other ear at the same time. People have been taught to control skin temperature in the palm of their hand, so that two different spots an inch apart will vary by five degrees. So far it seems that any physical system we can monitor is capable of being influenced by the human mind.

Biofeedback is very often used to teach a person to relax. Brain research indicates that most of the time when we are awake and alert, we operate mentally at a high brain-wave frequency called beta, using the left hemisphere of the brain. Through deep relaxation and/or meditation, we can alter our brain-wave activity to a slower frequency, tapping the right hemisphere of the brain, which is emotional, spatial, creative, nonlinear, and nonlogical. The right hemisphere also controls the autonomic nervous system. This explains why an individual can tap into the right hemisphere of the brain and use an image like the little girl swinging to actually influence his heart rate. We began to wonder whether individuals could be taught to influence their own immune systems.

The surveillance theory holds that the immune system does in fact produce "killer cells" which seek out and destroy stray cancer cells many times in our lives, and it is when this system breaks down that the disease can take hold. When most patients are diagnosed with cancer, surgery, radiation, and/or chemotherapy are used to destroy as much of the tumor as possible. But once the cancer is reduced, we wondered if the immune system could be reactivated to seek out and destroy the remaining cells. Since people could learn to influence their blood flow and heart rate, could they learn to influence their immune systems? After all, it too is under the influence of the right hemisphere of the brain.

Unfortunately, even today we have no way to directly monitor the immune system and show a patient whether his imagery is actually activating that system. Very recently, however, new research has demonstrated that the mind can increase the immune response. But at the time of our initial research, we had to depend on X-rays and other measures to give a patient feedback. The will to live in the patients we studied who had conquered their disease was connected to deeply felt goals. We hypothesized that perhaps we could teach a patient to develop such goals and to form an image of his immune system activating and defeating the cancer. We thought that working with that image might be very effective. Our studies of biofeedback led us to decide that this should take place three times a day since regularity and repetition were important in the effectiveness of biofeedback techniques.

Imagery—The First Patient

With this background, Carl approached the first patient, Jim McKenna, a sixty-three-year-old man who was literally choking and starving to death with advanced cancer of the throat. He was a tough case with which to start. His weight had already dropped from 135 pounds down to 98. Because of his age and the location and size of his tumor, the physicians had debated whether he should even receive treatment at all. Radiation in the throat can result in some very severe side effects. Jim was treated, but his prognosis was poor. The treatment was only palliative, a small dose intended to shrink the tumor and make him more comfortable.

Carl approached Jim with our ideas about influencing the immune system through imagery. He listened intently. As a very determined man, he hated the feeling that his body was out of control and that he could do nothing about his disease. He had smoked four packs a day until he quit in disgust one day after he burned a hole in his pants—an illustration of his determination. Jim liked the idea that he could help himself.

Imagery was explained to him and he was asked to picture his cancer with white cells attacking it and overcoming it and to do this three times a day during the six weeks he received radiation. He agreed and became so determined that during that time he missed only one session. That happened through the intrusion of a friend, and Jim was furious and swore it would never happen again. He had a very intuitive feel for how the imagery was working and told us, "Up until now I felt I was getting control of this, and when I missed that session I felt the control slip away. I'll never let it happen again."

The radiation was effective in shrinking Jim's tumor; moreover, he had almost no side effects. During the treatment he actually gained weight. He regained enough energy to arrange to have his treatments early in the morning so he could go fishing.

The amazing thing to us—remember, Jim was the first patient with this technique—was his ability to know what was going on with his cancer. He could not see the disease, yet he could draw us pictures of what he saw the tumor doing in his imagery, and we could match the drawing with an actual photograph of the tumor. Once, for instance, he told us "There's a sore right here," drawing it in, and we found there really was an ulceration on the tumor. Since that time, I've seen other patients who had tuned in to their bodies just as accurately, apparently through some kind of mental-biological communication.

We were really excited by Jim's progress, and Carl would have coffee or lunch with him every day that he came in for treatment. Although we came to know him well, he was nevertheless full of surprises. One day he announced that his arthritis was acting up and interfering with his fishing. "I've decided to turn those white cells loose on that arthritis," he stated.

Immediately we were alarmed. Carl suggested that Jim's arthritis was probably incurable and couldn't be influenced by the mind. We were afraid that if he failed to affect the arthritis, he might lose faith in the imagery he was using on his cancer. But our skepticism only challenged Jim. He had always seen his white blood cells as a pulsating snowstorm that bombarded the tumor; now he gave them a sandpaper edge and sent them down to sand off the arthritic spurs on his knees. His arthritic symptoms cleared!

By now, Carl was having a hard time explaining to other people in the department what was happening. Jim was eating again and showing none of the typical symptoms, nausea, diarrhea, and so on, of the radiation treatment. Then, after less than four weeks, he came up with an amazing idea. He was so confident in his ability to control his white cells that he announced, "Well, I've only got one more physical problem.

Those white cells are doing such a good job on my cancer and my arthritis that I'm going to turn them loose on this one."

What now? we wondered.

"I've been sexually impotent for the last twenty years," he told us. "I'm going to fix that."

"Oh, no!" Carl and I said to each other.

The fact was that his impotence was psychogenic. It had no physiological basis but rather dated back to a traumatic event in his past. Carl explained to him that white cells would have no effect on a psychological problem. But he was undaunted. And he taught us that an individual doesn't have to understand his physiology correctly—he just has to believe that the imagery will help. Why Jim thought white cells would help in this matter was beyond me, but he did, and he sent them to the area of the problem to go to work. Again, his innate awareness of his body was revealed. He came back and said, "It's real weird. Those white cells can't find anything wrong with me." Apparently that was reassuring, for within a week he was able to have and maintain an erection. Soon he was teasingly asking us never to call him early in the morning because he and his wife would be making love. We kept in touch with him, and until he died, they apparently maintained a very active sex life.

Jim lived nine more years after he was told he would not live much longer. We kept in touch during those years, and he sometimes flew to our Center to tell his story to groups of our patients. When, at seventy-two, he had a recurrence, he called us long distance to talk about how he had come to terms with his approaching death. He also told us that those nine years had been some of the best of his life.

The Development of the Simonton Approach

Following the work with Jim and other patients in Portland, Carl and I married. Following his residency, he fulfilled his military obligation at Travis Air Force Base in California, where he became head of the radiation therapy department in the hospital. Here he had a golden opportunity to continue working with our ideas. Since it was a brand new department, we were able to shape it around our approach. Standard procedure was for a radiation technician to take the patient into the radiation room, lead him through imagery, and then administer the treatment. In-patients' charts specifically asked nurses to make sure the patients did imagery three times a day.

When Carl's military commitment was over, we moved to Fort Worth, Texas, where Carl entered a private practice of radiation oncology, and I set up a counseling service for his patients. A year later, in 1974, we formed the Cancer Counseling and Research Center. Although we were divorced in 1980, we both felt a deep commitment to the Center and have continued to work together for its growth, much as divorced parents cooperate in raising their children.

Today, the Center is located in Dallas. It is a nonprofit organization that focuses on the psychological treatment of cancer patients. The Center is also involved in research dealing with the psychological effect of cancer on patients.

In addition to our primary work with cancer patients, we have also trained several thousand other professionals in the use of our methods. The Simonton approach has been widely received, and today counselors using these methods can be found in most of the United States and in several other countries.

Another branch of our work involves research. Several years ago we obtained a substantial grant to work with the University of Texas Medical School in Galveston on a project attempting to identify blood markers in the immune system so we could apply traditional biofeedback techniques to cancer patients who are working with imagery. When these markers are identified and can be monitored, it will be a major breakthrough because it will allow us to quantify how much "killer cell" activity the patient's immune system is generating to fight the disease.

A Psychological Approach to Cancer

When Carl and I began our work, little was being done on the psychological aspects of cancer. Today this area is receiving a great deal of attention. By way of illustration, the 1978 World Cancer Congress, attended by over 8,000 oncologists from thirty-six countries, offered a symposium on the psychological aspects of cancer. The fact that this presentation was the single best attended event at the entire conference demonstrated the keen international interest in psychosocial approaches to cancer. The conference was also an occasion for trading information across national boundaries. We learned, for instance, that a Japanese study on spontaneous remission validated our own findings about the psychology of people who get well.

As research of this kind accelerates around the world, more and more data confirm the direct link between the emotions and the immune response. The influence of the mind on the immune response is gaining acceptance faster than I had ever anticipated. It has been very gratifying to see this positive reception, especially because at one time I thought it would take twenty-five years to get this far, not fourteen.

Until the last ten or twelve years, we as a culture have been slow to accept the psychological element of illness. Ulcer disease, for instance, is accepted by almost every physician as a psychogenic illness, caused by a combination of physical and emotional factors. Nevertheless, in many cases patients with ulcers are given antacids, and perhaps tranquilizers, and told to stop worrying so much. Happily, a growing number of physicians do take the psychogenic aspect of the disease seriously and refer the patients to a psychologist to learn to cope more effectively with their emotions.

It is understandable that some physicians are reluctant to make these referrals since it means confronting many people with one of their worst prejudices. In very conservative communities, it is tantamount to character suicide to openly see a mental health professional. In some places people believe that if you're unhappy, it's because you're not straight with God, and you need to see a minister, not a therapist. Many other people hold to the bootstrap theory that this country was built on and feel that no matter how ill or troubled you are, you ought to be able to pull yourself up by yourself. (As we shall discuss later in the book, this attitude is one that cancer patients cannot afford to hold.) The whole discipline of psychology is little more than a hundred years old, so this antipsychiatric attitude is somewhat understandable in that light. As a result of this prejudice, the person suffering from a stress-related illness who seeks a psychologist must sometimes battle very negative attitudes of family and friends.

During our years at the Center, we have not only developed imagery techniques but have also studied the personality patterns and life histories of cancer patients. Again and again in our research and that of others, we find that they are people under significant stress. A major emphasis of our work with patients is in helping them learn to cope more effectively with the stress in their lives.

Psychological studies show the typical person with cancer has a life history pattern that has led to hopelessness and low self-esteem—feelings that are directly opposed to the will to live. Because it is important for family members to understand the psychological as well as physical battle the patient faces, I want to give a brief explanation of this personality profile that shows what the patient is fighting.

In one classic study of persons with cancer, Dr. Lawrence LeShan found that 76 percent of them had shared a basic "emotional life history" in which they felt isolated, neglected, and despairing during their youth and early adulthood. Furthermore, they characteristically bottled up their despair and did not communicate hurt, anger, or hostility to others. This, of course, was extremely stressful. But the inner hopelessness was usually concealed. Others often saw these people as wonderful, always smiling and pleasant. According to LeShan, "The benign quality, the 'goodness' of these people was in fact a sign of their failure to believe in themselves sufficiently and their lack of hope."

Their hopelessness was displayed in an attitude toward their illness that LeShan characterized as " unconsciously waiting to die." One patient told him, "Last time I hoped, and look what happened. As soon as my defenses were down, of course, I was left alone again. I'll never hope again. It's too much. It's better to stay in a shell." This hopelessness, LeShan found, occurred in patients who had experienced stressful childhoods, characterized by poor parent/child relationships and abuse of some kind; many came from broken homes. The consequence of this early suffering was low self-esteem, leading to hopelessness. Seventy-six percent of LeShan's cancer patients showed these characteristics, a sharp contrast to the fact that only 10 percent of his control group of noncancer patients showed this pattern.

LeShan's work has been confirmed by other major studies. Caroline B. Thomas, a psychologist at Johns Hopkins University, interviewed and evaluated medical students in the 1940s. In a thirty-year study, she did extensive follow-up interviews with over 1,300 of these subjects. Her data on the history of their illnesses again shows a most distinctive psychological profile in those who developed cancer. Like LeShan's study, Thomas's reveals that many people with cancer experienced a lack of closeness with their parents when growing up, seldom demonstrated strong emotion, and were generally very "low gear." This evidence suggested that those who developed cancer had a life history that led to chronic depression, lasting sometimes twenty years or more, in which many of their feelings were suppressed. They were notably people who put other people first, because of their low self-esteem, and who discounted themselves and ignored their own needs in many ways.

The stress of chronic depression and low self-esteem is a significant problem for many people with cancer. Depression, in fact, has been shown to be correlated with death from cancer. In a study reported by St. Luke's Hospital in Chicago, several thousand factory workers were given the Minnesota Multiphasic Personality Inventory, a standard psychological test. Thirty years later researchers reviewed the files and noted the cause of death for those subjects who had died. When causes of death were matched against the personality profiles, there was a significant correlation between death from cancer and an elevated depression level.

Understandably, many families of patients who come to work with us at the Center are initially astonished at this. Their loved one, they tell us, has always been a happy person. It's not uncommon for us to hear, "Joe might have cancer, but he's always smiling. At least he's had a happy life." Even the patient is very often unaware of his own depression.

If someone you love is suffering from cancer and works with the Simonton approach, through a Simonton-trained therapist or through my book, you may be shocked to find that he is being encouraged to be expressive with his anger and even to be "selfish." But there is good reason for this. The low self-esteem confirmed by so many studies immediately begins to rise when a patient becomes *I-oriented* and emotionally expressive.

Once he begins to focus on doing that, he makes progress in his life and his healing. Many people with cancer were so criticized and abused as children that they seek acceptance everywhere and believe that the real person inside them isn't worthy of acceptance. You needn't be a psychologist to see how hopeless a person feels who lives that way. One task your loved one faces is to become "selfish," putting more attention into his own life and, for the time being, giving less to others.

The reason it is so important for someone with cancer to develop a more fulfilling, less stressful emotional life is that chronic depression and stress depress the immune response. As I've commented, we know of no drugs or therapies that are as effective against cancer as the specific antigens an individual's body can create. We also know the mind can affect this immune activity. In a 1982 study at Pennsylvania State University, Dr. Hall and his associates took preliminary blood measures of subjects to determine the general activity of their immune systems. They then did just one hypnosis session with each patient, asking them to imagine their white cells increasing in number and becoming more active. An hour later, they again did blood measures and found a significant difference. Moreover, the following week when they took blood measures a third time, they found white cell quantity and activity were still elevated. Right now a great deal of research is being done in this area.

The realization that the immune system is intimately linked to an individual's mind and emotions is very exciting, and yet should not surprise us. When someone lives on who should have died from a fatal disease, we commonly talk about a strong will to live. Now science is actually documenting that concept. This is a real breakthrough because until recently our culture viewed the body as a machine, separated from the mind and the feelings. This is a peculiar concept. It essentially sees a person as two distinct organisms existing side by side but rarely interacting. Today we are learning that every emotion causes a concomitant physiological response, either positive or negative; the body and the mind are intimately intertwined.

Conclusion

All this is important background for the family of a person who has cancer. The material in this book is aimed at helping you create a healing environment within which the patient can work on changing his response to stress and learn to enjoy his life. This is one of the elements that affects the immune system and aids the healing process. The family's support for this change is so important that we ask patients who come to the Center to bring their families into one of their first sessions. Out-of-town patients who are married are required to bring their spouses; if unmarried, we ask them to bring a close person who will be intimately involved in their battle against cancer.

The Simonton approach is a very positive one, involving a combined attack on cancer using mental imagery, learning to live a richer, more assertive life, and cooperating with medical treatment. A person with cancer faces one of the most important tasks of his life, and needs every bit of help and support he can get. There is a great deal the family can do to help, and in my experience, almost all family members genuinely want to help—if they can only figure out what to do. But there hasn't been a great deal of information available on the family's role in creating the healing environment. As a result the patient's family and friends may not have enough information to really understand and give support. That's why I've written this book.

Chapter 2

Coming to Terms
with Cancer

For years, the media blitzed us with the phrase, "cancer kills." This well-intentioned message seemed to play a part in motivating people to stop smoking, which was its purpose. Unfortunately, it also reinforced our cultural belief that cancer and death are synonymous. This belief adds greatly to the shock and anxiety a person with cancer and his or her family feel upon receiving the diagnosis. The idea that cancer inevitably kills deeply affects the way we respond to the disease and can add to our sense of helplessness and hopelessness. This is a real pity, because today many cancer patients get well again.

A family faced with cancer is often working from the deep belief that the disease is necessarily fatal. To add to the shock, the patient and family may be confronting the idea of human mortality for the first time. Depending on the particular form of cancer and the stage at which it is discovered, a patient may be given a very good prognosis. He is still, however, dealing with an illness that is potentially life-threatening. No matter how optimistic the doctors are, the patient comes up against the realization that he is mortal and that his body has limits. This sense of our own mortality is not something we have automatically. Often we gain it only through a personal encounter with something that threatens life, either our life or someone's we love. While the patient must deal with the understanding that sooner or later he will die, family members may come to the same realization. In addition, the family confronts the possible loss of a member and the disruption of the family as they know it. For each member, the question is raised: "Can our family survive this loss if it happens? Can *I* survive it and go on?"

The Initial Reaction: Shock and Denial

The mistaken idea that cancer always kills, the need to come to terms with one's vulnerability, and the fear of losing a loved one usually lead a person with cancer and his family into the first stage of coping with major crisis—shock and denial. In her classic work, *On Death and Dying*, Elisabeth Kübler-Ross breaks down the process of accepting death into five stages, which are also roughly the stages each of us goes through in reacting to any major life crisis. Please note, however, that none of us neatly fits any category; we are all individuals, and we cope and adjust in our own ways. Nevertheless, most people experience a progression similar to that described by Kübler-Ross: denial and isolation, anger, bargaining, depression, and acceptance.

In her intensive survey of more than 200 dying patients, Kübler-Ross found that the most common initial reaction to the diagnosis of terminal illness was, "Not me! It can't be true." This is denial, which is often accompanied by some degree of shock for a day or more. For many of her patients, denial took an intellectual form. They became convinced, for example, that their X-rays had gotten confused with someone else's. Some decided the doctor was totally wrong and began "shopping around" for a better prognosis, one that would be more reassuring and easier to tolerate. (Such frantic "shopping" is very different from methodically seeking second and third opinions and gathering information, a process that I recommend.)

For patients, denial is very common since quite often cancer is discovered in an individual who is feeling healthy and has no pain or other symptoms. Earl Deacon, one of my patients, learned of his cancer through a routine physical examination in 1975. A sixty-three-year-old Texan and very successful agricultural entrepreneur, Earl was able to spend seventeen minutes on the treadmill during the exam, a remarkable achievement for a man of his age. He felt very well and had no complaints about his health. But a blood test showed a suspiciously high protein content, and a follow-up bone marrow biopsy by a hematologist indicated a fast-moving form of cancer of the bone marrow. The doctors concluded that Earl probably had less than two years to live.

Naturally, Earl's initial reaction was denial. "I was feeling great—it just *couldn't* be true." Fear ran beneath this denial. A close friend had died of the same disease (its technical name is multiple myeloma) just a few years previously. Earl and his wife, Marge, had seen their friend's rapid deterioration. Marge too kept repeating, "Not Earl! How could it be Earl! He jogs three or four miles at a time, several times a week. He's in great health!" Marge also felt what she describes as "a mixture of disbelief and horror at the same time. I wanted to reject the whole idea."

Marge is evidence that no matter how much you know, accepting a diagnosis of cancer is still difficult. For the next two years she and Earl worked together to battle his cancer. They did everything they could think of, including learning to communicate with one another and creating a more enjoyable and less stressful lifestyle. Yet, when in 1977 she was hit with a diagnosis of cancer of the uterus, Marge went into shock. "To think that with all my background on the subject of cancer, I was as vulnerable as anybody!"

The extent of the shock a patient and family experience varies widely. Bob Gilley, a successful insurance broker in North Carolina, also learned of his cancer through a routine physical. The doctor found a lump in Bob's groin and called in three other doctors to examine it. Asked to go in for a biopsy, Bob refused until he returned from a national convention at which he was a speaker. When he did ten days later, the tumor had grown from the size of a walnut to that of a tangerine. What was to be a biopsy became an extensive operation in which the malignant tumor was removed. Bob's fear was so great that shock moved in to give him time to cope. "I really wasn't functional for several days," he admits.

Bob's wife, BJ, also felt shock and denial. "I didn't want to think about it when they found the tumor," she said. "Only after the surgery was I frightened, and then I was very frightened."

While bad news is hard to cope with, people have equal difficulty coping with uncertainty. For people with cancer, the period of shock and denial is often lengthened because of initial uncertainty about the disease. A suspicious tumor may have to be tested several ways and then biopsied. A laparotomy may be necessary to determine the stage of the disease, as well as sophisticated X-rays and scans. Patient and family may wait still longer until all this data is reviewed by a tumor board. In the meantime, everyone concerned is in a holding pattern with very little idea of what to expect. During this time both patient and loved ones may naturally be obsessed with such fear of the unknown that it becomes difficult to function. It is likely to be a period of some denial of feelings.

Parents of children who are diagnosed with cancer have a special task in maintaining their own courage as reassurance for the child. This can mean the parents choose to withhold information from their child until they have coped with their personal denial, anger, and fear. I witnessed this in Pamela and Bob Mang, a Palo Alto, California, couple whose daughter, Jessica, developed a limp in 1980. When Jessica's leg was X-rayed by an orthopedist and further tests were ordered, it was found that the ten-year-old had osteogenic sarcoma or bone cancer. A quiet, strong man, Bob discussed this calmly until the doctor told him that the usual treatment was amputation, perhaps followed by chemotherapy.

Bob, who had been standing all this time, said, "I think I'll sit down." He characterizes his reaction as shock. Despite his shock, he was able to discuss with the doctor how to handle Jessica, and he agreed that the child would be given a pair of crutches to use but not told the diagnosis until after the biopsy. As for Pamela, when Bob told her what the doctor said, "my mental processes just stopped for about 24 hours." The next day, healthy feelings of grief began to break through this shock, and Pamela found herself crying as she peeled potatoes for dinner.

Before they told their daughter, the Mangs gathered the best medical advice they could, including the results of the biopsy.

COMING TO TERMS WITH CANCER

They also came to terms personally with the devastating diagnosis, and with the doctor's help, made the decision to permit amputation. During this time they made an important decision, following a confused telephone call from the doctor, who had a strong foreign accent and who had left them with the idea that Jessica had only a 25 percent chance of survival. They decided that Jessica's death was unacceptable: they would fight the prognosis with everything they had. For them, as for many patients and families, this decision was significantly helpful in getting them through this most difficult time. As they gathered information on Jessica's illness and talked to doctors all over the country, the Mangs became better able to face their crisis. As it turned out, they learned that, with amputation, their daughter's prognosis would be very good. Working as a team, the Mangs helped each other through the initial period of shock.

Expressing Grief

Because Pamela and Bob had come to terms with Jessica's illness before they told her, they were able to help her express her grief. They told her the diagnosis and explained the options. She could have partial removal of the bone and an implant, which would periodically have to be replaced, or she could have an amputation, which would leave her with more mobility. Jessica, now twelve, remembers, "I figured my parents knew a lot more than I did, and I said I'd go along with whatever they thought was best for me. Then I cried.

Jessica's healthy tears also led her to an early acceptance of her condition. Pamela recalls Jessica looking at her leg and saying, "You've been a good leg, and we've had a lot of fun together. But we're going to do this." In saying goodbye to her leg, Jessica was coming to terms with the reality of her illness.

Many adults, particularly men, are unable to simply burst into tears as Jessica did and thus move toward acceptance of their illness. Unfortunately, our culture teaches us that tears are a sign of weakness, and, while women are permitted to cry, many strong women also find crying very difficult and embarrassing. Yet crying is a natural and wholly human response to pain. We may think that "a stiff upper lip" is a sign of strength, but in reality, the person who cannot express sadness and fear in the beginning is the one who is more apt to fall apart later on. Coming to terms with cancer means that denial must give way to the free, healthy expression of grief and fear.

Anger and Resentment

Anger is often a part of our response to cancer. This feeling, too, is one people may attempt to stifle, believing that it is somehow not nice or appropriate. Yet, it is normal to feel a sense of betrayal and anger at one's body after receiving the diagnosis. The person diagnosed with cancer, particularly one who has displayed no symptoms, may have felt an almost superhuman control over his life, an ability to do anything, including maintain perfect health. Now the body has shown him that he is finite, vulnerable, that maybe he hasn't controlled or taken care of everything.

The family's anger is likely to focus on somewhat different issues. If the patient is the breadwinner, for instance, family members may inwardly cry, "We've been depending on you for all these years! How dare you let us down? How will we survive without you to take care of us?" This anger is a result of very real fear and insecurity. When somebody loves and cares for us in many ways, the relationship may be so close that we feel we cannot survive without them.

That fear and insecurity can be expressed in a number of ways. Anger, as I've said, is common. Sometimes the anger is expressed in attempts to control the patient. A family member may, in effect, say, "You have to get well! And you have to do it *my* way. Here's what I want you to do. . . ." This behavior is both parenting and controlling and certainly may express love, as well as the family member's need to avoid feeling sad or scared.

Anger and resentment may also lead to a family pulling away from the patient—abandoning him. Such people are so frightened of losing the person that they unconsciously decide, "I better back away now." Since their need is so great, they feel unsafe relating to someone who may not always be there. More than unsafe, they may feel terrified. They say to themselves, "The thought that he won't always be here is so frightening to me, I don't even want to be around him. I can't accept the idea that he may be taken away." These people, in effect, are dealing with the loss too soon by withdrawing. In doing so, they become isolated, and as a result the patient becomes isolated, too. A husband who is emotionally withdrawing from his wife may become more intensely involved in his work and spend less time at home. People may engage in activities of every kind, so long as what they do enables them to run away from their feelings and avoid the possibility of the loss of their loved one.

The patient is equally capable of this kind of flight from the reality of the cancer. He may suddenly find himself feeling emotionally needy and reject that neediness by rejecting his family. I've known patients who tell their spouses and children not to visit them in the hospital. Others permit visits but turn their backs and go to sleep. These patients are fighting their new realization that they are really very dependent upon their loved ones. That dependence may evoke much fear and they respond to their insecurity by demonstrating that they need no one. It is as if they are clearly saying to the family, "I don't need you—I'll show you I don't need you." Again, such isolation is unhealthy. It increases the patient's alienation, and adds to his depression and anxiety—all of which can have a physiological effect on the disease process, reducing the possibility of recovery.

Patients and families who move from denial into realizing their fear and anger can, however, respond in much more positive ways. One reaction may be, "I never stopped to realize how important my husband (or wife, father, mother, etc.) was to me until now." Frequently this can lead to a real outburst of love and affection within the family. Family members can express need and fear together and comfort one another: "I love you so much, and I don't know how I could survive without you."

Depression and Hopelessness

While Kübler-Ross's concept suggests that in a life crisis we move through several stages, depression being one of them, I have found that many cancer patients and their families are depressed from the very beginning. A man who has been diagnosed just after his retirement may say, "I've been cheated! I worked hard all my life to get here, and now I finally have a chance to enjoy myself—and I've got cancer!" His anger and hopelessness may lead him to become depressed and simply give up. Many people tell me that they've stopped buying clothes, for instance, because they won't have the opportunity to wear them out. They refuse to plan trips that are too far ahead. In fact, they stop living long before their symptoms would confine them to that extent. These people invest less than ever in the quality of their lives. One such patient told me, "It's like I've seen the dark at the end of the tunnel." While she did not actually realize she was depressed, her attitude was, "What's the difference? I'm going to die anyway."

Depression and hopelessness, feelings that are not uncommon, easily strike those with cancer. Initially, both patient and family may decide, "What's the use? There's nothing we can do." Oddly enough, this stance is comforting for them because it removes the necessity to make choices. The victim's role expressed in this attitude is totally passive, and, therefore, it is assumed it relieves anxiety. If you don't make choices, you can't make wrong choices.

Fortunately, in our culture we have a strong distaste for the role of victim. We would rather participate in the event, just as Pamela and Bob Mang chose to fight Jessica's poor prognosis. Cancer patients and their families are often helped out of their depression by the information that comes flooding in from outside sources, information on cancer that they may consider. They are forced into activity by the need to make informed decisions: What kind of doctor should they go to? Which doctor should they see? How many other opinions should they get? Which of these doctors do they feel most comfortable with? The patient and family also have to decide immediately who to tell about the disease and how much to tell. It is impossible to avoid decisions about whether to tell the children, aging parents, business associates. In the process of making these decisions, the family often begins to feel a sense of moving forward and gaining purpose and even hopefulness.

Why Me? Why Us?

A family that begins to move away from depression and fear by active involvement in the healing process is well on the road toward acceptance, the final stage of the process of coming to terms with cancer. Now they are likely to continue an active search for a way to understand what has happened. They attempt, usually, to assign meaning to the illness and make it comprehensible. That effort may begin with the question, "Why me?" or, in the case of the family, "Why us? Why did this happen to us?" This searching gives these individuals a sense that their lives have some meaning and predictability. They choose to believe that everything happens for a reason, and once they discover the reason, they can have some control over their disease. They are on the other extreme from patients who say, "The world is unjust, there's no reason this should happen to me, poor me." The idea that this unfairness appears to be chaotic and beyond understanding is one very few humans can tolerate. If we decide an illness is a meaningless accident or a trick of genetics, we feel we are truly victims of something beyond our control.

Although I believe neither of these extremes is healthy, I encourage patients to think through the question, "Why me?" I have found that those who do usually arrive at a middle ground. Very little, if anything, that happens to us is totally outside our influence, and seldom, if ever, do we totally control anything. Patients who examine the many factors that entered into their becoming ill usually find that there are things they can change about their lives and that they can find ways to make this experience have meaning. In much of our work, we focus on how patients can do this so that they find a way to gain some benefit from the experience, to grow and change in positive ways. This understanding makes any bad experience more tolerable and valuable.

In asking, "Why me?" patients are also asking a theological question. It may be stated as, "Why is there evil in the world?" or "Is this really God's will?" or "What did I do to deserve this?" Often people who examine this question conclude with outrage that they did nothing to deserve cancer. A typical response might be: "I've always lived the way other people told me to. I've been a good little girl, a good wife, a good mother. I've taken care of other people all my life. I've always done what they told me were the right things. I might not have figured out who I am or what I want in life, but I did follow the rules and now *this* happens." Very naturally, such people now question whether the rules they have followed really work. A great deal of anger may result from thinking through this question.

For others, the diagnosis of life-threatening disease throws doubt on their concept of the divine. They want to know why painful things happen to good people if there is an all-perfect, all-loving God. Some people may have operated under a kind of childlike belief in a God who is a perfect parent and who protects, loves, and takes care of them. If so, that belief is now shaky, to say the least, and the person with cancer is forced to reconsider his understanding of God and the universe.

Another aspect of this theology is that the patient and family may feel the all-powerful God "visits bad things on them." Just like the idea that God totally protects us, this idea may throw all responsibility for our welfare onto the divine—and permits us to see ourselves as helpless victims. My concern here is not with whether this theology is right or wrong, but with whether it is healthy. Ultimately, an individual who believes his fate is entirely out of his hands may not take responsibility for himself or fight for his own life. We often find that cancer patients who begin wrestling with this problem come to a mature middle ground—without sacrificing their religious devotion. This means one might believe that God created human beings as a complex system of interacting biological and psychological processes, and when these processes interact, there are certain consequences. For instance, a human being who lives in a polluted environment, seldom relaxes, and is unhappy is going to be less healthy than one who breathes fresh air, relaxes and manages stress well, and enjoys life. This doesn't say that God had no role in this; it says that as individuals, each of us must take some responsibility for our own lives.

For Earl Deacon, "Why me?" was never a questioning of God. "First I said, 'Not me,' " he remembers. "Then a couple of weeks later I began asking, 'Why me?' I consider myself a very religious man, but I don't believe in an all-powerful God, more in a loving and just Father. And I think the reason I never questioned God was that I never thought He gave me cancer—I believe we have control of our own minds and bodies. So when I asked, 'Why me?' I was wondering, 'How could this happen to me when I was doing all the right things?' I ate well, I exercised regularly, I had a full life. I loved to fly my plane and fish, I had lots of friends. My life was exciting. I didn't feel ready to die—so it just didn't make sense."

Because Earl believed he was doing what he should to have good health, he persisted in asking *why* he had developed cancer. This was part of his personal belief in individual responsibility. Earl believes that, "Instead of blaming God for getting sick, a person ought to look at how he didn't take care of his God-given instrument—which is his body. If you do take care of yourself and your health still gives out, *then* you can say it's God's will." Earl's self-examination led to the insight that there *were* ways he could change to build his health, including learning to express his feelings, working fewer hours, and becoming more affectionate with people. Most of all, he and his wife Marge have focused in the seven years since his diagnosis on building a better quality of life. In this way, Earl's response to his own question, "Why me?" has led not to self-pity but to a richer, more fulfilling life.

Such acceptance signals the end of the process of coming to terms with cancer. Certainly we cannot expect to move from shock to acceptance and positive action overnight. Yet Earl's case is only one of many which demonstrate that coming to terms with cancer, rather than fleeing from the truth through denial or depression, is well worth the struggle. Many patients and families I work with have created beauty and meaning out of the realization that they may die. These individuals feel the effect of the possible loss, and then decide, if they are not going to live forever, it's high time they got serious about how they are going to use the time they have. Both the patients and their families learn to take time to smell the flowers and look at the changing colors of the trees. They make a serious business of thinking about the quality of their lives; they have more fun, and they stay more in the present. Until the diagnosis, they were much like most of us, putting off until tomorrow those things they wanted for themselves. Ours is a culture that dictates that we postpone gratification, but cancer is an eye-opener for most people, teaching us that life is too short to postpone everything we really want.

You might call this a reordering of priorities. It is a rather natural thing to happen once you begin asking yourself, "If I'm going to die, how do I feel about the way I've lived? If I might have only a few more days to live, how do I feel about today?" Once each moment becomes precious, we become more conscious of our interactions with people, of whether we are really making contact and expressing our affection. We begin to think about how much we enjoy life. And this kind of thinking is not just confined to a person with cancer. It also extends to the family that encourages and takes part in this exploration.

It would be pollyannaish to suggest that cancer is a positive experience; of course, it is not. But those who truly come to terms with it *use* it in positive ways, to grow and change toward better lives. Often they realize that they have given their lives over to making it in the world—making money, earning some kind of external success that they believe will validate them as worthwhile people. But they haven't spent time with their children. They haven't laughed and talked and shared the little and big things that have meaning for them. Until the diagnosis, every member of the family got up in the morning and rushed out to school or the office, never taking time to see what a pretty day it was. One patient told me that her youngest son used to frequently go outside in the morning and come back with a flower for her. She always accepted it with thanks, but until cancer showed her she was mortal, she never realized how loving and sensitive that little boy was.

If the patient and family are to learn new ways of responding to life and to create the most healing environment possible, they must come to terms with the illness as a family, working through the whole range of feelings together. When they reach the point of acceptance, it becomes possible to focus on positive action and arrive at family decisions on how to handle the many problems that surround this illness. The family can support the patient's decisions about how best to create a healing environment in his own body. And the family and patient as a unit can map out the future, draw up a strategy or game plan for handling the time ahead. While this kind of positive, decisive action takes courage, it also bestows courage and a sense of control and hope.

Chapter 3

Developing a Family
Game Plan

A fter a diagnosis of cancer, every family faces a multitude of decisions. One way or another, these decisions are made, and the family adopts an attitude toward the illness, as well as an overall strategy. In many families, the game plan for dealing with cancer is allowed to develop without careful thought or communication between the members, perhaps because the family is not used to working together toward a goal or because members don't want to talk openly about the illness and confront their feelings, or for numerous other reasons. Nevertheless, these families do adopt attitudes and develop ways of coping.

Having Direction—A Course of Action

It is far more helpful to both the family and the patient if the strategy is openly discussed and defined so that all members understand it. For one thing, this gives each member a sense of direction and control over his destiny, which is very comforting and strengthening when we are dealing with a life-threatening disease. Moreover, an open game plan will incorporate more information and thought than an unspoken one and so will give each member of the family, including the patient, better ways to handle the stress of this long illness. And cancer is often a relatively long illness.

A patient with heart disease, for instance, may be in the intensive care unit for only a few hours or days and is then past the critical period. Someone with cancer, however, can live on for many years with the knowledge that the outcome is uncertain. So the sheer length of time a family may live with cancer means that an open, well thought-out strategy for living with it is very desirable.

How formal should the game plan be? The more the family defines its course of action, the less confusion individual members will experience. To some people the idea of writing down family strategies for coping with illness seems rather impersonal and businesslike. On the contrary, it is an excellent way to organize thoughts and give each member something concrete to hold on to. When cancer is diagnosed, patient and family members are typically thrown into shock and confusion. Sitting down together to decide how to handle the following weeks helps pull the family together and reassures each individual.

A family's strategy must be flexible enough to change over time as the patient's situation changes and as other members' needs change, too. And, of course, each family brings to its decision-making process unique and special needs. In beginning to form its game plan, however, every family initially considers three important areas: gathering information, forming a family belief and attitude toward cancer, and making numerous practical decisions based on this information and attitude. Work in all three areas usually takes place simultaneously until the game plan has been formed.

Gathering Medical Information

One of the initial decisions a family confronts and must share in concerns the question of who should be told about the diagnosis, and how much should be told? In general, those who do best share their crisis with family and friends and thus build a support network. (At the same time, of course, some families have to give careful consideration as to how much to tell young children or elderly parents.) Once others know about the illness, the patient and family will almost always be flooded with information: books about cancer, clippings from newspapers and magazines, anything people think will be helpful.

This information *is* helpful, but it can also be somewhat overwhelming at first. As much as energy permits, the patient will feel more of a sense of power if he is in charge of the information, but it may be useful to designate certain areas to other family members. So much usually comes in that I recommend a file box or drawer so that new clippings can be slipped into the appropriate categories. Usually these will include nutrition, exercise, psychological resourses (such as counseling, meditation, and imagery), community resources (cancer self-help groups), medical treatment, and alternative treatment.

Sometimes so much information comes in that the family decides to delegate research and review in certain areas to specific family members. A teenager, for instance, could read the available material on the benefits of exercise and report to the patient on what is most widely recommended. An adult family member might want to make phone calls investigating local self-help groups, such as Reach To Recovery, an organization for mastectomy patients, the ostomy groups, and the more general groups such as Make Today Count and I Can Cope. Many cancer patients find these groups very supportive and enabling, and they should certainly be explored if the patient has any interest in them at all.

Decisions on alternative treatment can be among the most difficult to handle. Hardly a week goes by that the press does not announce some new and exotic treatment that is as yet unproven but may seem to offer hope. Morcover, the family and patient are likely to hear stories about people who recovered using these treatments. Many families decide not to consider alternative treatments; others find this anxiety-provoking, and wonder, "Is there something we're missing?" If a patient wants to consider alternative treatment, the information should be read by adult family members and discussed. I recommend that if a patient decides to try an alternative treatment, he still remain under the care of a medical doctor.

Information-gathering in general is a very good way to allay anxiety about cancer. When Bob and Pamela Mang learned that ten-year-old Jessica probably had bone cancer, they almost immediately began to learn everything they could about their daughter's illness. At the same time, they began forming a game plan and defining their areas of responsibility. Bob explains, "My focus was gathering information, and Pamela's was keeping Jessica comfortable during the three days before her biopsy." Bob and Pamela shared the information he gathered. Pamela comments, "We found that the more we knew, the more in control we were to deal with the situation. With a diagnosis of cancer you feel you have totally lost control, and for us it was important to get some part of our control back."

Perhaps the most important information the family gathers comes through doctors, and it usually bears directly on decisions about treatment. Typically a patient will first receive a series of tests from a doctor, who is sometimes an internist or family practitioner who first discovered the illness. As a general rule, the patient may feel more confident if there are at least two more opinions, preferably from oncologists (doctors who specialize in the treatment of cancer), before making a decision on treatment. If possible, the patient may choose to have all the information reviewed by a tumor board at a cancer center hospital where several specialists will discuss the case and make informed recommendations. All this is somewhat tedious, but in general, those who do it feel more secure in their choices, and, therefore, more hopeful about the outcome of their treatment.

Gathering information from doctors is both important and difficult. Usually the patient and any family member who is there are so anxious and distracted that they misinterpret what the doctor says. I have known emotionally upset patients and their spouses to leave the doctor's office with completely different memories of what was said. For this reason I recommend— unconventional as it may seem—that the patient take a tape recorder in for the conference, and explain the reason to the doctor. Failing this, the patient and/or the person who accompanies him may want to take notes *during* the conference.

Even in the case of an adult patient, it will be helpful if another adult (the spouse, if the patient is married) goes along for all visits to the doctor. This is not only comforting and reassuring, but it helps in gathering accurate information. Under the best of circumstances, most of us are relatively poor listeners. We comprehend and remember very little of what we hear. When faced with the anxiety of a life-threatening illness, we are even more likely to miss important statements and misinterpret others. The patient and companion can make notes on the doctor's findings and advice and discuss them immediately after the visit. These can be collected in a loose-leaf notebook or filed, dated, and kept together for future reference.

The reason all this medical information-gathering is so important is that for many forms of cancer, there is not necessarily one "best" treatment. Often combinations of treatment are recommended, and these may vary from one oncologist to another, since there are so many gray areas in our understanding of cancer. Not only may the results vary from treatment to treatment, but so may the side effects. With this in mind, physicians should fully describe both the benefits and the risks of proposed treatment as well as obtain the patient's written consent.

As medical information is gathered, the patient and family can begin the decision-making process that is a significant part of dealing with cancer. With most illnesses, we are accustomed to hearing the doctor say, "This is the illness you have, and this is the treatment for it." With cancer, however, this is often not the case. Instead, a patient is likely to be told, "These are the treatments used for this type of tumor. Let me tell you the potential outcomes, and we can decide which option is best." Because we are so unused to making medical decisions of this magnitude, we are likely to feel confused at this point, and ask the physician what he would do in our situation. Asking for this opinion may be helpful, but I would caution that it is wise to ask at least two other doctors the same question, and then to assess these responses. In looking at the alternatives at home with other informed adults, the patient may decide that the cut-and-dried recommendation of a particular doctor is not what he or she wishes to follow. One physician, for instance, may not be interested in the quality of the patient's life but only in defeating the patient's slow growing cancer. He may therefore recommend a harsh therapy with numerous side effects. A seventy-year-old patient has the right to respond with, "What you advise is good for someone who's thirty-five, but I'm seventy. I may only live another five years anyway, and I don't want to endure two years of being that sick."

A patient who sees several doctors is likely to find, on discussing it with his spouse, that one doctor seems to have a belief system and attitude he feels comfortable with. For those who are uncomfortable sorting through the medical information to make their own treatment decision, one way to decide is to consult several doctors and choose the one you think is most competent. In the process, patient and family will gather crucial information since each physician will be found to have a slightly different attitude toward the same data—sometimes a very different attitude.

Maintaining Hope in the Face of Uncertainty

Without question, competence is very important in a physician, but equally important is his attitude toward the patient's future. If someone with cancer is to continue to live a good quality of life, he must be hopeful. Hope is difficult to sustain if the attending physician is grim. Unfortunately, many are. Among oncologists today, the prevailing philosophy appears to be, "Never offer false hope." While this is fine, it often goes too far, to the point where the doctor offers no hope at all! This is done with nothing but the best intentions and in the belief that the patient should be prepared for the worst. But it can have a very negative impact on healing. While it's important to be realistic, it is not helpful to be totally pessimistic.

Moreover, the total absence of hope is not actually very realistic either, particularly not before treatment has been given and evaluated. Almost no form of cancer, no matter how severe, is 100 percent fatal. A patient may have an advanced disease that statistics say is 99 percent likely to lead to death in two years. But until treatment is completed, we have no way of knowing whether a patient will be in the 1 percent that survives. Many things influence the possibility of "beating the odds," such as how much the patient participates in getting well by living a vital life, getting good nutrition, exercising, and using such psychological supports as relaxation and visualization to build health and strength. Ironically, the motivation behind these actions has to be hope. The patient must believe these things will work—and a grim attitude on the part of the physician works against this hope. Physicians who discourage patients sometimes tell me they don't want to offer false hope. In fact, hope is merely an attitude one takes toward an uncertain outcome—and that is almost always the case with cancer. Logically, therefore, there can't be such a thing as "false" hope in dealing with a diagnosis of cancer. There is only hope, and it is a positive force for health.

As the patient and family members seek medical information and make treatment decisions, they are also involved in the formation of attitudes toward the disease that I mentioned earlier. In choosing a physician, I believe it is vital to bear in mind the importance of *his* attitude, and the effect it can have on the patient's recovery. One doctor may consider the data regarding the illness and say, "We're talking about a very serious disease. There is a 95 percent chance of the patient dying in two years." A second doctor may more suitably respond to the same data with, "We don't know how this will progress. We do have treatment options to look at. And we want to do the best we can to help you deal with this and maintain a good quality of life at the same time."

Hope is essential; human beings can't live long without it. It can be given in several ways. A physician can offer encouragement about the possibility of recovery, or the possibility that treatment will arrest or slow down the disease, or the possibility of maintaining a fairly pain-free, symptom-free life for as long as possible. Even in that rare case where statistics hold out no hope for recovery, there is always something to legitimately hope for. When hope is taken away, people become so depressed that no matter what the outcome, their lives are miserable. This is why I believe it's important to choose a physician whose attitude is positive. His belief system can have a dramatic effect on the patient's attitude and on the outcome of the disease.

The unstated foundation of every family game plan for dealing with cancer is the degree of hope in the family's attitude. That attitude will range somewhere from bleak to hopeful. It is usually based on medical information—sometimes on too little information. And yet, as important as medical information is, it is possible to hope in the face of an extremely discouraging prognosis. Through a misunderstanding, the Mangs were initially led to believe that Jessica had only a 25 percent chance of survival. As soon as she learned that, Pamela told her husband, "I just won't accept that." The couple took a silent walk together, during which Pamela's determination grew. "That helped me," Bob recounts. "From then on I just concentrated on the most effective thing I could do next." They had made a realistic decision to hope for and work toward Jessica's survival.

This hope was based on, as it must be, an acceptance of the uncertainty of the outcome. As a family formulates its attitude toward the cancer, it must deal with this unsettling lack of certainty, which often becomes strikingly clear when medical options are proposed. Very seldom is there a cut-and-dried treatment for cancer. In fact, many patients are rather disturbed to find that even the physician is indecisive or that physicians disagree radically. One may recommend surgery while a second recommends radiation treatments, a third holds out for chemotherapy, and a fourth suggests a combination of these treatments. In all this, no one can tell the patient the definitive treatment. For many, making such an important decision is difficult and frightening; these people are sometimes more comfortable choosing the doctor who seems the most competent and whose attitude agrees most with theirs and letting him make treatment decisions.

Even so, there remains an uncertainty about outcome. Often the first attitudinal decision the family makes is generated, like the Mangs', by the prognosis and concerns the question of whether or not the patient will survive their disease. For some families this issue is brought to the forefront by a friend or relative who brings a book on dying. Such material can sometimes jolt the family into saying, "Wait a minute! We're not preparing for that now. Dying isn't our goal!" In that case, the family has chosen a positive, hopeful stance. This is not easy in the face of uncertainty. Sometimes the reaction to the unknown future is to decide the patient *is* going to die, as a way of gaining relief from the anxiety of not knowing. So it is obviously important for a family to discuss its attitude together and to deal openly with the uncertainty: "How are we going to handle not knowing?" Those patients and families often do best who acknowledge that they don't know what's going to happen but are willing to hope for the best. Often it is necessary to fully discuss old feelings about cancer that may be heavily influenced by experience with relatives or friends.

Adapting to Cancer as a Family

As important as medical treatment is, it is only one aspect of the health of the patient and family. As I've mentioned, much of the information flooding into the household will deal with other possible ways of building health. Some of these affect the family as a whole and can be taken on cooperatively. Nutrition is an example. If the patient decides to eliminate sugar from their diet, for instance, it may be important for the family to encourage him or even to eat the same way.

While the family as a team decides how to support the patient's efforts at recovery, it is also very important that family members consider their own well-being. The diagnosis of cancer creates a serious stress on every member of the household, and each individual must pay attention to maintaining his own total health. When there is a life-threatening illness in the family, everyone, not just the patient, needs additional nourishment and support. Otherwise, they too are likely to become ill eventually, and when the patient is one of the parents, life can be very difficult when the other parent becomes overly stressed and finally sick.

One very important way to avert this is for the family to go about changing its lifestyle and priorities slowly. Certain changes are inevitable. Perhaps the patient is too ill to cook in which case other arrangements will have to be made. They will need to be accompanied to treatment sessions. And various other demands will be made on the family's time and resources. I recommend that family members try to keep life as normal in as many ways as possible. Change itself is one of the most stressful things human beings have to deal with, and there will already be changes taking place because of the diagnosis, information gathering, and treatment decisions. When, on top of all this, family members stop working or drop out of school or change major daily habits, it only increases the stress. In essence, the family should look at ways to improve life but go about changing slowly. If at all possible, the children should go to camp as always, the family should continue to give dinner parties, and so on. In the initial period after the diagnosis, some people do take time off to cope with the shock; perhaps they don't go to work for a week, see friends, or play golf. But as soon as possible, people may want to pick up their lives again. Cancer is a long-term disease, and it's often best not to make drastic changes immediately—and certainly not to withdraw from life.

One of the most important things family members need to attend to is their sleep. Because of the shock of the diagnosis and their anxiety, it is natural for the first night or so for people to stay awake at night talking or worrying. But eventually they will wear themselves out and will be of little good to anyone because they just don't have the energy. Paying attention to sleep may sound unimportant, but it is vital. People whose sleep pattern is significantly disrupted eventually experience many emotional difficulties such as depression, anxiety, and other serious problems. In addition to making rest a priority, family members may find that increasing their exercise will help them sleep better. Just getting out in the evening and walking around decreases anxiety as well as helping the body relax and grow tired.

Sleep is likely to be disrupted by the initial anxiety of coping with the diagnosis. If that persists for any length of time, individuals may want to seek someone who is understanding to talk to about their feelings—their doctor, therapist, pastor, friend, or each other. In talking to one another and sharing their common feelings, family members strengthen the bonds within the family and release these natural feelings. Relaxation is another aid to sleep. Many patients learn how to relax as a way to aid visualization, release stress, and build strength. Family members can learn relaxation techniques from tapes, books, or through a therapist. A ten minute nap or period of deep relaxation after lunch may be a good idea too. In short, family members should remember they are in a crisis too. Too often everybody in a family feels as if the patient were the only one under stress and the rest of the family is expendable. But a spouse of a person with cancer, for example, should firmly say to himself, "I'm under severe stress. I need to take even better care of myself than I used to."

Another important part of the family game plan is increasing the amount of physical touch and affection within the family. In dealing with this crisis and the anxiety it brings, touch is very reassuring and important. Family members can seek out each other and friends to literally hold their hands, to hug them and hold them, to rub their backs. Equally important is the expression of sheer affection. This happens spontaneously to the person who is sick; friends send flowers and cards to help create a healing environment. Certainly, family members will be renewed if they allow their friends and relatives to help and support them as well as the patient.

Depending on the circumstances, individuals may find that time management is now more important to them. It may help them cope with increased responsibilities and with anxiety in general. Walter Greenblatt of Dallas had to figure out better ways to allot his time when his wife, Carol Ann, was diagnosed with cancer of the bone. Her diagnosis meant that rapidly more areas of responsibility within the family became his. In the office, he decided to limit his work to forty hours a week, hired an intern to handle some of his clients, and hired a third secretary. This gave him the time he needed to run his household, which had four young teenagers, and to fit in the recreation he needed. In finding ways to ease up his workload, Walter did not sacrifice his career, which was important not only because he was a breadwinner but because it represented one of his own personal priorities. In 1981, he qualified for Top of the Table, one of the top five hundred members of the Million Dollar Roundtable in the insurance industry, in only seven months. This achievement was satisfying in several ways. He notes, "Your business can be therapy. You can relieve some of your anxiety by helping others solve their problems."

Aware of the stress Carol Ann's illness placed on him, Walter gave great importance to taking care of himself. He read literature on the various areas of health mentioned earlier, and his routine would include meditation twice a day and exercise, which was varied; swimming, jogging, bike riding, and racquetball. He has changed his diet significantly, eliminating sugar and extra salt and generally stressing protein, fresh fruits and vegetables, and low cholesterol. He also takes megavitamin and protein supplements. And, he adds, "I have fun, even if it's only a few minutes when I find something to laugh about."

Walter is an example of an individual within a family who is learning to care for himself and manage the stress of a long illness. This is far from selfish since a family is made of individuals who need to work as a team but should also always maintain their individuality. Because the family is a team, or system, when any one member becomes healthier in an overall way, the whole team benefits. When *all* members of the family gain in health, we have a synergistic effect: the whole is greater than the sum of its parts.

In talking about a game plan, individuals in the family should think about both taking care of themselves *and* operating as a team. The attention to personal needs is a vital part of coping with cancer in the family. Walter Greenblatt's time management enables him to take one of his children out to dinner once a week and maintain one-on-one relationships with them. The personal satisfactions in his own life make him a better parent to his children and a more caring husband to his wife. In other words, within the family team, he is a more able "player" and a resource for the other members.

In developing a family attitude toward the illness, gathering information, making the many decisions required, and maintaining individual health and well-being, a family is taking on a major task. For some families, this working together as a unit is new and can be both rewarding and frustrating, as parents and teenagers try to arrive at mutually agreeable decisions, for instance. If developing the game plan is unduly difficult, the family can learn and grow by looking at what seems to stand in the way. It may be that it wasn't made at all clear who would do a certain task. Or it may be that one individual is taking on too much of the responsibility and controlling the decisions. Insofar as it is possible, it is the patient who should be central in the process of making decisions about his illness.

Chapter 4

The Family as a Team

O ne way family therapists evaluate the general health of a family is by looking at how well the members can work together as a team to accomplish a task. It is one thing for a family to set up the goals involved in a game plan and another thing to actually work together to reach them. Without teamwork, the best family plan is doomed to failure.

Teamwork in a family does not mean that each member has equal freedom and decision-making power. A healthy family has clear leadership from adult members; young children know that the parents are in charge. This is not to say parents are domineering and controlling, always on top of the kids. It means the parents set and enforce reasonable limits, and, in turn, the children respect the parents.

Adults in a healthy family may divide their responsibilities in a number of ways, including the traditional way of the man earning the money and the woman running the home. But this division of tasks does not mean they are not equal; ideally, they operate as a partnership with mutual respect for one another.

Autonomy and Individual Needs

With this brief background on the role of the parents, I'd like to look at the question of individual autonomy in a healthy family. Autonomy means that each member is encouraged to be responsible for himself, to think freely and express his own opinions. Without this respect for individuality, the family cannot operate well as a team.

Autonomy becomes particularly significant when a family sets out to work together around a serious crisis like cancer. The patient needs to maintain his autonomy and not assume a passive, child-like role. This means family members may need to resist a natural tendency to overprotect the patient. The more they protect, the more helpless he may feel and the less able to mobilize his resources toward healing. At the same time, the autonomy and the needs of every other member of the family are also important.

Once a family has adjusted to the shock of the diagnosis and is ready to make decisions about something other than the patient's treatment, it's time for the members to sit down and talk about the problem they have in common: "How can we continue to maintain our lifestyle? How can each of us go on fulfilling our individual needs?" In many families, no one has ever been encouraged to state his needs—and this may be most true of the person with cancer, who is often too helpful and giving for his own good. Now the members have an opportunity to discuss their own needs and to ask for help and give help to one another in meeting those needs.

The healing family can make a very determined effort to see to it that parents and children go on with the activities that are important to them. Many people tend to feel they should drop everything in the face of this crisis, but that is not often helpful. In the long run, it can even be harmful. The family can say, "Okay, let's everybody set aside their own needs and focus on giving the patient whatever he needs." But ultimately people will resent the patient, and it won't work. Somebody might suggest, "Mary Jane, now that Mom's sick there's nobody to cook dinner. You'll have to drop your cheerleading and come right home after school to take care of that." But this ignores Mary Jane's very real need for friends and for an activity that matters to her. A family with respect for each person's needs can find another solution, such as tapping into the resources of friends and other relatives who would be very willing to take turns providing dinner one night a week. Another solution, if it is financially realistic, is to hire a part-time cook. The point is that the family decides that if Mary Jane's need is important to her, then *the family as a team will find a way*. As a result, Mary Jane can recharge her own energy in this activity, relieve her stress about her mother's illness, and come home with more energy and support to give.

An important aspect of a healing family, then, is that each member is autonomous and is respected by the others; each member continues to get his or her needs met and to maintain his lifestyle as much as possible. When the family team adopts this philosophy, the ultimate result is that every individual has more strength to cope with the crisis of cancer and more warmth and support to give the patient.

The Team Captain

Obviously, this is a team of equal members—however, the patient should be the captain since his illness is what the game plan and the teamwork are all about. There are some exceptions, of course. An adult patient who is severely ill, semicomatose or just coming out of surgery, is going to have to turn over responsibility for a time. The patient who is facing surgery will have less anxiety if he discusses this situation with his spouse or other adult member of the family before the surgery and knows just who is going to take on his various responsibilities. If the patient is a woman who has always handled family finances, for instance, she may want to know who is going to pay the bills and balance the checkbook. In this way, even though the patient is going to be unable to make decisions or really be captain of the team for a while, he will have an easier mind. If the patient is a woman who is a homemaker, she may be better able to focus on recovery if she knows that family members are now handling the laundry or other tasks according to some agreed-upon plan. It would not be helpful to see confusion or fighting over a task or to see that it isn't really being handled at all.

Decision Making as a Team

In the decision-making process that surrounds the illness, the family should include the patient in all possible decisions. Even shielding the patient from bad news is something a family may want to consider very, very carefully. The family is only a team when every member joins in the making of decisions. The patient especially needs to feel in control. It is, after all, the patient's life that is on the line. Granted, the disease greatly affects everyone—but the patient is the one who must make the crucial decisions around his life or death. If he is despondent and does not want to hope, family members can encourage him to stay on the team, functioning as its captain. While the family may try to take pressure off the patient by reassigning chores, for instance, it is much better if the patient is in the driver's seat, stating his needs about these and other things. This certainly doesn't mean he has to *do* everything. One important function of the family right now is to give him time to rest and help relieve anxiety. So if he is interested in gathering information about cancer treatment centers, and this would involve lengthy research at the library, another family member can volunteer to gather the material. Others can also participate in reading it and talking it over. But when it comes down to, "Should I go to a cancer center and, if so, which one?" then the patient will generally want to make this *I* decision for himself.

In questions about treatment, family members may rightly have strong feelings and opinions. It is healthy for them to express these in discussing treatment as long as they don't attempt to steamroll the patient into doing it their way. For example, I have worked with women who had breast cancer and had to choose between a lumpectomy or a mastectomy. In one case, the husband went with his wife to talk with the doctor. He was convinced that a removal of the lump alone would be adequate, and for emotional reasons, he preferred that treatment. His wife, however, had seen a relative die of cancer which began in the breast and was very frightened that the lumpectomy would not be enough. While he thought her anxiety was irrational, to her it was very real. She believed she would never rest easy unless she had a mastectomy. Fortunately, her husband loved and respected her enough to recognize that this was her decision and that her feelings about it were most important. He was able to take a genuinely supportive attitude, once he had worked through his own feelings, and accept her decision. This kind of communication and acceptance is immensely helpful to a patient facing a difficult and important choice like this. As this husband's willingness to go along with his wife's decision illustrates, teamwork can mean that a support person must compromise his feelings for the patient's. This does not imply, however, that a support person cannot voice an opposing opinion, and implicitly express it to the patient.

Sharing Hope

An equally important part of teamwork is a shared belief in hope. It is very hard for any patient to direct his energy toward recovery when ever-present family members project a secret hopelessness. However they try to conceal their feelings, the patient may sense that they are patronizing him, giving nothing more than lip service to his efforts. The result is that at a time when he needs to feel warmth and support the most, he feels alienated, misunderstood, and even betrayed. The family attitude toward recovery is fundamental to teamwork in this matter; the best intentions in the world will not conceal secret despair. For family members who are finding it very difficult to hope or to talk over their feelings about this, seeing a therapist or counselor may be a necessity, not only to make their personal adjustment easier, but to be able to support the loved one in this crucial way.

Supporting Visualization

The general idea of family teamwork is that the patient decides what he needs, and the family supports those needs while seeing to it that they meet their own individual needs. Often, in supporting the patient, family members gain benefits for themselves. We have seen this at the Center in regard to one process we teach, mobilizing the immune center through imagery. We recommend that family members take time to gain a clear understanding of what the patient is doing in practicing imagery. Moreover, we suggest that family members, especially the spouse, try imagery; they too are in a difficult time, and need to maintain their health. Similarly, we suggest patients *and* their spouses learn relaxation techniques. They may even set aside time each day for relaxation and visualization, both valuable ways to relieve and discharge stress.

Unless the family gets involved in these processes too, they usually find it difficult to really understand their importance to the patient as well as the self-discipline and personal strength the patient must have to practice them. They may see the patient letting imagery slide and find this really hard to understand. Tom McNamara, from Merced, California, whose wife Pat is a patient of mine, told me, "I had my share of initial scepticism, but I decided to try this stuff along with Pat. It's not hard to get into it, it's interesting and even fun. *But* I learned that it can also be a big pain to set aside time to do it two or three times a day, which Pat does. I don't do it that often, although I would if my life were on the line." Spouses who understand the value of imagery can become alarmed when their mate stops. The spouse can begin to nag and worry, which only deepens the patient's sense of failure and guilt. Tom, on the other hand, does become concerned. As he says, "When she lets up, I worry, but I don't nag. I discuss it with her. I'll ask her, 'What's up? We both know that it's important to you, so what's bothering you?' And we talked about it." This supportiveness has helped Pat meditate regularly. Tom reports with a smile that his only complaint about it is, "As soon as we get in the car to go someplace, she starts to meditate. She's not exactly the world's best company!"

Often a patient's spouse or an older teenager in the family is interested in meditating for themselves and will agree to meditate at a certain time each evening with the patient. When a whole family makes a commitment to do this, it can create a wonderful family ritual and time of closeness in which everyone relaxes and discharges the anxiety so natural to people who are dealing with illness. Moreover, members who participate learn quickly that relaxing and sitting quietly for twenty minutes is not as easy to do every day as it may seem. They develop empathy with the patient's efforts and respect for the patient's success.

BJ Gilley made a major commitment to her husband Bob's time for visualization. At first her support took the form of keeping the household quiet during that time.

"Our children got to know how important it was not to disturb him," she explains. "If there was any noise at all, Sean, who was four years old at the time, would say, 'Shh, Daddy's messitating.'" Finally BJ made a commitment to meditate with Bob. "That showed me how much self-discipline it took. But I did it and was very glad I did, later, when I found a lump in my breast and one under my arm. The doctor said he would do a biopsy if they didn't go away in six weeks. I knew about imagery, and I sat down to do it on my own—and when I went back in six weeks, they were gone."

Whatever the family does to support the patient, nobody can do the meditation for him. I had one interesting case, however, where a wife virtually *did* do imagery for her husband. He was receiving radiation therapy for a brain tumor that was affecting that part of the brain that controls imagery and communication; moreover, his medication made him so drowsy he would fall asleep during imagery. He badly wanted to use this technique, because he really believed it could help the treatment shrink the tumor, but he was completely unable to visualize and stay awake. His wife, however, was a very creative person. Knowing that he still had acute tactile and auditory senses and knowing what his imagery was because they had discussed it, she set out to help him. Each day she sat by him while he relaxed and then talked him through his image, drawing it with a fingertip on the back of his hand as she talked. Because his hearing and his sense of touch were acute, this kept him awake and focused on the process. It was amazingly helpful to him, and they kept it up until his tumor was reduced to the point where he could do the imagery on his own.

Supporting Exercise

The above is a good illustration, I think, of the power a loving family member can have to help a patient achieve what he wants to. This works well when it is also good for the family member. Exercise is a prime example of something others can join the patient in doing. It can benefit them and also provide encouragement for the patient. When Pat and Tom McNamara came to the Center for the first time, Pat joined me and some of the other patients in running every morning; I had decided to run in a marathon and was committed to daily jogging. Pat was excited about her running the first morning "until," she said, "I found out I had only run a quarter of a mile." She had never been very athletic, but now she was convinced she had to exercise to get well and decided to keep running. Her husband and children were all athletic and very encouraging. Tom, in fact, joined her every morning. After a month she was running almost three miles each time.

"But I was a 'closet runner,' " she says with a little laugh. "I didn't want anybody to see how bad I was, so we'd sneak over to the track early in the morning." After about a year, Pat enjoyed running so much she decided she, too, would try a marathon. In December 1978, just twenty months after that first quarter mile jog at our Center, Pat and Tom completed the Honolulu Marathon. In preparation for that 26.3 mile race, Tom enthusiastically joined her in running the Bay-To-Breakers Race in San Francisco, a 7.6 mile annual event that is the largest footrace in the world. Pat got so much enjoyment out of this that she and Tom have run it every year since, and are now joined by a large group of runners they know. So Pat's family, friends, and neighbors—her support system—have encouraged her to exercise, and they have gained something in the process.

Other patients, of course, are not able to begin their exercise programs with something as demanding as jogging. Many who visit our Center take brisk walks together. Others can manage only a leisurely walk once or twice a week, which is still valuable for exercise, fresh air, and a change of scene. Whatever the patient decides to do in the way of exercise, it is a good way for the family to work together. Even young children can be a great help in motivating the patient to exercise by showing up for it at the regular time and providing company. I've known patients whose teenage sons took them out on the tennis courts for the first time; others had daughters who had been busy and distant, but now began to take an evening walk with them. These things once again show that in supporting the

patient in positive ways—by participating rather than nagging—
the family can grow closer. Teamwork of this kind forges
bonds that may never have existed in the family before.

Other Ways to Support the Patient

I like to be careful about making specific suggestions on
teamwork. Patients have certain needs in common, like the
needs to exercise, meditate, and know that the household is
going on in an orderly way, but each patient also has individual
needs that he or she must express. The important thing to take
from the examples I've given is the inspiration to be creative.
Whatever the need, there are several ways to meet it.

Families should also bear in mind that almost every member
can help, even fairly young children. Children can obviously
pick up on such chores as dishes, lawn work, and dusting. They
can run errands. Older children can drive the patient who needs
transportation and can often do things they may have never
done, such as the grocery shopping.

Sometimes more consideration is in order around the house,
although this should be distinguished from overprotecting the
patient. But if a patient feels uncomfortable or is in pain and
feels irritated by loud rock music, obviously the stereo should
be turned down. A positive approach can be taken to problems
like this one, too. The patient can say, "I really feel anxious
and unsettled. Can you choose some soft, relaxing music for me
and keep records on for the next hour?" This focuses on
meeting the patient's needs, not on depriving the person of his
pleasure or accusing him of doing something wrong.

Children can also do many nurturing things for the patient.
Bearing in mind that touch and intimacy are particularly important at this time, a child can rub the patient's back, hands, or
feet. Any child old enough to read can sit close to the patient
and read aloud; a patient who is feeling unwell after treatment
may feel comforted by the closeness and distracted from his
symptoms. Older children can also be asked to babysit one
evening a week or even over a weekend so that the parents can
spend some time alone with each other.

The catalog of things family members can do to help the

patient feel well and get well is endless, and the list is limited only by the creativity of the family. Supporting the patient, of course, often depends on the patient stating his needs in the first place. Communication remains important, so that the patient never begins to think he is burdening people. When the family members are autonomous, they do their teamwork willingly. Families who feel they aren't quite this cooperative shouldn't be disheartened; in many families, people have never been encouraged to state their needs and work together. This will be a learning process. An important goal to remember is: to create a team in which each member can state his needs, can receive support for them, and can choose to give support to the patient and the rest of the family. After all, this is what teamwork is all about.

Chapter 5

Developing Outside
Support Systems

E veryone has at least one family—even people who live
alone. If this seems paradoxical, consider that most of us
limit our definition of *family* to the nuclear family, that is, to a
husband, wife and perhaps children who live together in the
same household. But most of us also have a family of origin,
the family into which we were born. For many people, these
immediate relatives are a great source of support and strength
during an illness.

The third category of family is the one this chapter will deal
with, the extended family. At one time the extended family
referred to the network of aunts, uncles, cousins, and so on that
surrounded most Americans. In today's highly mobile culture,
many adults leave their birthplaces and lose their connections
with these relatives, making the traditional extended family
rather unusual. And yet these were the very people who came
with casseroles and flowers and helping hands when a family
faced an illness such as cancer.

Extended Families

As the extended family began to disappear in society, it was replaced. Its functions were vital; very few of us can live in comfort without the support of numerous others. It has been replaced, for most of us, by a new network of caring people, who are not relatives, but instead are friends, neighbors, and co-workers. This group is often called an extended family because its role in the individual's life is so important. For the person who lives alone, it is especially vital to a healing environment. But for every patient, this extended family can be a significant resource. While its members can do much to reduce the stress experienced by the nuclear family, they may need to be asked.

Asking, of course, is not always easy. Most families facing cancer have many people in their extended networks who are available and often willing to help fill all kinds of needs, both emotional and physical. But many families are reluctant to seek these people out and actually make a request. Sometimes these extended family members have never said in so many words, "Give me a call and tell me what I can do." Most often this is not because they don't want to help but because they don't know how to say so. Frequently, they *have* offered help to the patient and family, and still nobody calls them. This problem is common in our culture; we all tend to have difficulty asking for help, as if need were a sign of weakness.

In general, it is helpful for a household dealing with a long-term illness to call on the extended family, that is, on the support system outside the home. Patients who withdraw from these friends, instead, sometimes do so because of a problem. It may be that the patient feels nobody cares for him now that he's not up and cheerful and feeling good. It may be that the extended family is really not being very helpful but is instead "cheerleading" or, on the other hand, acting gloomy around the patient and his family. The patient concludes, sometimes, that he'd rather do without them. Another cause of this withdrawal from friends is that the patient may be denying his illness and doesn't want to confront his own feelings about it by talking to others. This is an emotional difficulty that should be dealt with.

In fact, we know that the broader and more intimate a person's support system, and the more they rely on it during times of stress, the healthier they are likely to be. Developing support systems outside the nuclear family, then, is an important part of building the total environment that makes healing possible.

Is Outside Support Available?

As soon as a patient lets others know about his diagnosis, there is almost always a landslide of support. In fact, many families are overwhelmed by the calls, visits, and reading material they receive in that first week from people who genuinely want to be helpful. But these friends are usually limited by the fact that they don't know what to do.

Such supporters have various relationships with the family and patient, ranging from intimate friendships to more distant social contacts. Almost every one of them can be genuinely helpful in this crisis; it is up to the patient and family to tell them how. Often the family is initially so upset and frightened by the diagnosis that it doesn't respond to offers of help. As a result, the supporters fade away, not knowing how to take the initiative.

As soon as possible, the patient and family may want to list those tasks they could use some outside help with. Early on, families often feel they don't want to seek this help but want to manage everything themselves. Cancer is frequently a long-term illness, however, and ultimately they may wear themselves out. The tasks to be considered can be physical efforts that go toward helping the patient recover, such as transportation to and from a distant cancer center for treatment. They can be tasks the patient used to do, such as mow the lawn or shop for groceries, but he cannot do now because he is feeling weak from radiation treatment. They can be tasks related to the everyday survival of the family, such as young Johnny's car pool or Susie's need to be driven to her dance class. When these survival and comfort needs are being met, the family will be much better able to cope with the larger issues of the illness.

Asking people for this kind of help seems very gutsy to some, but I think it helps to bear in mind that the extended family *wants* to give support. It is much easier on friends when they have some concrete way to help. If you ask a friend to pick up and deliver the cleaning once a week, he can do that specific task and feel the satisfaction of contributing.

When Pamela and Bob Mang learned of their daughter's bone cancer, they sought support from a large extended family. First, because they were going to be using the ideas in our book, *Getting Well Again,* they sent letters to about two dozen close friends and relatives, along with copies of the book. The letters explained that the book represented their philosophy of working for Jessica's recovery and that they wanted close friends to know their approach to cancer. The people who received that letter and book responded by supporting this affirmative approach.

The Mangs also wrote down the names of all their other friends and acquaintances who wanted to help in some way. Then they listed every task someone else could do that would lift their burden so they could concentrate on helping Jessica. This included taking care of the garden, since Pamela and Bob were now spending weekends with Jessica while she received chemotherapy. It included transportation for Nicholas, their youngest child, as well as special events for him, since they would often be unavailable for such things.

Next, Pamela and Bob broke down the lists, until they had the names of close friends, a list of things close friends could do, the names of acquaintances, and a list of tasks they might do. One close friend, Carol Sanford, helped them with this process and undertook to write letters to all the people on both lists, explaining what was going on in the Mang family. The letters added, "It would be helpful if you could do any of these things." Almost everyone responded, choosing items off the list. One close friend replied that she would rather be there for anything and not be boxed in by the list. That worked very well, too.

"People *do* want to help," Bob says. "I think those who draw away from a person with cancer often do so because they feel helpless and don't know what to do."

Pamela and Bob feel they have grown through this exercise in asking for outside support. Pamela explains that "before this, we were terrible at asking for help. We were the kind of people who would do everything for ourselves. We figured a family should deal with its own problems from within. Thankfully, we realized we needed help. And I don't know what we would have done without it."

Every patient and family has individual needs. The patient can define these to ask for the kind of help he wants most. One of my patients, Joe Ayoob, set up a network of six friends to help him in a very special way when he learned he had a brain tumor. Joe, who believes deeply in his daily meditation, asked each of his friends to drop whatever they were doing at a certain time each day and "give me five minutes of meditation." Joe adds, "I asked them during this to visualize me as being healed." He chose friends he thought would understand and support this request, and they all did.

In talking about this experience, Joe hits the nail squarely on the head, "People are eager to help. It's just a matter of seeking them out and asking them. They want to help, but most of the time they just don't know how."

Close Friends

Regardless of how close the patient and family members may be to one another, it is essential to receive emotional support from sources outside the family. Often a patient is so close to his spouse that he has no really intimate friend; this can be a mistake. Seeking to have all of our needs satisfied through one source may make us too dependent on that person. In a sense, that person is our single lifeline—what if he, too, becomes ill and is not available to nurture us? It is also very hard on a spouse to be totally depended upon. If you know someone is relying on you alone for their emotional support, it is easy to see how burdensome this can become. These are some of the reasons why psychologists urge individuals to develop several intimate friendships with people who care and accept them.

Sometimes a close friend or outside support person may abandon the patient in a time of need, and this action may be interpreted as a sign of disloyalty when, in fact, it is not. For example, one of my patients was deeply disappointed when a close friend began avoiding her more and more as the cancer advanced. The patient was very hurt by this seemingly disloyal conduct until she learned that her friend was behaving this way out of her own personal fear. Three years earlier the friend's sister had died of cancer. Now she feared the loss of another loved one. This fear—not disloyalty—led her to stop seeing her good friend. With this story in mind, I suggest that patients and family carefully examine why a good friend may uncharacteristically fail to support the patient.

It should also be noted that because cancer is often a prolonged illness, there may be a point where support people simply reduce the time and effort they devote to the patient. Again, it may not be accurate to interpret this as disloyalty. After a period of time, many people will no longer react to the patient's illness with the same sense of urgency as when they first learned of the diagnosis. Often they have come to accept the disease as a chronic problem rather than an acute catastrophe. Once people develop this frame of mind, they may tend to reduce their support. Here again, the patient and family may reach conclusions about a support person's concern and loyalty that are unwarranted.

No matter how close the patient and spouse may be, it is now more important than ever that each of them seek outside friends to talk to and be comforted by—not just one intimate friend, but several. The strain of hearing about the illness can be too much for one friend; again, if he is a dear friend of the patient, he may be very upset about the illness and may even begin to avoid the patient altogether because of his painful feelings.

Sometimes patients and family members begin to experience difficulty with certain friends during the illness. These people whose pessimism may have been tolerable in the past are now very difficult for a patient who is struggling to work toward recovery. Often the initial reaction is, "She's so gloomy and hopeless about me, I'd better just avoid her altogether." But another solution is to really examine both oneself and the relationship. Exactly what is it this friend says or does that makes you so uncomfortable? It may be something rather simple. One patient told me her friend always approached her very solicitously and asked, "How *are* you?" The patient felt this friendship was worth trying to preserve, and made an effort to "retrain" her friend. She told her, "I would appreciate something you could do that would help me out. I do have cancer, and you and I both know it. But there are a lot of other things in my life that are important to me, and sometimes I like to forget about my illness. So if something new develops, I'll be sure to tell you. But I'd rather you wouldn't ask me about it all the time. I'd so much more enjoy talking about our tennis game!"

In this instance, the friend was very responsive—again, she had only wanted to help and still did. The patient felt this investment in the friendship was well worth it. So it is important, during this family crisis, not to discard friendships lightly. At the same time, it is only realistic to note that some relationships can't be changed.

I have been talking of intimate friendships, but relationships with friends take many, forms. As the family looks at its needs and considers asking for outside support, it's a good idea to think as Bob and Pamela Mang did about whether people are close friends or friends on some other level. In this way, you can avoid asking people for something you and they are not really comfortable with. When you have a realistic perception of what a friend likes to share with you, you can be more nourished by that friendship. One friend, for instance, may like to laugh and joke and almost always puts you in a happy mood. While laughter can be very good medicine, laughter at inappropriate times may promote denial of your feelings. When you're feeling frightened or sad, you may not wish to call on this cheerful companion but on another friend who is comfortable with more difficult feelings. This doesn't mean that a laughing friend is not a good friend; some people can't hear you cry—but they can sure make you laugh.

Among the people offering their support to the family at this time will probably be some who are acquaintances or social friends. They can offer the patient companionship, which may be very welcome at times when symptoms are bothersome. A friend who is famous for his backrubs might enjoy coming over and giving the patient a backrub once a week. Another might like to take a walk with the patient on a regular basis, which can help in getting into an exercise routine. (Some patients schedule three friends on three different evenings.) Much of what family members do to help the patient recover, people from the extended family can also do—if they are asked.

For family members, it is equally important to share with friends during this time and to maintain a life away from the illness. Walter Greenblatt, whose wife Carol had cancer of the bone, has found that many of his friends have become supportive since Carol became ill. For Walter, getting together with these people for lunch has a high priority. "I make sure I do," he says. "I'll call them, I'll make a note of the date, and I'll follow through. It's really important to be able to sit and talk with someone about my problems—and in turn, to listen to his. We both feel better for it."

Bob Gilley, like many cancer patients, found he received tremendous support from friends during his illness. One expression of friendship he treasures came from the partners in his insurance agency. The morning after Bob's operation the two men appeared by his bed at 6:00 A.M., the earliest the hospital allowed visitors. Bob woke up to see them there. They told him, "We don't want you to worry about *anything* but getting well. We'll run the business, and you'll take your one-third share of the profits." Bob adds, "Both of them are multimillion dollar producers, so that was a real chunk of money they were talking about. Let me tell you, that took a real load off me." Bob's partners were also supportive of his special health needs; as soon as possible, he took a cot into the office, where he lay down and rested when he got tired. During the ten month period Bob received chemotherapy, his partners' continued support enabled him to concentrate on his sales enough so that he was named the number one agent in the United States that year by the major insurance company with which he was affiliated.

People who become ill are often amazed at the friends and acquaintances who offer their concern and help. Many times we live our daily lives not perceiving and appreciating how much affection others have for us. A serious crisis can show us how much support we have. And by sharing the crisis with friends, we can enrich our friendships.

Groups and Organizations

Many patients and families receive wonderful support from groups they belong to. The groups may be religious, work-related, or social. Here again, the family often finds an affection and concern they didn't realize was there, and deeper, more intimate relationships form with people in the group.

Since 1968 Walter Greenblatt has belonged to a study group of ten insurance agents from all over the country who meet several times a year to exchange information. When Walter's wife Carol was diagnosed with cancer of the bone, the professionals in this group and their wives immediately showed their concern and support by calling both Walter and Carol, writing, and sending flowers every week. When Carol was hospitalized in Philadelphia, group members from the east traveled to visit her. Since then, others stop by if they are in the Dallas area. "Their loving support has been tremendous," Walter says. "I feel very close to them, and I don't hesitate to call them when I need advice, or just need someone to serve as a sounding board."

Bob Gilley, who is also in insurance, found the same support from the Million Dollar Roundtable. This organization paused in its national meeting to give a silent prayer for Bob. Spiritual support of this kind was a significant comfort to him. His friends in the insurance business also set up prayer chains throughout the country that were followed by phone calls from other agents in every state in the Union and Canada. The Gilleys belonged to a small, interdenominational religious society, and its members also focused time and energy on Bob and his recovery. Of course, it is not my intention or province to recommend any religious body or to recommend any religious activity to patients or families. This is an entirely personal decision and one that most often has been made some time before the diagnosis of cancer. Those who do have religious affiliations, however, can freely accept whatever support they get from these groups, which, like other groups, can be deeply nourishing.

For Bob Gilley, spiritual and emotional support was so important that he went on to found a supportive group called Dayspring for other cancer patients. Like numerous recovered patients in other cities who have formed similar groups, Bob has been helped by putting his creative energy into building the organization. Bob's spiritual orientation is reflected in the name of his group. Dayspring is derived from an Anglo-Saxon word that means "new dawn, new hope, new life, new light." Bob took the word from the gospel of St. Luke, in which Zacharias refers to Jesus as "the dayspring from on high . . . come among us to bring light to them that sit in darkness and in the shadow of death." Bob explains, "I interpret this to mean that new energy must be brought to people who are really down—and that's what we try to do."

While some find supportive groups through their work and others through their religious affiliation, many find group caring in social organizations. Some people with cancer make the decision to seek out social groups after their diagnosis, not necessarily to receive extended family support but to broaden and enrich their lives through enjoyment and involvement. Earl Deacon is one patient of mine who did this. After his diagnosis (he was in his midsixties), he decided to cut back on his work hours and devote some time to a nearby summer theater group consisting of aspiring young actors. A successful businessman, Earl brought to the group his expertise as well as some financial backing.

His growing enthusiasm for this theater group was in itself a sign of Earl's personal change. His wife Marge confides, "There was a time when Earl would have thought a group like that was just foolishness. But since his illness, he's learned to express affection more openly and reach out to people in a loving way. He's a magnet to those young people! They come just to sit at his feet and hear him talk. I believe they see something in him that they don't see in a lot of older people." For Earl, this involvement with the group has had equally rich personal benefits, Marge adds. "I'm sure he gets even more back from those young people than he gives."

Earl Deacon's involvement in the theater group has not been particularly focused on his illness. Both patients and their family members would do well to remember that it is both strengthening and healing to be involved in something you enjoy as an individual. This, too, is a significant form of outside support.

I have already touched on the many kinds of community

organizations that exist to help the person with cancer. Some are general, such as Make Today Count, and some are geared toward coping with recovery from specific forms of cancer. The American Cancer Society is likely to have a list of local groups. I am unable to endorse any particular organization because in each community these groups are operated by different individuals, and can have very different orientations. I do know that groups of this kind are extremely helpful to many patients. Any patient who is interested should see what is available locally and consider giving one or more of the groups a try.

There are some real benefits inherent in cancer self-help groups. One is the opportunity to talk to other patients who are going through the same experience. This sharing can be truly supportive. Sometimes patients and families feel that the illness somehow makes the family alien and different from all others. In cancer organizations, patients and family members meet others who are facing the same problems and going through the same changes. Another way these groups help is through bringing in fully recovered ex-cancer patients as speakers. Witnessing the health and joy of those who have gotten well again is a very inspiring, positive experience. For most patients, the only other place to meet people with the same illness is in the waiting room of an oncology clinic or chemotherapy ward. People in these settings tend to be upset and anxious, and under those circumstances the conversation is seldom uplifting. So this is another reason why families may want to explore such organizations.

In coping with a diagnosis of cancer, or perhaps with a patient who is recovering from surgery, the family can help itself *and* the patient by accepting the support of groups. With organizations, as with friends, most families find that a great deal of encouragement is offered, the family's only responsibility then is to accept that offer and make sure the group knows how to help.

Psychotherapists

Since a long-term illness is so stressful, professional help in dealing with it is frequently invaluable. Because of his perspective, the therapist is sometimes more helpful with difficult feelings and problems than friends are able to be.

The patient or family member who is considering psychotherapy may begin by defining what he wants. Some professionals specialize in hypnosis and can augment imagery. Some work with hypnosis and other tools that diminish pain. Some are skilled in biofeedback and methods of relaxation. Some are expert in family relationships.

If the patient or a family member is already working with a therapist individually, it is sometimes not wise for that therapist to begin seeing the whole family. A family therapist works not with an individual but with the entire family system. You might say that the family is the "patient." These specialists look at how the people in the family interact and communicate. They try to share their insight and help individuals in the family change constructively. For instance, in a family therapy session, a patient may express his anger at family members who seem unsupportive to him. A spouse or child, who are more able to communicate under the guidance of the therapist, may reply that the patient isn't showing any need for support. The patient may then be able to express his fear and sadness and let go of his anger. In this way, during the hour of therapy, a family can begin to communicate more openly so that the family system changes and becomes more responsive to everyone's needs. Working with a family in this delicate learning process demands a special set of skills. For this reason, it is wise to seek a therapist who concentrates on working with families.

In choosing any therapist, the family or individual should take the same attitude they take toward choosing any professional consultant. Therapists *are* consultants. As educated professionals, they are taught a body of skills that pertain to communicating, asserting needs, and so on. Much of the antipsychiatric mystique in this country derives from the fact that many people don't understand the therapist's role as consultant. Certainly it is not a sign of failure to hire a tax accountant or lawyer for help with special problems; in the same way, it is not a sign of failure to seek a therapist but rather a sign of willingness to grow.

A first step in locating a good therapist might be to check with people you know and respect who have had good results in therapy. The local psychological association is also a source of the names of licensed psychologists and psychiatrists. A doctor or other health professional may know someone whose reputation is good. A health professional is an especially good source for the names of therapists who work with individuals and families coping with life-threatening illness.

Once you have several names, you may want to schedule the first meeting with the idea in mind that you are investigating this particular therapist. Most therapists, in fact, consider the first session to be a time for patient and therapist to evaluate one another. In your evaluation, you can ask about the therapist's experience in dealing with serious illness and note whether or not he seems to be comfortable discussing cancer. A therapist, after all, is only human; some have had personal experiences with cancer that left them frightened of the disease. The therapist's skill and ease with people who are ill are not the only things to consider. It is important that you like, respect, and trust him. This is a special need associated with therapy. You may hire a plumber whose personality you dislike, but whose skills are good. With a therapist, however, you will do well only if you feel that he genuinely cares about you and is someone you can trust.

At the end of your first meeting with a therapist, he will probably bring up the question of whether you can work together. It is appropriate and common for patients to say, "I'd like to go home and think about this session and about my reaction to you. I'll call you in a day or two." This also gives the therapist a chance to think about making a commitment to work with you. It is certainly a decision he can be expected to respect.

If you are not sure you or your family would gain from therapy, you can use the above method to try one session and see what it seems to offer. Certainly, therapy can be one of the most powerful supports a patient or a family can have, and it should be seen as a possibility for the future.

For Patients Who Live Alone

The patient who lives alone has to create his own healing environment without the help of a nuclear family. This means he has a more urgent need to seek support from his extended family, from groups, and perhaps from a therapist. When we are dealing with frightening crisis situations, we need to rely on others. Isolation only increases the patient's depression and anxiety and can work against healing. All this means that it is very important for a patient who lives alone to develop ample sources of support.

One simple and interesting way to gain some comfort is to grow plants or adopt a pet. A recent research project at the University of California at San Francisco found that patients suffering from heart attacks who had pets or plants to care for recuperated significantly faster than those who didn't. Evidently, living things that depend on us for survival give us a purpose and a feeling of being needed.

Most people who live alone, if they examine their lives, find that they have one primary relationship. While it may be a romantic bond with someone of the opposite sex, it can also be a close tie to a relative or a friend. In dealing with the effects of cancer on their lives, single people can consider everything said in this book about the impact of the diagnosis on spouses and families. Those who are your "surrogate family" outside the home will experience the same shock, fear, and denial and will need to talk through their feelings about the illness.

The single person has a greater need to get together regularly with other people than does the patient with a family. There are innumerable ways to do this. One excellent ritual to establish with a small group of friends is a dinner or get-together on the same evening every week. Singles can also spend time with married friends or relatives and their children.

The person who lives alone can get outside support for exercising by either joining or forming a group to jog, bicycle, play racquetball, or some other sport. Teaming up for regular tennis games is another good idea. Singles can seek out bridge clubs or establish their own card-playing groups. Those who have children can work in the PTA or attend meetings of Parents Without Partners. Most churches also offer a variety of activities and ways to get involved with other people. The important thing is that a patient who lives alone needs to take the initiative in gathering a support system.

* * *

It's especially important for the single person to be willing to ask for help. If you simply feel a need for companionship, it's easier to ask for it when you bear in mind that your single friends have the same need and probably welcome the company just as much as you will. It usually deepens a relationship, too, when you call to say, "I'm feeling kind of lonely tonight. Would you mind coming over?" Or even, "Would you mind coming over to spend the night? It would be really nice to have somebody near." An important kind of help to have available is that of a friend or two who will help you in an emergency. Ideally, this is a reciprocal agreement: "If you ever need to go to the hospital in the middle of the night, call me. And if I need somebody, I'll call you." A nearby neighbor is also a good person to make this arrangement with. Some single people exchange keys with a friend, which can simplify things if someone is suddenly hospitalized or incapacitated.

Joe Ayoob, the single patient mentioned earlier, found that his request for meditation time from his friends led to other kinds of help and consideration on their part. They visited him often and brought or sent books they thought would inspire him. One of these friends became very close and supportive—"a true friend, there at my side, telling me I would get well again, telling me how much I had to live for." Joe's experience demonstrates very well that the patient who asks for support usually gets it in even greater measure than he hopes.

People Who Need People

A popular song claims that "people who need people are the luckiest people in the world." We might revise that line to read, "People who *know* they need people. . . ." for we all need other people, and we need them even more when we are dealing with illness.

Both single patients and families sometimes want to rely on themselves for everything after the diagnosis of cancer. But, because of its chronic nature, cancer makes it necessary to seek the help of outside support systems and of a more extended family. In the early stages, families can often meet their own needs without help, but if they persist in doing this, they may eventually wear themselves out. There are so many new, time consuming activities, treatment, exploring nutrition, exercising, and on and on, that those who "go it alone" simply exhaust their own resources.

With this in mind, every patient and family may want to develop outside support. There are countless ways to do this, and no one can say that this cancer self-help group, or this religion, or this team sport is the right one for any particular individual. Each family and each patient can find what is right for them. Only one thing is certain: outside support is essential.

Chapter 6

Dealing with the
Doctor

People with cancer work closely, and often for a long period of time, with their physicians. To some extent, a patient's comfort, as well as his belief in the effectiveness of his treatment, will depend on his relationship with the doctor. This patient-physician relationship is a vital element in the healing process. Obviously, choosing the doctor is one of the most important decisions the patient and his family make. While it is ultimately the patient's decision, the family can help him gather information to make the choice. If difficulties with the doctor develop later, the family can support the patient's efforts to work them through.

Choosing a Doctor

The process of selecting a physician logically begins when the patient seeks out second and third medical opinions. As I have emphasized, this is infinitely preferable to accepting the diagnosis of the original physician for two reasons: First, it is always possible that doctors will interpret the data differently and arrive at different diagnoses. Second, even though they may agree on the diagnosis, they may very well have different approaches to treatment.

As the patient and spouse or other family member confer with several doctors, the patient has the opportunity to evaluate these doctors with an eye to selecting his primary physician. In order to make this evaluation, the patient must know what he wants in a doctor. Expertise is obviously very important (although I would caution that "the best surgeon in town" may not be significantly more skilled than many others—just better-known). In terms of expertise, most cancer patients want to be under the care of a specialist, an oncologist. But perhaps as important as expertise, for most patients, is the nature of their relationship with the physician.

The patient who knows in advance what kind of relationship he wants is more likely to be satisfied with his final choice. The possibilities range from the traditional, directive relationship to one in which the physician acts like a consultant and the patient directs the treatment. For some, anxiety is vastly diminished by this kind of active participation in their own treatment. Such patients want to make the final decisions regarding their treatment and how to deal with their side effects. They want to read every available piece of literature and even to come up with their own suggestions. Some patients need a doctor who is willing to negotiate, who will offer several choices in medical treatment and discuss in detail the potential advantages and the possible side effects.

Other people feel this sort of responsibility would simply escalate their anxiety. They may be people who are not comfortable making major decisions regarding their health, particularly with an illness like cancer. These patients sometimes feel very comforted by working with a directive physician who tells them in no uncertain terms, "This is what you need." They can then relax and follow orders with a sense of security. This people relationship feels right to them while other people might feel constricted and angered by the same treatment. So the degree of directiveness you prefer in a doctor is one element to think about.

Another element that's important to many people is the doctor's personality. While personality may seem irrelevant, it matters greatly to some patients, especially when they're not feeling well. One person is very soothed by a doctor with a traditional sort of bedside manner—one who's gentle and loving and pats his patient's hand. Another patient feels more secure with a straightforward, unemotional doctor who just gives the facts. A third patient is downright uncomfortable with either extreme and prefers a doctor who's friendly and chatty. If personality is important to the patient, it should definitely be considered in the choice. I had one patient who was working with "the best" doctor in the field but found his impossible personality left him constantly depressed. When that kind of thing happens, a patient may consider another good doctor whose personality is more suitable to him.

Most of the time the patient will not have clearly formulated preferences in terms of physicians when the search process begins. Instead, these criteria and values will tend to emerge as the patient and spouse talk over what each doctor said and how they feel about him or her. After seeing several doctors, the patient can sit down and actually define criteria on paper and see how well each physician matches up. This is another occasion when the family will be glad to have written notes from these conferences and even tape recordings of the doctor's conclusions. Getting further opinions, then, not only gives more medical information, but also gives the patient a chance to select the right primary physician for him.

Getting Information from Doctors

Almost everyone who receives a diagnosis of cancer is confronting something quite unknown—and has a need for a great deal of information. When Pamela and Bob Mang were told their daughter had osteogenic sarcoma, they had a typical reaction: "We felt entirely out of control; we were so *shocked* to think Jessica's life was in jeopardy," Pamela says. "Then we realized that the more information we had, the more power we had to deal with the situation. By gaining knowledge, we could get back some of our control."

The Mangs also knew that Jessica had the same disease Ted Kennedy's son had had, and that the boy's leg had been amputated. Amputation was a treatment decision they had to face, and they didn't want to make decisions of this magnitude without information. Bob decided to gather this information from top physicians all over the country by telephone. He asked each doctor he talked to for the names of several specialists who were obviously considered experts by their peers. He didn't hesitate to call these physicians, identify himself, and tell them he wanted a telephone consultation and wanted to be billed for it. "Their time is worth money, after all," he says. Every doctor talked to him, some at great length, and as it turned out, only a few sent bills.

The Mangs gathered this information in an orderly way. Bob took notes the whole time he talked to the doctors, and afterward he and Pamela sat down and reviewed the conversation. They also began a collection of medical reference books that helped them understand terminology and the disease itself.

In gathering information directly from physicians, the Mangs came equipped with this background knowledge; they were therefore able to ask sophisticated questions and understand the complicated answers they received. One of their ongoing concerns as Jessica began treatment was, "What are the possible side effects? What is the worst possibility?" This became crucial knowledge when one drug did cause heart toxicity, a fairly improbable side effect, but one which they knew could happen. "If we'd had no idea that was a possibility," Pamela says, "It would have been awful. Even knowing it was, it was still a heavy blow."

The Mangs had learned just enough about this possibility to know where to look for more information. One thing they decided after their research was that high doses of Vitamin E might help repair the damage to Jessica's heart. Vitamin E is an anti-oxidant, and the adriamyacin she took is an oxidant. They discussed this with the primary physician they had chosen, who agreed that at least the vitamin supplement couldn't do any harm.

The Mangs also learned that Jessica's heart medicine robbed her body of potassium, which made necessary the use of diuretics. "It became a chemical mish-mash," Pamela says. "The minute she was off her chemo, I told the cardiologist we wanted these medications reduced a little. We knew from our research that this wouldn't cause any sudden, dramatic problems, and could be monitored. And it worked. We reduced her medication little by little until she was off everything. Today Jessica takes no medication—which the cardiologists said would never happen—and she has total heart function."

The Mangs were able to assume the responsibility they did for Jessica's treatment because they had thoroughly researched the possibilities—they were informed. In addition, they understood the nature of medical treatment. Particularly when cancer is involved, every treatment decision is a calculated risk. "Nobody knows for sure what will work best," Pamela emphasizes, "and that includes the physicians. They may have more information than we do, but they are still making human judgments. They don't have any God-given power for making those decisions. Recognizing that made a fundamental difference in our approach because we understood that we also had the ability to make careful, informed decisions, and we felt we had both the right and the responsibility to do that for Jessica."

Even though she was only ten years old, the Mangs felt that Jessica needed information, too, and therefore she must also participate in the process of becoming knowledgeable about the disease. They believed information would help her feel some personal control and security during the treatment, and when she asked questions about her cancer, they answered as well as they could. But they always encouraged her to put the questions on her list and to ask the doctor during her consultation with him. In this way Jessica gained a sense of her own rights and responsibility in her illness. Family members who are dealing with children, or with adult patients who are for some reason unable to control their own treatment, can similarly encourage the patient to seek information.

Approaching physicians with numerous questions is a relatively assertive act, and one not all patients are fully comfortable with. For these people, it helps to remember that the peace of mind gained by knowledge is an important factor in healing. And, of course, since it is the patient's body, he is entitled to make decisions about himself and to gather the information to make good decisions. This process can be made easier by good communication techniques with the physician, which are essential to any smooth relationship and are a key element in dealing with the doctor.

Communicating with the Doctor

A common complaint among patients is that they don't get a chance to really talk with their doctors. Communication is a two-way street, and it can indeed be true that the physician is not allowing time for this vital interchange of information. The doctor may have a hectic schedule, especially in a large hospital, and too many patients to be as sensitive as he might to a patient's emotional needs. Whatever the case, the patient can change the situation.

The first thing the patient can do is let the doctor know that he needs more time to talk. It is possible to do this in a way that is frank without being hostile: "Doctor, there are some things I want to talk to you about. I need fifteen minutes of your time." This is a specific request to which the doctor can respond. If the patient is setting up an appointment through the doctor's nurse, he should tell her, "I'd like the doctor to schedule an extra fifteen minutes with me so I can ask him some questions." This is only fair, since otherwise the physician's appointments will probably be clocked out in such a way that he will be very inconvenienced by giving the patient extra time. What I am suggesting is that it is really not a good idea to expect a busy doctor to drop everything for questions on the spur of the moment. Scheduling that communication time is both thoughtful and practical. It is also a good idea to stick within the allotted time and not insist on thirty minutes of questions and answers when you've asked for fifteen.

Getting time with the doctor is not the only problem some patients have. There can be more difficult communication problems that are derived from the emotional stress surrounding cancer. One patient I treated had a physician who told her flatly, "We're going to try this combination of treatments, but your prognosis is extremely poor. Frankly, I believe it's unrealistic to expect recovery." The patient first had to grapple with whether or not to continue with this physician, for whose expertise she had great respect. She decided to continue with him, but found that every time she talked to him he made gloomy references to her prognosis.

We discussed her dilemma. These references were depressing to her. She felt she could not let the situation continue. But she decided to give this relationship a chance to change by expressing her feelings. The next time she saw her doctor, she said, "Look, you've told me more than once what my prognosis is, and I know what you believe is going to happen. But it's very depressing for me to hear it over and over. I do understand what you think, and now I'd like you to not talk about my prognosis anymore." The doctor, who had apparently never been told anything like this before, was a little startled, but thereafter he tried very hard to cooperate with her request.

If the patient finds it just impossible to be this direct with the doctor, he can try another approach, by discussing the problem with his internist or family doctor. This other physician may agree to call the oncologist and say, "Look, what you're saying to this patient is really disturbing him. I think he'd do better if none of us mentions his prognosis in the future." Since doctors are often acquainted with one another, this approach can make sense to the family doctor. If it doesn't, a family member can seek a few minutes alone with the physician and explain. Whatever approach is used, it is important for a patient to express his feelings if discussions of this kind are deeply upsetting.

I would never want to imply that patient-physician problems are always the physician's fault. The physician is trained to cure disease, not necessarily to deal with the highly charged emotions and communication problems that can arise around a disease like cancer. Working with life-threatening illness does lead to difficulties for physicians. I have found most patients relate better to their doctors when they develop empathy for the doctor's problems.

One difficulty physicians who work with people who have cancer must contend with is their own frustration. Most physicians are attracted to medicine to relieve suffering and heal the sick, but with cancer they must work with great uncertainty as to the outcome. This is very stressful for the physician. He is also often asked by patients to shoulder the entire responsibility for the treatment. One reason Pamela and Bob Mang got along so smoothly with the various physicians who attended Jessica was that they understood this difficult situation and empathized. Pamela explains, "Although we were personally in a very stressful place, we kept in mind that doctors are human too. Whenever I got very upset with a doctor, I'd make myself stop and imagine what it was like to be in his shoes—how he was seeing it. I came to understand that doctors have fears, too, as many as anyone else. In particular, oncologists who work with children are in a very difficult position. During Jessica's treatment I watched a number of physicians burn out and leave the field because they just couldn't take it. And I couldn't blame them."

Some cancer specialists deal with their personal discomfort and frustration by emotionally distancing themselves from patients. Every physician feels a degree of personal connection to his patients, and when he is constantly seeing death among these people he cares for, he is almost always experiencing grief, although it may be at a deep, perhaps unconscious, level. This grieving can sap a doctor's emotional energy and make it harder for him to be patient and understanding. It can also make him take a cold and distant stance for his own self-protection. There's nothing malicious about this; it is a way of coping with a very difficult profession. Again, a patient who is upset with a doctor's behavior may feel more tolerant by imagining the position the doctor is in.

While doctors can inadvertently create poor medical relationships because of the difficulty of their profession, patients can equally create problems through their expectations. Many of us approach doctors as if they were God. Unfortunately, the medical system of the past reinforced that very attitude. Until recently, both doctors and patients believed doctors should be directive. This was displayed in many ways, such as the fact that prescriptions were written in the venerable language of Latin, which patients usually couldn't read. When this attitude prevailed, it was not common for a doctor to discuss side effects, and the concept of informed consent was not emphasized. The doctor simply told the patient what he was going to do. Patients, in turn, accepted the rather comfortable position of being treated like children who had no responsibility for their own bodies. Furthermore, they participated in putting their doctors on pedestals: the doctor had all the answers.

With cancer as with many other illnesses, the doctors do not have all the answers. Patients who have up until now relied on their doctors for their health sometimes become extremely angry when they confront this fact. "Doctor, you *should* be able to cure me." In a sense, the patient blames the doctor for his illness. And this anger is rooted in the patient's hidden belief that doctors are infallible.

There are other characteristics of cancer that tend to make some patients grow angry with the doctor. One is the fact that cancer is frequently "a silent disease," meaning that the patient goes in to see the doctor for a physical, feeling perfectly well, and is hit with a diagnosis of cancer. Some patients tell me bitterly, "I was feeling great until *he* told me I had cancer." What can happen next is that the patient feels a natural anger at the disease itself, and at the fact that he has cancer—but instead of admitting this anger, he may displace it onto the doctor. This phenomenon is common enough to have warranted a study at one cancer research center. The results showed that often patients leave the doctor who made their original diagnosis, and choose someone else for their primary care. The researchers concluded that the first doctor who said, "You have cancer" was often seen by the patient as the executioner. Even patients who stayed with this doctor frequently had so much anger and resentment that they were very uncooperative in treatment. Family members, of course, can take the same attitude. When either the patient or family feels a great deal of anger at the physician, it is worth examining whether this is really anger at the illness itself. Such anger is quite natural—but, if displaced onto the doctor, may significantly disrupt the doctor-patient relationship.

It is also natural for a patient to become angry if his treatment results in uncomfortable side effects, such as loss of hair, nausea, or weakness. With the best intentions, the patient has accepted this treatment plan, understanding that these symptoms might result. But two weeks later when he's not feeling well, he is likely to start thinking, "The hell with this! I want out!" It is generally not helpful for a patient not to ventilate this natural anger. We all do this when we have a distasteful chore; we may complain bitterly, but we get the resentment out of our systems and then go on and do it. Expressing your dislike of the whole thing makes it easier to accept the necessity.

Although such treatments as chemotherapy and radiation therapy may be clearly desirable in the beginning, the patient can lose sight of that fact when things get tough. Here is another time when communication with the doctor is very important. It's a good idea for the patient to go back and ask,

"Doc, are you *sure* I have to have this much treatment?" The patient may rapidly feel reassured that it is worth his while to go through this. On the other hand, he may find that his doctor considers the amount of treatment negotiable—which it sometimes is. Whether or not the patient decides to modify the treatment plan, discussing it will help him feel in charge. In fact, the patient *is* in charge and is choosing to take this treatment. It is easy to lose sight of this and feel that somehow the doctor is doing this to you. When that happens, the patient has a sense of losing control, of *having* to do it—even though this is not true since it is his body and his choice.

The patient who decides to follow a treatment plan and experiences uncomfortable side effects should not assume that there's no way around his misery. Many patients never communicate their problems with side effects to their doctors. Instead they take a stoic position. They need to remember that the doctor is there to deal with *any* physical problem, not just to combat the illness proper. They could say something like, "You know, this nausea is really awful, and it's very debilitating. Is there something else you can give me for it?" Physicians have a number of options in treating side effects and can often prescribe something or manipulate the treatment to make the patient more comfortable.

Communicating with the doctor, I know, can be difficult. Sometimes the patient's efforts to change the relationship are not successful, yet the patient feels the doctor's expertise is so valuable that he is reluctant to change to another physician. I have known patients who kept vacillating on this issue, saying to themselves over and over, "I don't like him, maybe he'll change, maybe I'll leave him, I don't like this." This uncommitted attitude can make a patient very frustrated. It's generally better when the patient makes a clear choice of some kind and relieves his mind of the anxiety of indecision. It can be something as limited as, "Okay, I don't like him, but I'm going to stick with him for the next six months. Then I'll reconsider."

A patient in this situation can also feel better after expressing his negative feelings to his family and support people. This releases some of the frustration and anger, even though it doesn't change the relationship. If the patient is going to stay with the doctor, suppressing these feelings will not help. It's better to come home and say, "Damn it, I don't like that guy! I think he knows what he's doing, but he's very insensitive and nasty!" If the patient is allowed to vent his frustration, he will feel better for it.

On Being Depersonalized

Some patients complain that their doctors and other medical staff treat them coldly and without respect. These complaints are frequent enough that I feel obliged to address this issue.

A typical example of this problem is time spent in the waiting room. Some doctors or clinics indeed seem to have little ability to schedule patients well; it is not uncommon to hear, "I had to wait three hours in the reception area for a ten minute visit with my doctor." Certainly, if this happens, the patient is entitled to ask that his own time be respected in the future.

Some people get very angry in this kind of situation, but repressing the anger and then abruptly spilling it out on the doctor may not yield very good results. More direct communication can be quite effective. You can say, "Doctor, it just doesn't work for me to come and sit for three hours. What can we do so this doesn't happen again?"

It can be more difficult to resolve complaints about impersonal treatment from an institution, and it is the large hospitals patients complain most about. They go because these large cancer centers give some of the most sophisticated care available and are often staffed with very experienced physicians. Many of these institutions, of course, offer personalized care. But some patients have expressed great anger at the stark, impersonal treatment they received during a time that was already very difficult for them. They have also found it difficult to have an effect on what was happening. One of my patients, Bob Gilley, reacted to such depersonalization in aggressive and imaginative ways. While he did not effect great change in the way he was treated, he did have an impact, and he felt much better for having expressed himself. Bob's style, as you will see, is his own. His response to the depersonalization he experienced was forthright and expressive.

Bob initially became upset during the nine hours it took the hospital to process him in. First of all, it frightened him and his wife, BJ, to sit so long in a waiting room with people in advanced stages of cancer. "We assumed the same thing would happen to me that was happening to them," he says. Finally Bob was given a double room and a bathtub to share with thirty-five other patients. In itself that wasn't a problem, but a young doctor had just told Bob off-handedly, "Do you know the latest findings suggest cancer might be contagious?" Thoroughly upset, Bob always sterilized the bathtub twice before he got in it.

In no time Bob was telling the staff, "If I ran my business the way you run yours, I wouldn't be in business." He explains, "Their scheduling was absurd. They wanted me to stay nine days to get test results, and by rearranging the test schedules I was able to compact everything into four days. They were prepared to just totally waste my time."

Bob was also confrontive with the medical staff. "One time a chemotherapist came into my room to check me out, and he was smoking and dropped ashes on me! I was infuriated, and he just went about his business without any apology. I told him, 'You get out of my room, and don't you ever come back.'

"This cancer center was also a teaching hospital, and the longer the white robe a doctor wears there, the more status he has. Well, one day in comes this doctor with a robe down to his ankles, and all these other guys following him with their little notepads. He said not one word to me, not even 'Good morning.' He just started punching my body and telling them my history. It really hacked me off.

" 'Don't do that to me,' I told him. Of course, he was taken aback. He said, 'I beg your pardon?'

"I said, 'Don't you touch me until you introduce yourself and ask my permission to do that to me.' You could see this really burned him up, because he was the great doctor.

"I added, 'I want you to understand something. I want to be nice, but I'm here as a paying customer, so don't do that to me. I don't like it.' "

In this instance, perhaps predictably, Bob's feelings were not respected. He reports, "That doctor got infuriated, and told me *I* was arrogant and insolent. And I told him to get out of my room. I didn't bother to say it in a nice way, either."

Perhaps Bob's greatest difficulty was with the casual attitude in this institution toward his personal needs—in other words, a conspicuous absence of tender, loving care.

This became a major issue one day when he was driven from his room that was located in an annex to the main hospital for testing, and another stay while he received chemotherapy. Bob had already found that the orderlies who picked him up and drove him the three miles back were extremely casual about their scheduling. "They'd tell me they'd be back at 11:00, and then they wouldn't show up until 1:00. Well, I was having some strong side effects right then, and I didn't like waiting so long— I just wanted to get back in my own bed.

"So this time, when they took me I asked when they'd be back. And once again they said, 'Oh, around 11:00.'

"This time I said, 'Guys, you've been telling me this, but you haven't done it. I want to tell you to set your watch by that big clock up on the wall because when that clock hits 11:00, I'm going to walk back.'

"Of course they said, 'We'll be back for you on time. Don't worry.'

"I explained this to the head nurse too. I told her, 'I'm tired of being sick and turning green in your waiting room.'

"After my tests I lay in that waiting room in kind of a fetal position, with my legs pulled up against my stomach—it makes you feel better when you're nauseated—and I watched that clock. At 11:00 I said, 'Are the orderlies here?'

"The head nurse said they weren't. So I said, 'Well, I'm getting out of here.'

"She said, 'You can't do that!'

" 'Yeah I can, 'cause I'm a lot bigger than you are.' "

The nurse tried to take hold of Bob's arm, but he pulled loose and said, "Don't you do that!" She then began calling for help, while Bob, in pajamas and bathrobe, walked out the door and three miles up the road to the main hospital to the astonishment of people driving past. When he got there, he got in bed. And, he says, "I really felt good about doing what I did."

Bob complained about things many hospital patients endure as inevitable—being wakened unnecessarily at 5:00 a.m. by bright room lights, being impersonally poked by nameless doctors. Breaking through to an institution that depersonalizes you is not necessarily easy, as evidenced by Bob's experience. When it is a question of getting vital care or essential personal respect, it may be necessary to repeatedly assert your desires, both verbally and nonverbally. In fact, there are indications that it is necessary to do this to get superior care in some hospitals. A sociologist studied patient-staff interactions at Stanford Hospital, and in his dissertation, he documented one of his findings on this subject: essentially he found that it's the squeaky wheel that gets the grease. If you are dealing with medical personnel who tend to treat all patients like numbers, you may have to be a "squeaky wheel" to get the respect and care you need.

A word of caution, however, to would-be squeaky wheels. There is sometimes a very fine line between a squeaky wheel and a pain in the neck! While I advocate speaking out and making sure your needs are attended to, a patient must be careful not to unduly antagonize doctors and nurses and, perhaps, damage otherwise good relationships.

It's also important to remember that in many hospitals the medical staff is overworked. Doctors and nurses with extremely busy schedules don't have time to give unlimited individual attention—such as patients receive from television's Dr. Marcus Welby—and rarely do real-life medical people have Welby's bedside manner. This is especially true in hospital wards that are sometimes understaffed.

At the same time, it is helpful to bear in mind that what we have said about the stress experienced by doctors is equally true of other medical personnel. Those who work in cancer centers, especially, can be overwhelmed by their grief and their inability to help patients as they would like. They may find it very draining to see patients as human beings and relate warmly to them in the midst of all the uncertainty of cancer.

While this chapter has dealt with problems patients and family members have in communicating with physicians, this should not be taken to mean these problems are universal. Many of my patients have excellent relationships with their doctors, governed by mutual respect. The ideas here are for those who are having difficulties in this critical area. If the patient in your family is having problems of this kind, by all means, he should be supported in his efforts to overcome them. A rereading of this chapter will show that in one way or another, all the problems mentioned center on communication. In attempts to create a healthy environment, good communication is always a key. In the following chapter, this topic will be looked at with emphasis on communicating feelings—a skill of great importance in every family and needed even more when the family is under the stress of a crisis.

Chapter 7

Communicating Feelings

T he open expression of feelings within a family is so crucial
to the overall health of its members that the subject has
come up repeatedly in this book—and will continue to be
discussed. This chapter is exclusively devoted to the communication of feelings: why we deny them, why we need to express them,
how to encourage expression, and how to respond. The reason
for my emphasis on this subject is that communicating feelings
within the family is paramount in creating a healing atmosphere and helping the patient gain the psychological strength
to work toward recovery.

If the examples in this book have convinced you that your
family has communication problems, don't be alarmed—every
family does in some areas, even the healthiest. But communication is a matter of learned behavior, and bad habits can be
replaced with good ones. Bear in mind, too, that problems
within a family are usually magnified by a crisis such as the
diagnosis of cancer. Crisis makes communication far more
important, and we often become acutely aware of our difficulty
talking with one another only when we have something really
important to talk over.

It is well established that the communication of our feelings
to others is necessary to mental and emotional well-being. For

people with cancer this is doubly true. Many people who are experiencing cancer seem, on the surface, to communicate well, but a closer look shows that the only feelings they communicate are cheerfulness, optimism, and hope about getting better. What they don't communicate is the whole range of natural feelings we sometimes call "negative," including anxiety, depression, hopelessness, and anger at the fact that they have cancer. This bottling-up of feelings, as I mentioned in chapter 1, has been found to correlate with cancer. People diagnosed with cancer frequently suffer from suppressed feelings, and this suppression of feelings seems to impair the efficient operation of the immune system. Undoubtedly it impairs the quality of life itself since repressed feelings lead to depression.

Patients and families who understand how intimately health is related to the free expression of feelings may consider changing family patterns of communication. While the family got along up until now, the crisis of illness may make change a necessity. Those families that do change ironically realize a benefit from the crisis—without it they might have gone on forever living "lives of quiet desperation."

Cancer Patients and the Denial of Feelings

In our culture many people deny "negative" emotions. We are learning more each day about the significant impact this denial has on health. Heart disease, for instance, has been associated with the denial of anxiety. Cancer is often associated with the denial of anger. This denial usually means that patients don't just refrain from talking about the anger, they refrain from feeling it. Note, however, that such denial can be present in other family members; seldom is the patient the only member of the household who holds back feelings since our culture as a whole encourages us to deny a certain range of feelings.

The person in the family facing cancer may not only mask his anger but he may also cover up and deny the resulting depression. Instead, he may appear to be pleasant, content, and generally on top of the world. I had one such patient who agreed to take psychologcal tests that revealed an extremely depressed inner self. When I talked with her and her husband about this, she sat silent, thinking it over, but he was irate. "Depression—Julie? She's the most carefree, happy-go-lucky woman . . . she doesn't have a problem in the world!" To the one who was closest to her, Julie seemed to be an unusually cheerful person. But to me, the cause of her depression—denial of feelings—was fairly obvious as her husband talked. "She never gets upset about anything!" he proclaimed. "We've had some serious financial problems, thought we might lose the house, had one son who was getting in scrapes with the law. She *never* got upset. I'm the one who gets upset and lets it all out. Julie never loses her cool."

Julie herself finally chimed in to affirm that all he said was true, and she really couldn't see how the test results could be right. I knew she was sincere. Typically, a person's denial is not only hidden from family members but hidden from the person himself. This means that someone who begins to communicate long-denied feelings to the family is acting very courageously by discovering "a new me." He is often more surprised than anyone at the feelings that emerge.

We do not unlearn denial overnight but through day by day attention to our feelings. It would be surprising if it were simple to overcome since the roots of denial usually lie deep in childhood, sometimes in the earliest years. Usually, it is the result of some degree of rejection as a young child. Ideally, a child receives unconditional acceptance from his parents, which encourages him to freely assert his needs and express his feelings. But a disapproving parent, or one who withholds significant nurturing, can cause a child to feel unsafe. A toddler soon learns, for instance, that if he gets angry with his mother and yells, "No!" she will get very angry back and not hold him all afternoon. Such a child may learn to repress his assertive anger, and usually a number of other feelings, too. Perhaps his father's acceptance is conditional upon the child smiling and acting happy, so he learns to "put on a happy face." Such a child grows up to be an adult who rarely feels angry, expresses sadness, or looks to other people for caretaking. "Don't worry about me," he'll say. "I don't need a thing. I'm fine." He is sincere, of course, but inside he may also be very unhappy.

Such a person may internally reject not only his anger but another part of him that I think of as his vulnerable, needy self.

The child who was discouraged from crying often grows up to be the adult who doesn't want to be a bother to anyone. As a result, when he is under a lot of stress and feels sad, needy, and vulnerable, he will suppress these feelings rather than seek out somebody to listen to and hold him. This may result in an image of strength and self-sufficiency, "Nothing gets John down— he's got it together." Neither John nor those closest to him know how needy and sad he really feels. Since he never lets himself cry on somebody's shoulder, he never gets the support he needs under stress.

There is a very important consequence of his denial, however. Because he denies his anger and doesn't let off steam, he may well become depressed or experience one of the "stress-related" diseases. Current research in the field of psychosomatic medicine indicates that denial of feelings can trigger a variety of illnesses, including heart disease, ulcerative colitis, and ulcer disease as well as cancer. Denial has been shown to exacerbate an existing disease. In one of the early psychological studies of cancer, Bruno Klopfer was able to predict which patients would have fast versus slow growing tumors by measuring the amount of denial the person used. Those with a strong need to maintain an image of "looking good" when they were in emotional pain had the fastest growing tumors.

A person is more likely to suffer from the syndrome I've described if he is a first-born. This is significant because statistics indicate a higher incidence of cancer in people who were first-born children. One reason for this is thought to be that families are more likely to put pressure on the first-born to grow up quickly; thus the child is encouraged to deny his vulnerable self at a very early age. Typically, the second child, who may be born when the first-born is between eighteen and thirty-six months old, suddenly gets all the attention. Naturally, the first-born feels quite frightened and rejected by all this. He is at an age where he should be acting defiant and assertive, saying "No!" to his mother in an effort to define himself. Children who are encouraged to do this and who meet firm adult limits, but are not rejected for their feelings, learn that it is safe to be separate from their mother and angry with her. But with the new baby around, all this takes on a different light. Now it's *not* safe to yell at Mother. Things become too uncertain. These factors

may be compounded, of course, by the parents' own tempera-
ments and beliefs about anger and vulnerability. If they were
raised stereotypically, little Johnny might be encouraged to "act
like a man" from the time he can walk—meaning don't cry and
don't be needy. Or, if the mother is overwhelmed with the care
of a difficult second infant, she may encourage the oldest girl
child to be a "little mother" at two. At any rate, these are some
of the factors that go toward creating an adult who denies his
feelings and often develops physical symptoms under stress.

Encouraging the Expression of Feelings

Anger and depression tend to dissipate when we fully experience and express them. For many people learning to let out
feelings will seem risky and frightening. One of my patients felt
a great deal of grief over the loss of her daughter who had died
some months before. Dorothy, like many, had borne the loss
with a stiff upper lip, handled arrangements, and tried to cope
bravely. When she became very sad, she went off alone to cry.
And she couldn't get over her depression. I encouraged her,
"Go ahead and let yourself cry. Let somebody hold and support you. When you do, you'll find that a lot of your tiredness
and lack of energy will start to lift." Finally Dorothy did make
this breakthrough, and she felt much less depressed the next
time I saw her. Suppressing her feelings had only deepened her
depression.

One common feeling people face with cancer, and one they
are likely to suppress, is fear about their illness. Some acknowledge their fear to themselves but hide it from family members in
order not to burden them. This often results in the patient
feeling isolated and alone, which compounds his fear. Hiding
his "unseemly" emotion, the patient becomes more and more
emotionally removed so that the fear builds rather than being
diminished by the comforting of a loved one. The spouses of
patients sometimes do the same thing. "The last thing my wife
needs is to have to worry about me," a husband might say. The
irony of such concealment is that it frequently invites the patient to worry much more than she ever would have. She may
sense something is wrong and begin to wonder: "Does he know

something I don't know about my diagnosis? Is his business running into real trouble? Maybe he's thinking about leaving me now that I'm so sick." Whatever her speculations, they will provoke much more anxiety than would a simple expression of her husband's fear about losing her.

Men often have more difficulty than women with expressing fear because of the role imposed on them by cultural stereotypes. A man with a "John Wayne" notion of how he ought to act may be very frightened at the thought of cancer undermining his strength and equally frightened at the idea of revealing his fear to anyone. A wife who senses this sort of difficulty needs to be sensitive and caring in her approach. She may think he's feeling scared, but it's not very effective to ask, "Are you scared?" The patient has a need to define and express his own feelings. A better way to encourage this is to simply open the door for that expression. So she might ask, "John, is anything bothering you?" If he doesn't answer, she can go on with something like, "Are you having any difficulties?" This gives him the opportunity to get in touch with his feelings, something that people who bottle up their emotions usually don't do. John is probably not aware that his fear is affecting him so deeply. In fact, his image of himself has caused him to deny any feelings of fear. However, his wife understands that he is frightened, and she wants John to come to terms with his fear—and realize that there's nothing wrong with feeling that way.

There are many ways to open the door to feeling communication so long as the question is asked in an open-ended way, without pressure or expectation of immediate response. "Is there anything going on with you right now you want to talk about?" is the kind of question that gives the patient an opening to answer, "Yes, maybe there is now that you ask."

Just as likely, a person who is unused to expressing feelings may say, "No! Nothing's wrong with me." If the response is this defensive, chances are something *is* wrong, but the only thing to do with such an answer is respect it. Let the person know you are not going to push or try to define his feelings for him. So the answer should be something like, "Okay. I hear you. It just looked to me like you might be feeling bad. If you ever have feelings you want to talk about, I'm here." And then let it go.

In essence, the family member who invites expression in this manner and shows respect for the patient's limits has created the environment in which the patient can talk about difficult feelings in the future. The patient may even go away and think through what happened, realizing that he has not been pursued or pressured to talk, and then come back to take up the invitation. "You know, I thought about what you said, and I guess I am feeling anxious."

Helping a patient open up to denied feelings is a delicate process and one that demands the understanding and patience of love. Asking about feelings is never a wasted gesture; even if the patient doesn't return to talk about them, he has learned that you do have concern, you do respect his limits, and you are willing to listen if he ever needs to talk. Needless to say, such an invitation to self-expression is also appropriate for other members of the family who seem troubled. The mere offer to talk *is* good communication and helps to create a healthier, more intimate family.

The Cheerleading Impulse

Many people in our culture believe that the best way to deal with cancer emotionally is to project a "positive mental attitude" at all times. But rather than being helpful, this behavior can be harmful. If the patient or family is not feeling "positive," this can encourage the suppression of feelings. For instance, a patient may say to his wife, "I'm worried sick about how you and the kids are going to survive if I'm not here."

The "positive" wife may ignore the feeling message of this statement, which communicates fear, anxiety, and concern, and respond "Don't worry, dear—you're not going to die. You'll get well again." She may sincerely believe this, but that isn't the issue, and it may not be helpful to her husband to respond to his anxiety with denial. He certainly has grounds for feeling uncertain about his future and he needs to deal directly with that anxiety. Looking at the possibility of death is something all of us find upsetting, but denying the anxiety of this unknown future is unrealistic. People generally feel better when they sit down and take a look at the uncertainty and try to prepare to some extent for what might happen. If the man in this example is able to examine the financial future of his family and feel assured that they would be able to manage, no matter what, he will be a good deal more relaxed. Then he and his wife will have more energy to defend against the worst and work hard for his recovery.

When a patient expresses his fear of dying—or when any family member expresses anxiety about the patient's future—it should be accepted that these fears are real and important, even though some people may believe they're exaggerated. So a sensitive answer might be something like, "I understand you're frightened by this. It's a really difficult situation." This gives the patient an opening to talk more about his fear, cry, be angry, or otherwise express his anxiety. He may even feel much better about just being heard. Once he has had his chance to talk, *then* he may move to a more positive vein, and this time it's more likely to be true optimism, not a brittle denial or "whistling in the dark." Then a family member can say, "I know how you feel, and I still want to keep doing everything we know how to help you recover. I know you might not recover; you might die. But I still want to give it our best shot."

I think it's obvious that this is a very different way of handling the expression of a patient's fear than saying, "Oh, you're not going to die, don't even think about it," a response that encourages denial and hopelessness. The more open response offers a realistic optimism while acknowledging that death is a possibility. It offers something else to the patient that denial does not—the genuine support of a loving family member who is willing to work with him and be there, whatever happens. If we put ourselves in the patient's shoes, it's easy to imagine just how comforting and warming that support would be.

Family members, of course, are not the only people who are likely to play cheerleader and discount the patient's difficult feelings. Unfortunately, friends may do this, and even medical professionals. When Pat McNamara's doctor was talking to her and her husband Tom just after her second mastectomy, they displayed the anxiety and grief natural to anyone who undergoes such a traumatic change. The doctor quickly supplied a very dubious piece of positive thinking: "Don't be so concerned about losing a breast. Other parts of the body can be attractive, too."

Tom's comment on this exchange was, "I know he was trying to cheer us up. But we were overcome with grief and confusion. We needed supportive understanding of those feelings, not out-and-out denial, as if our feelings were trivial and foolish."

The positive attitude is one some people sustain to the bitter end; in its extreme form, this cheerleading denies the patient the right to experience any of his difficult feelings and to work them through by communicating them to someone. An adult has more power to seek out someone to talk to when this happens than a child does. Often, too, parents of children with cancer decide that it's best to shield the young person from all emotional pain—which, of course, is not possible. Denying a child the right to experience his fear and anger only drives these feelings underground and can lead to extreme helplessness and depression. During the course of my research, I have met parents who encouraged "optimism" to a pathological degree.

One mother, whom I will call Mary Ann, had a twelve-year-old daughter, Lisa, whose bone cancer was fairly advanced when it was diagnosed. This mother's reaction was to deny her own and Lisa's grief. "My daughter and I had the same kind of happy personalities," she says. "When the doctors gave us bad news, no matter how terrible it was, we'd find something to laugh about. You won't believe it, but I had Lisa laughing within five minutes of telling her that her leg would probably have to be amputated."

An amputation, needless to say, is nothing to laugh about. By way of contrast, Bob and Pamela Mang helped their daughter express her feelings when they told her she would have to have an amputation or a partial removal of bone from her leg. They even allowed her to help make the decision. At first stunned, Jessica asked questions, and they talked about the decision. Then, as Jessica tells it, "I cried a lot, we all sat around and cried and hugged and talked. Finally I stopped crying and said, 'That's over. I'll just let this be and I can sleep on it.'" While she did, her father sobbed.

The Mangs were able to move on from this point with

realistic optimism and boundless determination. Unfortunately, Mary Ann and her daughter were caught in an unrealistic denial of their grief and fear. Moreover, Mary Ann prevented the possibility of intimate communication with her husband during this time by bringing Lisa into their double bed at night during her last several months of life. "I didn't want her to be alone to think any bad thoughts," Mary Ann says calmly. While this took away any chance Lisa might have had to get in touch with her feelings, it also meant Bill and Mary Ann had no intimate time, during these months.

This family's denial of feelings was evident in Mary Ann and Bill's relationship throughout the crisis of Lisa's dying. "We weren't getting along very well during her last days," Mary Ann says, "but we never argued. He knew he had to go along with me, and as long as he did, everything was fine. If he didn't agree, I didn't want to hear it. I don't fight. If he pushes me, I blow up, that's all. I'm sure Lisa never sensed any of the friction between us though."

Tragically, Lisa was denied any opportunity to express her feelings as she neared death. When her mother told her she was soon going to die, the little girl said, "I'm not frightened." After that, they didn't talk.

Mary Ann is an example of the person who rigidly denies her own grief and fear. During the illness, she forbade her husband to show sadness with such statements as, "Come on, there's no need to have such a long face!" when of course there was a need. At the funeral, she did not cry, and as far as I know has never cried on the shoulder of anyone, including her husband, since then. She explained that she comes from a family that taught her this kind of "strength." "It's an unwritten rule that none of us ever cry. So I stayed very strong throughout the entire ordeal, and I know how proud my parents were of me. . . ."

This pride is gained at a very high price. While Mary Ann's rigorous denial of "negative" feelings alienated her husband and committed her daughter to isolation and silence, it is now literally making Mary Ann sick; she is being treated for dangerously high blood pressure. She never went back to work since Lisa's diagnosis and now spends her life in a darkened living room, trying to defend herself against a host of painful feelings that refuse to stay suppressed. Both her physical and her mental health are in jeopardy.

Mary Ann's case is certainly extreme, but it illustrates how a family member's denial of feelings can have a profound impact on the patient, all other family members, and themselves. Whether the patient is a child or an adult, family members can be tremendously helpful in encouraging the expression of all the range of feelings natural to this illness. During the course of Jessica's illness, the Mangs learned how dangerous suppressed feelings were to the child. They taught her to express her anger by listening for it and accepting it. When Jessica periodically burst out with, "It's not fair!" her parents promptly reacted with, "You're damn right it's not!" Rather than trying to calm her down, they acted as sounding boards. This kind of help met one of Jessica's deepest needs just then and expressed brave and authentic love on the part of her parents. I believe it contributed to the quality of Jessica's experience. She maintained an incredible self-image, particularly considering she was a twelve-year-old who had been through an amputation of her leg and a disease like cancer.

How Do We Tell the Children?

When the patient is a child, parents face a special challenge in helping the child express the anger, fear, grief, and uncertainty every cancer patient feels. There is seldom any question about whether or not to tell the young patient since medical treatment usually makes this necessary. But when the patient is a parent or beloved grandparent, adults must deal with how to tell the children in the household, a question that is often complicated by the children's ages. Many adults use a form of denial by deciding not to tell the children what's happening. In doing this, they establish a pretense of normalcy in the household that denies the obvious truth.

Children, as we tend to forget, are very observant. When adults are suddenly silent, serious, or get involved in long secret discussions, or disappear for unspecified appointments, any child knows something major has happened. An older child may sleuth out the truth one way or another while a younger child may just become extremely anxious and threatened at this inexplicable change. Any child in this situation is likely to take a cue from the adults and deny his fear of this unknown trouble. But for children, as for adults, the unknown is almost always more frightening than the known.

Parents may make a serious mistake when they exclude their children from an open discussion about the patient's disease and prevent them from expressing their feelings about it. Sometimes parents keep silent even when the illness is making apparent physical changes in the patient. A child in this situation can see that their mother or father is sick and go on to develop a belief that it is somehow his fault. "I made too much noise," or "I shouldn't have been such a bother." Ironically, when parents try to protect their children from the responsibility of knowing about the illness, the children usually proceed to take on too much responsibility for the illness.

Providing children with information about the disease helps allay their anxiety and protects them from irrational fears. This does not mean they should be given a college course in cancer, however, nor should adults dump a great deal of their own anxiety on the children. Instead, the children can be given as much information as they ask for, not unlike telling children about sex for the first time. You begin by giving them a little essential information, such as "We've learned Mommy has cancer." Then allow the child to ask as many questions as he wants. Your children will let you know how much they're ready to handle. In the case of a smaller child, it's often helpful to let him know he is not responsible for the illness and to let him express his anger and fear at having a mother or father who's sick and not as available to him. This alleviates any guilt that may result from the child having these natural feelings.

Communicating Feelings in a Healthy Way

You may recall that Mary Ann's strategy for letting her husband know she was angry was to "blow up." As most people know, habitually losing your temper is not a healthy way of communicating anger, even though it expresses feelings. Feelings within a family are best expressed in ways that are respectful and that leave the door open for other members to communicate their feelings on the issue. The goal is to be open and direct while maintaining respect for other people's autonomy—for their right to their own opinions and emotions.

The cheerleading I've talked about in this chapter is an example of failure to respect the other person's feelings and will often occur in families where individual autonomy is not promoted. In other words, the family member wants to fix the patient's feelings, so when the patient says, "I'm sad," the family member may say, "Nonsense! You can't be sad—look what you've got going for you!" In families that don't promote autonomy, a similar disrespect is shown by members who routinely speak for other members. I may ask a patient, "How are you feeling today?" and her husband will answer, "Oh, she's fine." In doing this repeatedly, he demonstrates that the boundaries between them are not clearly drawn, and they don't allow one another to be separate individuals. Good communication can be best promoted when everyone is permitted to express their own feelings and is encouraged not to let others speak for them.

When something like this is a problem, families can develop healthy ways of communicating about it. The McNamara family is a good example. After Pat learned of her cancer, she began to realize that her close-knit, loving family also had a tendency to insist that each individual go along with the majority, regardless of his or her feelings. In learning to take care of her own needs and protect her health, Pat had to confront this problem. "For instance," she explains, "I might have been extremely tired, but the family expected me to prepare Sunday dinner for ten people. And it used to be that I'd do it, just to please everyone, and it could be that they'd be a little pushy about it, too. Well, today we have an expression in our family that we all use when we feel that happening: 'Quit the steamrolling.' Now they all understand that if I really don't want to prepare that big dinner, they're not to roll over me. I might be in the minority, but they have to respect my rights. And the same rule applies to my husband and the children; nobody gets steamrolled anymore."

Learning better communication inevitably means that there may be times when your expression of feeling is not responded to or is shunted aside by cheerleading or some other reaction. If you need to express painful feelings but find another family member trying to "fix" them, it's important to let him know how you feel about that while bearing in mind that he probably finds it quite difficult to listen to your feelings. You might say, "Wait a minute. Telling me not to worry about my cancer isn't very helpful to me. It would be better if you would just listen to my feelings. If you can't do that right now, okay. But what you are doing really isn't helpful." And then *stop*. At that point, you've said enough.

The basic pattern of communicating feelings is very simple: someone expresses them openly, and someone hears them and acknowledges them. Notice that the listener doesn't have to "fix" them. Many a well-meaning person who hears a family member express sadness will jump in and say, "I'll tell you what—let's go to a funny movie!" There's a time and place for this suggestion, but it is not when someone is expressing sadness. A healthy respect for autonomy means assuming that the other person—especially one who is ill—can take care of himself.

Paradoxically, really "fixing it" for someone means simply hearing them out and empathizing with that difficult feeling, rather than trying to fix anything. "Of course you're scared—I'd be scared." Or, "I know you're really sad." This is best followed by an affirmation of your love and sympathy: "I'm so sorry this is so hard for you right now." Probably the most valuable thing any of us can add at this point is the assurance of our love and support. "I want you to know I love you and care about you. And I'll try to talk to you about this anytime you need to." This is communicating feelings at its best—and it will do more to "fix things," to ease painful emotions, than anything else you can do.

Chapter 8

Surviving and Thriving
as a Family

E very chapter of *The Healing Family* is about how a family dealing with cancer can both survive and thrive, but this chapter has a special emphasis. It invites the family to consider not just how to effectively cope with this long-term illness but also how to put energy into building a joyful, satisfying life.

This idea is shocking to many people because in our culture people believe that when a life-threatening crisis occurs, we should all stop living and concentrate on grieving. When the crisis is a major illness, there can be subtle pressure on family members to abandon all their pleasures and focus on the patient. But that often serves no meaningful purpose; in fact, it can be self-defeating—life must go on.

Life is for Living

As I've discussed previously, when a family is under stress the members desperately need their own recreation and purposeful activities. Unfortunately, we live in a society that has a poor understanding of health and how it is related to stress. Sometimes family members feel considerable pressure to deny their own needs, drop everything they care about, and focus on the patient. One couple I worked with felt this pressure very directly. The wife, who had lung cancer, agreed that her husband should go golfing as usual on Saturday afternoons. He worked hard, spent evenings with her, and loved to unwind by playing a golf game.

No sooner was he on the course, however, than he began to get comments from acquaintances he ran into. "Well, I thought Marjorie was sick!" Some people said nothing, but their expressions were cold and judgmental. Poor Don already felt just a little bit guilty anyway; this was all it took to make him decide he just couldn't go golfing anymore. The message he inferred from these people was "Shame on you for having a good time when your wife is sick!"

The irony is that the opposite is often true. Family members who take good care of themselves are to be congratulated. I don't mean to imply that the family should just pick itself up after the diagnosis and say, "Oh well, we're all going to act as if nothing has happened." This denies the real strain of living with an illness. But the opposite, saying, "Oh my God, Mother has cancer, everything's got to stop," is at least as harmful. For every member of the family, including the patient, it is healthier to find a balance that helps each individual seek the highest possible quality of life.

In order for family members to do this, they must recognize that their constant presence is not essential to the patient. The spouse who is always at the patient's side may be both overcontrolling and overprotecting—and headed for a health breakdown of his own. I don't believe anyone sacrifices his own life for someone else out of any motive but caring, yet it's just not realistic to think that we are so needed that we can't take off time for our needs.

An extreme case of this was Mary Ann, the mother I talked about in the last chapter. She left the accounting office she worked in to take Lisa to the orthopedic surgeon. When the child's cancer was diagnosed, Mary Ann called in her resignation. She never went back to her job. During the first three weeks of Lisa's illness, both Mary Ann and her husband sat in the children's hospital beside their daughter. Thereafter, Bill went to work, while Mary Ann slept in Lisa's room every night. For the next eight months Mary Ann was at Lisa's side 24 hours a day. As the little girl got sicker and realized she was dying, she was burdened by this attention. On top of her own fear, she felt guilty for the grief her mother was experiencing. A patient in this position may actually feel guilty about dying. When the husband, for instance, has centered his whole life on his wife, she can only feel burdened by the responsibility to try to live for his sake. This is not the same thing as a will to live, and it is not healthy for anyone concerned. Mary Ann, as I mentioned, has been quite unable to resume life in the year since Lisa died.

Occasionally I see a spouse adopt an equally unhealthy attitude toward the diagnosis by cutting the patient out of his life. Believing that sadness and fear are unmanly, some men suddenly become extremely busy in an effort to try to distance themselves from these feelings. These are people who will often bury themselves in work as an escape. They spend less and less time with the patient. On the surface, they may seem cold and uncaring, but the truth is that they often feel so much need that they're quite frightened. In a sense, they can't stand to think their wife may die, so they abandon her before death occurs. "My wife is likely to die, so I'd better not depend on her for anything." In a way, they accept her death before it happens. "When she dies, I won't be bowled over. I'll survive without her." Certainly this long illness is a very lonely time for them and for their wives. But their avoidance of the illness is as unhealthy as the other extreme of martyrdom.

A middle position for a family member is of one who can be loving and supportive of the patient while maintaining his own life and his own satisfactions that are necessary to his health and well-being. Walter Greenblatt, the Dallas insurance agent, realized that his wife Carol's bone cancer would be a long illness. "For my own mental health," he says, "I needed to take some quick, get-away vacations by myself." Carol was entirely supportive of this idea, and periodically Walter took off for a day or two. One summer weekend, for instance, he spent two days backpacking in the mountains of Colorado. Walter and Carol also talked about his need for a social life, even though she began to feel too tired to go out in the evening. He kept up their friendships. He went with married couples to the theater or symphony, and he kept going to dinner parties. There was a marked difference between this and the avoidance behavior just mentioned. Walter always included Carol. He would sit down and talk with her about where he'd been, what had happened during the evening, and so on and give her little details she could enjoy. He says, "By talking with her, I included her, and I'd feel as though she'd been there with me."

Often we feel that taking care of ourselves and coping with a long-term illness means fundamental health care only. While sleep, relaxation, exercise, and nutrition are necessary, a key ingredient of health is recreation and pleasure. Life *is* for living, not just enduring. There's a very real need for joy and happiness in all families—*including* those that have a member who has cancer.

Dealing with the Secret Wish

Each of us has a strong need to keep his life stabilized and to fulfill his major needs. When family members sacrifice themselves, they will sooner or later become resentful of the cancer patient. Feeling they can't talk with anyone about this, they keep thoughts like, "I wish this were over with" to themselves. This thought, which I call the "the secret wish," is not unusual and is a natural response to extreme self-sacrifice. It is also natural for the family member to then become consumed with guilt. There is no way to thrive as an individual carrying such a burden; in fact, it may begin to feel difficult to even survive.

As complex as the problem of the Secret Wish may sound, the solution can be simple—do not give up those things that are really meaningful to you. Working as a family to see that everyone's needs are fulfilled, in the way I described in chapter 3, is good insurance that this won't happen. If it is already happening, the reason is usually that the family member believes the patient wants things this way. In that case, the best approach is to sit down and talk about it.

Very often when family members do this, they discover that the patient doesn't want their self-sacrifice at all. The husband of one of my patients had been spending all his time at home. Finally he got up his nerve to tell his wife that he really needed to play golf. He explained to her, "Judy, I really want to be supportive of you all the way. I've decided that to do that I need to get some outdoor exercise, to work off stress and relax. My golf game is a really good way for me to do that, and remember how refreshed I always felt afterwards? I like the guys I play with, and I think their company is good for me. I think if I go back to my weekly game, I'll have more to give you. How do you feel about that?"

Judy listened to this careful explanation and then said, "Oh, George, I never wanted you to give up that game! You're a lot nicer to be around after you've played." George, of course, could have just gone golfing, but this conversation let him do it without guilt or anxiety about Judy's reaction.

In all fairness, not every patient is initially supportive. Please bear in mind that communication is the objective, not the permission. One patient I worked with gave her husband somewhat of a hard time on this exact issue. She had a form of leukemia that meant she was confined to the hospital in isolation for many weeks on end; only her husband and older children were allowed to visit. After several weeks of spending literally every spare minute in Susan's room, Sam found himself going stir-crazy. In a therapy session, he brought up his need to get out on a sunny weekend and play tennis—and Susan didn't like it a bit. "I'm stuck in that room!" she said, "and you're the only company I have."

Sam acknowledged that he knew how hard it was for her, but he had to have some exercise and recreation—roughly the same arguments George gave. But no matter how much Sam explained his need, Susan was hurt and a little sulky. Sam played tennis, nevertheless, and did so every weekend thereafter. Gradually, Susan accepted his need, and in fact, out of sheer boredom, decided to learn to paint so she had something to do when he wasn't there. So, although Sam had some difficulty asserting his need for recreation, ultimately it was beneficial to both of them.

Sam had another problem to contend with: his friends. Since Susan was hospitalized, some were critical of his time off. He told them, "Susan and I sat down and talked about how we should handle this difficult time. We've found it works best for both of us if I try to continue some normal activities. And, by God, we're doing everything we can to manage her disease."

After this he had no resistance from friends. This was a far better solution than avoiding critics because it meant that Sam maintained his support network.

Another Look at Priorities

From the moment of the diagnosis of cancer, patients and families often begin reassessing their priorities. The sudden shock of realizing our mortality casts an entirely new light on daily life. The person who is seeking to survive and thrive during this crisis sometimes feels at a loss. I have known patients who said to me, "I don't even know what to do with myself now. I used to work six days a week. Now my work just isn't so important." Very often patients and their families lose their interest in values connected with money and achievement. Many times a new priority rises to take the place of the discarded ones. In this case it may be other people.

Sometimes a patient doesn't take a hard look at what counts to him until it is too late. One multi-millionaire told me, "Now that I'm lying here dying, you know what I'd do if I had it to do all over again? Instead of spending so much time making money, I'd get to know my son better ..." This wealthy man came to feel that he really had not enjoyed a very good quality of life.

Most patients and their families look at their priorities sooner than this—and the impulse to do so can be one of the positive effects of the disease. Serious illness can be a loud and clear message to slow down, if only because time now has to be given to the disease. That means that some activities are going to have to go. Priorities are going to be reordered. Almost always, family members now want to spend more time with the patient—time that isn't devoted to the illness but just to being together.

Just as many people unthinkingly give high priority to work, many others spend their spare time in activities that are not deeply satisfying. Those who are looking at how to reorder their lives usually discover that there are things they don't mind dropping. One man who was very active in civic work told me, "I looked at these committees, and I've been going every week for five years to this one—and I've been bored with it for a year. I think I've already contributed what I could to this, but I've just drifted along with it." He gladly resigned from the position he held on the committee to free up another weekday evening he could spend with his wife who had just had a mastectomy.

Walter Greenblatt not only wanted more time with Carol but he also wanted more time with their four children. He made a point of being alone with each one individually on a regular basis, often over dinner at the restaurant of their choice. When the children were away at college, he made regular weekend trips to see them. "I got to know them much better than I ever had," he says. "It's been very good for them as well as me."

While some new priorities are usually clear, other areas of life can be thrown into confusion by the presence of cancer in the family. For patients and family members who don't know quite what they most want, I suggest answering the question, "If this were the end of my life today, how would I feel about what I had done?" Other helpful questions to consider are: "What's been important to me?" "What have I achieved?" "Who have I loved?" "What mark will I leave behind?" The answers to these questions point the way to what really matters to you and what you may have been ignoring. A shift in priorities can create a better quality of life, and that's worth pursuing whether we're going to have twenty more years to enjoy it or just two more weeks.

The Will to Live

In my experience, the will to live is not some magical, unpredictable thing. It's an energy, a desire to fight for life because *there is something to live for*. It is normal for a cancer patient to temporarily lose this will after the diagnosis. The shock and uncertainty lead many people to suspend living for a few weeks while they adjust to the idea of the illness. For a while the patient may think, "It's no use. It's all over for me." and stop investing in life. His behavior communicates to everyone around him that he feels hopeless.

This is normally a limited period though. Once he has worked through his feelings, the patient usually accepts the fact that he has cancer, adjusts, and begins to work toward recovery. This is the point at which one can see the strength of his will to live. Invariably, that energy and fight will be stronger in patients who find their lives enjoyable, who have things in their lives they genuinely look forward to.

Some patients enter a period of intense review of their own priorities and activities. They find themselves waking up each morning, thinking about the day ahead, and saying, "What's the use of getting up? I don't want to do those things. That's not fun." These patients are receiving a significant message about their lives, now that they have a sense of their own mortality. Their will to live is often strengthened by their determined search for a better quality of life. "What is it I really enjoy? What would give me a sense of purpose?"

I encourage such patients to set goals that are three months, six months, and a year into the future. Sometimes they protest that they'll never live that long, but my reply is that none of us knows how long we will live. In the face of that uncertainty, it is still healthy to have things to look forward to, and commitments to the future can be powerfully energizing. I have seen very ill cancer patients live on several "extra" months in order to see their children graduate from college or be married. One patient held on until he completed a manuscript he had labored over for years; it was as if he did not give himself permission to die until it was done. This kind of behavior demonstrates the inner power we receive from working toward meaningful goals.

Family members cannot set goals for patients, but they can encourage plans for the future. Patients who simply refuse may be withdrawing from life. I have met many people who, from the moment of the diagnosis, begin saying, "There's no point in buying a new dress—I'll never have time to enjoy it." One patient's husband wanted to plan an extensive European trip in a year from the time she was diagnosed, but the patient only replied, "Oh, you know I can't make a commitment that far in advance." A patient with this attitude may have unconsciously decided that it's all over and more than anything needs to find purpose and enjoyment worth getting out of bed for.

In his studies of concentration camps, Victor Frankl found

that the survivors were those who had strong meaning and purpose in their lives. The will to live is strengthened by purpose.

Cancer is a serious crisis—but isn't life a matter of adapting to one change after another? I believe we must continually adapt to survive, and as life goes on, we can thrive on living. There's no reason we cannot maintain a fine quality of life during a life-threatening crisis. The diagnosis of cancer is not an automatic death warrant that demands that the patient and his family stop living.

Chapter 9

Supporting Emotional
Change in the Patient

A s the Greek philosopher Heraclitus said, "There is nothing permanent except change." Throughout our lives we experience change, both around us and within our own thoughts and feelings. Any significant event causes some change within us—and so it is reasonable to expect that a major event such as the diagnosis of cancer will change the patient and his family, sometimes dramatically. In many cases, this is the family's first encounter with the possibility of one of its members dying, and the very thought sets off a series of repercussions. Regardless of the outcome for the patient, changes inevitably occur within the patient and family. The family that expects change can be emotionally prepared to cope with it.

As a family works to create a healing environment, this too creates change in the entire family; most of all, it encourages the patient to grow in positive ways. Patients who respond to this environment by deciding to participate in getting well and assume more responsibility for their own lives can change a great deal, and the family can help this growth by understanding what the patient is going through.

The Patient's Need to Change

At the Cancer Counseling and Research Center, we work with patients who have decided to change in positive ways that they believe can help them in their effort to recover. They have decided to change a behavior that is part of a historical pattern associated with cancer. They want to break the habit of suppressing such feelings as hurt, anger, and vulnerability, and to learn to pay attention to their own needs—to begin to cut through the chronic depression and low self-esteem many of them have been living with. These are patients who have responded to their diagnosis with a determination to do what they can to aid their chances of recovery and to improve the quality of the time they have left. Other patients work with therapists in their own towns, often with counselors who have trained with us. Still others, even if they are not in therapy, find that their priorities are rapidly changing now that they have a sense of their own mortality; they want more satisfaction in their lives, and they begin to search for it.

At the Center, we try to facilitate change in patients through encouraging an attitude some families are not always initially comfortable with and may characterize as "selfishness." We emphasize to patients the need to be "I-oriented," focusing on their own lives rather than always trying to please others. The patient who succeeds in making this shift gains higher self-esteem and experiences less depression. In fact, it is not selfishness we believe in, but assertiveness and being in touch with one's own feelings and needs. Learning to do these things takes a great deal of commitment and work on the patient's part; the process is immensely aided by the support of receptive family members and friends.

Effects of the Patient's Change on the Family

When one member of a family changes, the whole family will be affected since a family is a system. It's hardly surprising that when some families see their mother for the first time express anger, or say no, or insist that *she* needs the car, they react with downright alarm! At the same time, however, when family members understand what she is trying to achieve, they are usually willing to cooperate and be supportive. Even so, responding in helpful ways to the patient's changes is no easy task.

First, it is bewildering to learn that the patient has a whole range of feelings, past and present, that he may never have expressed before. (One teenager said of his father, the patient, "Who *is* this guy?") Moreover, these feelings are often expressed with some force at first since the patient is letting down long-established barriers and has a great deal of feeling to let out. To the family, this may feel somewhat like seeing the dam blasted away and being inundated by the flood. The patient, impelled by the belief that he has to learn to let out pent-up feelings if he is to get well, may explode over seemingly trivial problems. After all, if he's been nice, self-sacrificing, and always willing to give in all these years; he's got some steam to let off.

It's much easier for a family to cope with this process when they understand how it is helping the patient. To review the mechanism, suppressed feelings are likely to bring on depression that, in turn, may depress the immune system. So, as the teenager I quoted above decided, "It's better to have Dad angry and *here*." Aside from questions of physical health, the patient who becomes more expressive and assertive begins to enjoy a better quality of life.

There is also a benefit for the whole family in responding to the patient's changes positively. When one member of a family has been psychologically unhealthy, it is often a symptom of problems within the entire family system. It is unlikely that one individual in a household is suffering alone. So it may be that if a mother develops her much-needed assertiveness, others in the family may take permission to become more assertive, too. When one member of the family gets healthier, the entire family can benefit.

Learning to Handle Anger

When we begin expressing our feelings, one of the most important and obvious emotions is likely to be anger. The typical person with cancer has not been very good at feeling and

expressing anger, so this will be new and different for him—
and for the family. His anger will probably be surprising, and
because he is in a learning process, he will make errors at first
and may not express himself appropriately. Sometimes families
find it hard to know how to respond to this new behavior.

One common mistake we make as we learn to express anger
is to blame others. The patient who begins tapping into his
own anger can start making accusations and blaming others for
all sorts of things, both present and past. He may do this
loudly, may do some name-calling, and, in short, he may be
very disagreeable company. The blaming may be a little more
subtle, too; he may say, "*You* make me mad," rather than
saying, "I'm mad." Family members usually try to make conces-
sions in the beginning, but ultimately there is a time for them to
express their feelings, too—not, it is hoped, by returning the
blame, however. In response to a loud, angry, accusatory
statement, the family member might say, "Look, what you just
said really hurt my feelings. I want you to know I understand
that you're working on expressing anger, and I know you are
angry with me—but it feels to me like you're more angry than
the situation really calls for. And that hurts my feelings. But I
still want you to keep on working on this." This supports the
patient's efforts while asserting the family member's needs.

When the patient expresses an emotion very intensely and
seems to overreact, it may help family members to bear in mind
that some of this anger is over events in the past that the
patient didn't deal with until now. Don't personalize the exces-
sive anger, in other words, but see it as part of the patient's
learning process. This perspective is an immense help in gaining
patience and compassion for the patient's struggle. The patient
needs this understanding. He is often frightened of what he's
doing and may be particularly afraid that if he releases his
hostile feelings, people will reject him. Sometimes, in fact, family members do get offended and come back at the patient with
something like, "This is just too much! This time is the last
straw. You stop being like that." This confirms the patient's
worst fears, and he says to himself, "See, I knew it! It isn't safe
to express my anger. That's the last time I do that." Back he
goes to ground zero: suppresses his feelings, doesn't get his
needs met, becomes depressed, and bottles up his emotions

again. As with blaming, family members do need to express their own feelings about overreaction, but in a way this encourages the patient to keep dealing with his anger.

The Newly Assertive Patient

A second area many patients will begin to work with is their assertiveness. If they have been "nice" people, always doing for others and rarely saying "no," they will be forced to look at how this has affected their lives and how it has taken a toll on their health. Now they may learn to ask for more from others. The woman who used to say, "I don't care what movie we go to, dear—you choose," is suddenly saying, "I'd really like to go to this movie, not that one." The man who ate anything that was set in front of him says to his wife, "I'd like chicken for dinner tonight," thus defining the menu for the first time in thirty years of marriage. He may even "give orders," such as, "Would you pick up my suit at the cleaners?" when she is accustomed to him doing that task. It is to be hoped that he will be asking for personal support, too: "Would you rub my back?"

All this seems innocent enough, but when a family is used to one member being mild and nonassertive, they can quickly become irritated at his new style. Some may even discourage the patient with, "Oh come on, don't be so greedy all the time!" Others may complain, "What happened to the sweet, lovable girl I married? You're changing everything I loved in you." Assertiveness also means expressing the "softer" more vulnerable needs and that too can frighten a family. One woman said to me, "I don't know. Joe was always so strong, nothing bothered him. Now all of a sudden he's crying! It's like he's falling apart." In our culture, crying by men is often considered taboo—it is "unmanly." But Joe was neither unmanly nor falling apart, he was merely expressing his fear and asserting his need for comforting. It is natural, however, for any of us to feel somewhat confused and upset when a loved one begins to act in new ways. Any temptation to tell the patient in no uncertain terms to stop this behavior is something the family member needs to think about. Talking to a friend about your feelings may help dissipate them.

While family members may sometimes resent the patient's new assertiveness, they may also go along with it to such an extent that they become burdened. When a family member feels burdened by a patient's request, it's certainly possible to say no. We don't have to agree just because it is a cancer patient who has asked. Saying no to the newly assertive person is all part of the process, for being assertive means we learn to take noes. Anytime we ask for anything, we risk being refused. I would caution, however, that the patient may be quite sensitive to rejection at this point for several reasons. A person may have the habit of not asking for anything until he is needy and desperate; if that is the case, the no hits hard. Other patients fall into the habit of asking only one person for things, perhaps the spouse. For example, if a wife refuses her husband's request for a backrub, saying she's really tired, he may have no one else to ask (he feels) and so the rejection is again very difficult to accept. In this case, his support system is not broad enough, and it may even be that there are older children who could fill this need for him, but he does not feel he can ask. When patients have a great sensitivity to rejection, family members can tell them, "I do want you to be more assertive—keep asking. But understand that I'm not going to say yes every time."

Saying no kindly is an important part of dealing with the newly assertive patient. For one thing, it prevents resentment from building up in overly compliant family members. For another, it means family members are attending to their own needs, which, of course, they are entitled to do. If they neglect their needs, they will begin to feel deprived, and deprived people are poor at giving to others. Ultimately, the patient suffers. A spouse who finds himself resentful of his wife's assertive requests may do well to talk to her about it; "I'm getting resentful of you asking me for so much. I feel like I must want something I'm not getting. I wonder what?" This kind of communication on the part of family members helps keep the patient in the position of a contributing member, which is beneficial in maintaining self-esteem.

Changes in the Family's Balance of Power

This cluster of changes the patient may be going through affects the entire family. One potential effect is worth noting: a change in the balance of power. If a husband is accustomed to ruling the roost and getting his way, it is threatening for him when his wife, the patient, starts becoming less submissive and more assertive. But, while it feels threatening, it can be healthier for him, too. If one dominant family member shoulders all the responsibility, he bears a heavy load, and may be pleasantly surprised at how good it feels to let go of some of it. Moreover, if this inequality of power is between husband and wife, it may damage their intimate relationship; if the husband examines his feeling, he will find that there have been times when he did not respect his wife because she let him dominate her. That lack of respect is a barrier to closeness. So is the guilt he may feel. It, too, may contribute to his distancing emotionally in ways he's not even aware of.

When someone becomes more assertive, it changes the homeostasis of the family and often the balance of power. This may be threatening and draining to other members—but it can also eventually be good for everyone concerned. If the family stays with it and deals with the feelings they have about this change, they can become a healthier family. When there is significant change in the balance of power between spouses, the husband may have to ask himself whether he's willing to tolerate a wife who isn't submissive anymore, but who's well—and who's *there*.

Change, even positive growth, brings about its own problems and confusion in the family. People must work with the change over time to realize the gains. In terms of the changes brought about by diagnosis and treatment, it can be very difficult to deal directly with the feelings involved, but then promoting good emotional health is not an easy task. When it comes to living with the patient who has decided to change personally, again, family members can find this difficult to live with since it demands some change on their part as well.

This process of change is rather like the process you go through in beginning an exercise program. During the first few weeks your muscles are sore and aching, and you wonder, "What am I *doing* this for?" If you thought about it, you would say that in no way did all that soreness feel healthy. Those who last out the initial hard times and keep on exercising usually have their eyes on a positive, healthy goal off in the future. In order to reach that goal, they are willing to go through the aches and pains. In the same way, psychological change can be difficult at first, but it is made easier by keeping in mind the ultimate goal of a richer, healthier life for the patient and the entire family.

Chapter 10

Taking a Family
Inventory

T*he healthier a family is emotionally, the better it can deal
with a diagnosis of cancer in one of its members.* This
premise is woven throughout the first nine chapters of this book.
With that in mind, this chapter will focus on defining an optimum
family, but don't be overly concerned if your family does not
meet this standard. As the very word "optimum" implies, the
perfect family and the ideal home environment are eternally
unattainable goals; even the best families fall short in some
areas. My intention is not to suggest that your family should
meet the ideal given in this chapter but instead to give you
guidelines against which to measure your family's strengths and
weaknesses. In doing so, you may discover one or two specific
areas that you feel need more of the family's attention than the
others. Remember that tackling just one area will improve the
quality of family life for everyone.

The material in this chapter is based on studies of healthy
families conducted by Drs. Beavers and Lewis at Timberlane
Psychiatric Hospital of Dallas. These studies have identified the
very specific, major characteristics given below. Much of my
explanation may seem to focus on the unhealthy ways in which
families operate since it is so important to clearly identify
unhealthy relating patterns. Be sure to bear in mind that most

families fall down sometimes in just about every area; it is the degree of the problem that is important. It is also important and healthy for the family to be aware of its areas of strength.

The nine categories listed below for family assessment are in no particular order. Each of them is a meaningful part of the overall functioning of the family.

Individual Responsibility

The degree to which each member takes responsibility for his own actions and feelings is an important determinant of the family's health. When people disown responsibility, it can often be seen in their language. A woman who says, "You never take me anywhere," is throwing responsibility for her recreation onto her husband. One who says, "I'd like to spend Sunday afternoon walking around in the park," is taking responsibility for her own needs in a more direct way. Accusatory "you" statements can be a sign that family members are blaming others, rather than setting out to solve their own problems or communicate their feelings and needs. Sometimes this is because the individual does not feel permitted to directly express himself with such a statement as, "I don't like what's happening right now." Instead, he says, "You're making me unhappy."

In essence, "you" statements often indicate that the speaker holds someone else responsible for his happiness. It's as though he depends on other people to take the responsibility of being aware of his needs and filling them. Someone else is given the duty of making his personal choices—and if things don't work, someone else gets the blame. In a healthy family, members tend to make "I" statements that express their own needs, feelings, likes, and dislikes. While people in such families are very supportive of one another, there is a clear understanding among them that each individual is responsible for determining how things go in his own life.

Family Leadership

In a family with optimum functioning there are clear generational boundaries; everyone knows that the parents are in charge and, furthermore, that they work together as a team. Being in charge does not mean that the parents are always domineering and authoritarian. It means their authority is so respected that they seldom have to exercise it.

Characteristically, parents share leadership in a healthy family, respecting one another's equality and making decisions together. This means there is not one domineering partner and one who is submissive, such as the mother who never confronts the father when he says, "This is how it's going to be." The parents work together as a team although they may very well define specific areas in which one or the other is in charge. The father may take care of the car and the yard while the mother prepares meals and looks after the house. But despite these divisions of labor, each parent shares decision-making responsibility, and the children understand that.

One common sign of unclear family leadership is that the parents can be "pitted against each other" by the children, sometimes causing considerable dissension. Parents may also endlessly dispute child-raising matters and issues of policy in such families.

Responding to the Outside World

In a healthy family, the boundaries are open; members know it's safe to venture beyond the family to the outside world. In contrast, there are those families that believe the outside world is unsafe. In such families, members depend only on one another and are constrained from sharing with anyone else. They may say such things as, "We take care of our own," and "Never trust anyone but your family."

A healthy family also believes that allegiance to the family is important, but it recognizes the value of having other relationships, too. The parents are not threatened when the children develop relationships with special teachers, aunts, uncles, neighbors, and other adults. They encourage the children's friendships with other children as well. Some unhealthy families consider these relationships to be disloyal, and members fear the unknown dangers of the outside world. When such families are confronted with a crisis like a diagnosis of cancer, they continue to expect members to meet all of each other's needs for nurturing without seeking outside support. This places an enormous pressure on the family members. The healthy family remains close-knit in crisis, but its members are accustomed to going to the outside world and to having extended support systems.

Autonomy

When autonomy is promoted in a family, each member has a clear self-awareness and is encouraged to express both thoughts and feelings. When autonomy is not promoted, members discourage the expression of certain feelings and ideas. One person might say, "Gee, I feel sad," and another will respond with, "Why are you feeling sad? Shame on you! You don't have anything to be sad about—be happy!" Families that promote autonomy, on the other hand, are characterized by respect for the individual's feelings and will ask open-ended questions, like, "How do you feel about that?"

Families that stifle autonomy often impose external role systems on individual members. In the example above, the member who expresses sadness is explicitly told not to feel that way. He may then be told, "Why don't you be happy like Johnny?" This is the same thing as saying, "Don't be yourself—be somebody else." Communication of this kind discourages people from focusing on who they are and what they feel. A healthier response to the expression of sadness would be, "Are you feeling sad? What's that about? Tell me some more." The individual is now encouraged to experience and express his feelings, which is the basis of an awareness of self. Only when the family environment is open to individual differences are members encouraged to express themselves freely and develop self-awareness and self-determination.

Expression of Opinions

A related characteristic of healthy families is that they encourage the free expression of individual opinions. There is no "party line" to which family members must adhere. In less wholesome families, members may be ignored or even ridiculed for expressing personal opinions. Some families are so severe in this regard that the members learn to have almost no opinions of their own. In these disturbed families, the simplest request for a preference can be met with apathy. If you ask, "Do you like chocolate or vanilla ice cream?" everyone in the family will murmur, "Oh, I don't know . . . It doesn't matter . . . I really don't care."

Another kind of family environment, less disturbed but still limited, permits the expression of opinions, but the general attitude is that there's a right and a wrong way to think about any given topic. A member might say, "I think it would be fun to have a picnic Saturday at noon," and the others will respond, "That's a dumb idea. You should be working around the house on Saturdays." In such a family there is no room for difference of opinion. While the members may be opinionated, the environment strongly demands that they all agree; there is no middle ground.

In the healthiest families, members are permitted to clearly express different opinions. There may be disagreement, but an individual's right to disagree is respected. Furthermore, the family does not require people to come to an agreement. It is understood that it is possible for two opposing opinions to be valid. This respect for varying points-of-view promotes each individual's self-determination and self-esteem.

Expression of Feelings

Another sign of a family's openness to individual autonomy is its willingness to allow the free expression of feelings within the family. Some families almost suppress emotional interchange altogether; the members exchange only information, facts about what went on in their day, and perhaps opinions. But they almost never express feelings of sadness, fear, anger, or even joy and tenderness. The atmosphere is emotionally sterile. Other families limit the expression of feelings to a certain range. Joy may be permissible, and even sadness or fear, but anger is not tolerated. If a member steps outside the boundaries and expresses anger, the others get very upset and may pout or withdraw. Quickly the angry member gets the message: he had better keep those feelings to himself. Some families permit and encourage anger to such an extent that members go around being angry at one another much of the time. But these families seldom or never express tenderness. They think, perhaps, that it is too intimate. In this way they keep from getting "too close" to one another. The same family may also forbid fear and use anger to cover up fear. In this sort of family, everybody has to seem tough and strong, rarely fearful or tender.

Families that restrict the expression of feeling do so in many different ways. The healthiest environment, of course, is one in which no feeling is out of bounds, and sadness, joy, fear, anger, and love are openly and frequently expressed.

Ability to Resolve Conflict

Healthy families not only tolerate differences of opinion but are able to resolve conflicts when a decision must be made. More limited families can be so poor at resolving conflict that opposing views are never expressed. For example, everyone knows Dad has extremely strong views on some question, and while the other members disagree, they never bring it up with him, knowing this would invite dissent. Other families allow each member to express strong, definite beliefs, but each member also feels, "My view is the right one, and there's something wrong with anyone who doesn't see things my way." In this kind of family, a conflict eternally rages, with each member saying, "I'm right," and others saying, "No, you're all wrong, I'm right." The members do not recognize the subjective reality of others but believe there is an absolute "right way." Consequently, conflict often ends up in a struggle and nothing is resolved because nobody is willing to budge from his position or recognize the opinions of others.

In these two types of families, either nobody expresses a

dissenting opinion or members express opposing views but don't listen to anyone else's. Healthy families characteristically allow their members to express opinions, including those that are diametrically opposed, and discourage polarizing attitudes such as, "My way is the right way, and you're wrong!" In healthy families, members can say, "This is what I think, and I might be wrong, but it is my opinion. Now, you have a different opinion, and I hear you." In this kind of family, it may be that Mom's a Democrat and Dad's a Republican, and everyone knows it. They have different views, and they may debate, but they respect each other's right to their own opinion.

Conflict resolution can be significant for a family dealing with cancer. In a healthy family, the patient and spouse may visit several doctors to make a selection, and in the end the patient prefers Dr. Smith while the spouse prefers Dr. Jones. They may both feel strongly yet understand that their opinions are based on their individual beliefs about what is important in a physician. The spouse may assert his beliefs clearly, and the couple may debate the question for quite some time, but neither one says, "I'm right and you're wrong—you've got to see it my way!" The patient may ultimately decide to stay with his choice, and both the patient and spouse know that it is ultimately the patient's decision to make. His response will show respect for his spouse's point of view: "Well, you know I'd choose Dr. Jones instead, but I understand that Dr. Smith is best for you, considering what you believe is important. I want you to know I will support your choice even though I have another opinion."

Cancer patients and their families may have conflict in a number of areas, such as the patient's nutritional choices. The patient may decide to go on a strict diet with a great many supplements, and a family member may not believe this will be helpful. But he is not likely to say, "That's stupid to think those vitamins are going to help." Instead, he may say, "You know I believe differently about this, but I respect your opinion and your choice. If this is what you think is important, then you should do it."

Empathy

Especially important for cancer patients is the family's ability to understand another person's feelings when they are expressed and to respond with warmth. Sometimes families permit the expression of feelings but fail to respond with empathy. For instance, the patient might say, "I really feel scared." It is not very helpful to respond with, "How come you're scared? You know everything's going well." This can be perceived as a rejection of the feeling the patient expressed. Sometimes feelings are dismissed very abruptly. The spouse might say, "You're scared? That's really silly." In other families, members do not reject feelings outright but simply fail to respond. The patient might say, "Sometimes I'm just terrified of dying," and the spouse might say, "Hmmm, really?" and go on reading the newspaper, or he might say nothing and quietly get up and leave the room. In yet another family, a member might say something like, "Yes, I can understand that you would be," but with no warmth or emotional response accompanying the words.

In healthy families the response to expressions of feelings is empathetic. In the example above, the patient's husband would hear her fear with concern and respond with something like, "Gee, I can understand that. It must be really tough on you. I wish I could fix it for you, I hate your being so frightened." Then he might express his empathy further with comforting physical contact, like sitting with her and holding her.

Intimacy

Empathy helps create intimacy within a family. Many families share very little of themselves with one another, and contrary to what they may believe, they are not close because they are not emotionally expressive and responsive. Sometimes the individual members are intimate with friends but cannot tolerate intimacy at home—it's too close.

At worst, families share nothing, not even the same values; they are separate and distant even though they live in the same house. Other families that lack intimacy believe in the same values and "rules of conduct," such as an ethic that everyone should work very hard, but no member shares intimacy with anyone else in the family.

In a healthy family, members are bonded by respectful intimacy. They express a desire to be close, and they work at promoting closeness. At the same time, they respect the boundaries of other members. This means that a patient might say to his wife, "I had something really sad happen to me today," and she would not feel obligated to listen. Instead, she can say, "I'd really like to talk with you about it, dear, but I've just got so much on my mind at work right now, I can't deal with anything else at the moment." The patient's respect for his wife's limitations may lead him to answer, "All right, I hear you," and to go find someone else to talk to, perhaps a friend. This respect for one another's needs promotes intimacy over time; if members feel they must listen and share when asked, they will eventually develop resentment, which makes it difficult for anyone to give emotional support.

By the same token, members of a healthy family allow one another privacy. A patient might come home from a visit with the therapist feeling obviously upset, but when his wife asks, "What's the matter?" he replies, "I'm having some feelings about what went on in my therapy, but I'm just not ready to talk about it yet." Rather than push the issue, his wife might hug him and say, "I understand, honey," and let it go at that.

Naturally, if someone is always saying, "I don't want to talk about it right now," then there's a problem. But in general, in healthy families members have the right to withhold sharing as well as sharing their feelings and thoughts with one another. They are warm, affectionate, and respectful, and this promotes intimacy. (In Chapter 16, "Intimacy and Affection," I will cover this subject in more detail.)

One Marker of a Healthy Family

In taking inventory of a family's health in various areas, a family therapist will often ask the family to work as a team on a given project for some defined period of time, perhaps fifteen minutes, while he observes them. The project might be to plan the next family vacation. In a healthy family, the discussion might begin:

"Well, what do you guys want to do?"
"I dunno. I keep wanting to see the Grand Canyon."
"Not me. I'd like Bermuda, sand and sun."
"I'd rather go to Cape Cod if we're going to the ocean."

In the beginning, each member may express his own desires but also listen to the desires of the others. If the family then gets down to the question, "Where can we go that will satisfy some of everyone's needs?" they're on the right track. Their ability to negotiate and arrive at a decision is based on whether, as a family, they can promote autonomy, respect one another's feelings, and give empathetic responses. The autonomy is indicated by the fact that each member has his own individual needs, and while this may at first seem to stand in the way of harmonious teamwork, just the opposite is true. In any team, people function as individuals. If each player on a basketball team, for instance, was a forward with no one filling any other positions, the team wouldn't work very well. A healthy family works well as a team while each member remains an individual.

In conclusion, it's important to remember that few of us were taught good ways of communicating or of being part of a family. As children many of us may have picked up some very poor habits, ones that we may unknowingly carry with us to our own families. So if your mental inventory of your own family suggests that it doesn't score very high, don't be dismayed— most families don't even come close to this ideal, and no family meets it perfectly. A family that is determined to change because of the diagnosis of cancer can find that this is a most opportune time. A crisis bounces people out of their ruts, which creates an opportunity for change. Even so, nobody should expect instant perfection. It's important for any individual or family that is working to change to keep in mind that this is a process that takes place over a long period of time. When patients begin therapy with us at the Center, we tell them to remember that change doesn't take place all at once. In the same way, the family that is growing and becoming healthier will find this a long process—but one with many rewards along the way.

Chapter 11

Managing Stress

The link between stress and illness has been well established. Many studies confirm the finding that our emotional responses to stress can trigger a physiological process that directly increases our susceptibility to disease. As I have indicated earlier, this knowledge is critically important to someone with cancer. Since stress may be related to the breaking down of the body's natural defenses, learning to manage it is a vital factor in working toward recovery.

In their research at the University of Washington, Drs. Holmes & Rahe's data indicated that illness is more likely to occur during or immediately following highly stressful events. Not only cancer but also ulcers, high blood pressure, heart disease, migraine headaches, infectious diseases, and backaches develop with greater frequency in individuals who are experiencing an unusual amount of change or stress. We all know that certain painful experiences are stressful, such as a death in the family, divorce, and loss of employment, but Holmes and Rahe's studies revealed that joyous events—marriage, pregnancy, and retirement, for instance—also generate considerable stress. What we surmise from this information is that *change* itself, whether positive or negative, causes emotional conflicts to surface, which can have an adverse physiological effect. In other words, when

we talk about stress, we are talking about the effect that any
major change has on our life.

People adapt to stressful events in different ways. For one
person, the changes brought about by retirement are exciting
and positive; for another, the experience is disastrous. Some
newly retired people relish the free time, but others feel bored
and useless. Most people expect to enjoy the change, but if you
think back on the people you know who have retired, you
probably know some whose health suddenly became poor not
long afterward. Divorce, another major change, can be bitter
and shattering for one person and relatively calm and amiable
for another. As you can see, it's hard to anticipate how stressful
a given experience will be for an individual.

We do know that a high level of stress increases the likelihood of illness. Moreover, we know that a diagnosis of cancer
brings about considerable change in the patient's life—and
therefore enormous stress. With this in mind, I will devote the
rest of this chapter to "self-help" methods of managing this
stress. These are specific methods we emphasize at the Cancer
Research and Counseling Center, and they have helped many
patients get through some very stressful times.

Relaxation

Needless to say, a diagnosis of cancer gives rise to a great
deal of fear and tension. Commonly, patients feel overwhelmed
with visions of a prolonged, painful death and of becoming a
great burden to their loved ones. These terrible feelings of
anxiety can bring on sleepless nights, which endanger health.
Without adequate sleep, people can become physically exhausted,
using up considerable nervous energy, and thus sapping the
strength they need to combat the disease. To counteract this
stress, the patient can learn to relax for a few minutes each day
and gain relief from his overriding, constant concern with cancer.
Patients who have learned to use a relaxation process and
formed the habit of doing so daily report that they have a
different perspective and renewed energy. In effect, they find
their batteries are recharged.

Before I go any further, let me point out that the kind of

relaxation I am referring to is not the same as relaxing with pleasurable activities like watching television, having a few drinks with friends, or playing a round of bridge. Recreation is a different form of relaxation. The physical effect of full relaxation is detailed by Dr. Herbert Benson of Harvard University in his book, *The Relaxation Response*. As his work shows, there are specific, positive physical benefits to certain relaxation techniques that may be superior to the benefits of conventional ways of relaxing.

Briefly, Dr. Benson advocates that the individual take ten to twenty minutes at least once a day, and preferably twice a day, find a quiet place, close his eyes, and relax. Then he in some way removes himself from all external stimuli. For some people, this results in a nap, but a meditative state produces better results. I recommend visualization as a way to achieve this state. If you close your eyes, relax your body, and focus your mind on a peaceful image, such as relaxing on the beach or by a brook in the mountains, you gradually tune into a "twilight zone" away from your present life. Practice being fully into the scene: feel the warmth of the sun on your skin, listen to the ocean waves or the rippling of the stream, and remember how relaxed you were then, and how wonderfully healthy you felt. After you have done this for ten to twenty minutes, your body has experienced a short vacation, you can get up and go about your day.

This brief and simple process has a profound, positive effect on the body, diffusing its overreaction to stress. Some of our difficulty with stress today is due to the body's primitive response system. The human nervous system has existed for thousands of years, and only in a very small portion of this time have human beings had to cope with civilized stress. For primitive people, survival was dependent upon an almost instantaneous physiological preparation to fight or flee when confronted by a threat. The nervous system helped with an upsurge of adrenaline and other endocrines to give energy. Today, our bodies still respond in much the same way, but we no longer discharge this energy in battle or in running for our lives; we just have to stand there and take it.

Because we seldom physically discharge this energy called forth by stress, the endocrine-hormone process can cause physiological damage in any of a number of ways. Blood vessels may constrict and cause high blood pressure—hypertension. Hyperacidity in the stomach can lead to ulcers. These and other health problems may result when the physiological effects of stress are allowed to accumulate. In order to protect our health, we can regularly clear away the results of the body's reaction to stress. It is believed that this "leveling out" is what happens when we put ourselves into a trance-like state of rest.

While meditative techniques have been used in Eastern cultures for many centuries, we still do not fully understand how they work to normalize the body. The effect seems to be related to the slower brain-wave activity of this condition of mental relaxation and is similar to the process by which the body rests and normalizes itself during sleep. Even more interesting is that for people who practice the relaxation ritual daily, the effect of each session lasts much longer than the short time of relaxation would lead one to anticipate. This is because the hormonal and endocrine levels actually change, settle down, and normalize. This is why many experts recommend daily relaxation as a way to maintain health.

At the Center, we recommend this process to each of our patients. Obviously, only the patient can make the decision to practice relaxation. If he does, the family can give him support. First, his need for uninterrupted time and a quiet setting can be respected. Second, he can be encouraged to take this time for himself. Third, family members can be helpful by letting the patient know they believe this is a good decision: "I really support your doing this for yourself. What can I do to help you?" One good form of support is for the spouse or other members of the family to begin practicing relaxation too. Certainly they are also experiencing unusual stress and have a real need to rest and let their bodies rejuvenate.

Although relaxation feels good, not everyone is able to stick with a commitment to practice it daily. It does take a certain amount of self-discipline, particularly for those who have the habit of being active and busy most of the time. Family members who at least try relaxation for a time will have more empathy with the patient who has some difficulty making it part of his daily routine. Of course, it generally doesn't help to make the patient feel like a child by nagging him if he should make this commitment and then lapse back. A family member can express concern and ask supportively if there is any way he can help the patient maintain the routine. When relaxation is practiced every day at a set time, it can eventually become as habitual as brushing one's teeth.

Exercise

Physical exercise is another excellent way to get rid of the effects of stress. Ever since researchers began examining the effects of physical exercise, it has been shown to have a significant relationship to health. In 1921, when Silversten and Dahlstrom analyzed the case histories of 86,000 deaths, they found that the death rate from cancer was highest among people whose work involved the least amount of physical exertion and lowest in those occupations with the highest amount of physical exertion. This, and the data that shows that cancer is much less prevalent among less "civilized" peoples, suggests that cancer is a disease of the machine age.

Later studies have shown that the correspondence between exercise and a lower rate of cancer may well be related to the fact that exercise seems to dissipate stress and help the body normalize. Studies of animals exposed to high stress have shown that when they are given a physical outlet to release their stress, they have much less disease than those which are not. These and many other studies suggest that vigorous exercise may stimulate the immune system as well as channel off the physiological effects of stress. An individual who exercises aerobically for twenty to thirty minutes, increasing his heart rate and oxygen intake, goes through a physical process that actually cleanses his system of any hormonal upset due to stress.

Less understood is the psychological "cleansing" that also takes place. Although we don't understand the mechanism, it has been established that people who exercise regularly are less depressed and less anxious. They also tend to have a greater sense of calm and self-worth.

For these reasons, exercise is another important aid to a cancer patient's recovery. Of course patients vary in their physical ability, but some form of exercise is almost always possible.

I have seen family members aid patients in simple arm and leg exercises within a few days after extensive surgery. Many patients can begin exercising with short walks, increasing both the distance and the pace little by little. I have known others who began with jogging and ended up running in marathons. One patient was so impatient to get back to his tennis after major surgery that he began by hobbling to the court to hit the ball gently against the backboard for a few minutes at a time. Today he plays tennis daily and enjoys the idea that it is not just fun but good for him.

This patient, as everyone with cancer should, consulted his doctor about his exercise program. When dealing with a disease process, it's not wise to move full speed ahead into exercise without medical supervision. On the other hand, it's not necessary to assume that exercise is out of the question. By working with a physician, and possibly a physical therapist, cancer patients can do a surprising amount of exercise.

Recreation

While recreational activities do not produce the same discharge of stress that relaxation does, they are definitely valuable. I recommend to my patients and their spouses that they make a point of setting aside time, preferably an hour each day, strictly for play. This can be anything from a sport like tennis to playing cards, going to a movie, or dining out. What is important is to break one's normal routine for the sake of doing something that simply gives pleasure. The mere act of doing something for one's own benefit alone is good therapy. This is not, as many may still believe, just being "selfish," but rather it is a way of making sure we take care of ourselves.

While the patient may need to establish some recreation that is his alone, it can be beneficial for the entire family to develop recreational activities together. In doing so, everyone can gain from the experience.

Expression of Feelings

Freely expressing feelings is so vital to health that I have emphasized it throughout this book and even devote Chapter 7 to the subject. The expression of feelings bears a clear relationship to stress and warrants discussion here.

As I've explained, our bodies are designed to get ready for "fight or flight" whenever we feel stressed. Often, however, we can do neither. You might be very angry during an encounter with your boss, but you really can't punch him out, leave the scene, or even tell him where to get off. You must just stand there and endure, withholding your feelings. This kind of bottling up of emotions is essential to surviving in our society. The trouble is, the emotion stays there, churning around, until you express it somehow. If you go through the whole day without talking to anyone about it, by the time you sit down to read the newspaper before dinner, you're likely to be recreating the scene in your mind. If you still don't express the feelings, you may tend to keep replaying the scene; and each time you do, you put stress on your body. So you end up experiencing the whole physiological mechanism of stress caused by this episode not once but many, many times.

Talking your feelings over with someone, however, allows you to feel them fully, which helps release them. You might come in the door and say to your spouse, "I had the most *rotten* time with my boss this morning! He said . . . and I said. . . ." By expressing your anger about the incident this way, you're less likely to keep obsessively replaying the scene and getting angry each time. It makes a difference how you talk about what happened. Itemizing what happened in a cool, rational way is not at all the same as *expressing* your anger, fear, or whatever you're feeling. A very direct statement of your feelings can be the most helpful. When a person with cancer can say, "I'm so scared," and he actually feels the fear as he expresses it, it helps discharge the emotion. The result is that the hormonal upset caused by this stressful feeling can begin to normalize.

Fear is an emotion that is very stressful when it is suppressed. It is a natural emotion for the family of someone with cancer to

134 THE HEALING FAMILY

feel. The wife of a patient increases her own stress if she tries to "act brave" and not share her own fears with anyone. Instead, she might confide in a close friend, "It's really awful for me to think about Jack having cancer. I'm so terrified he might die, I don't know what will happen to us then. I keep thinking about how I'd ever pay the bills, and I'm so scared." Expressing this fear certainly does not mean she is not behaving courageously; and it will help immeasurably to reduce her stress during this time.

When they think of expressing anger, many people picture an explosion of total rage. I don't believe anger needs to be expressed in that way. When anger is not bottled up and stockpiled, it can be expressed over a specific incident in a quiet, calm way—without a lot of fireworks. A person can say, "I am very angry about what you just said. . . ." People who do explode have often suppressed their feelings for too long. Often, the person who has a plain, old bad temper is carrying around an enormous load of pent-up anger that may have begun in his childhood. When someone comes along and provokes him, he has an excuse to dump the rage against his father that he's been holding back since he was ten years old! This kind of expression of feelings may be an indication that psychotherapy is needed.

In general, patients and family members who feel themselves to be anxious and under stress should bear in mind that expressing feelings during this time of crisis is an important way to reduce the effects of stress, as well as build intimacy and mutual support within the family.

When stress management becomes crucial, as it does with a diagnosis of cancer, relaxation, exercise, recreation, and expression of feelings are major ways to relieve stress. In addition, many other suggestions in this book function in the same way, including the development of a broad, intimate support system. If your efforts to deal with stress aren't successful, and particularly if pent-up feelings seem to be getting out of hand right now, consider seeing a therapist. Professionals are trained to help their clients come to terms with difficult feelings and cope with stress in productive ways.

While I have been discussing ways to manage stress, probably the single most important issue is knowing that you are under stress; until you recognize that, you can't begin to look at how best to deal with it. A diagnosis of cancer in the family means that for all members there has been an increase in stress—a major stress added to all the normal, everyday problems of life. Even though you may feel you are coping, it can be important to evaluate what you are doing to relieve stress and how you are adjusting to new priorities and responsibilities. Above all, this is a time to avoid taking on any unnecessary burdens—your goal during this crisis is to relieve stress, not to increase it.

Chapter 12

Dealing with Fear

S ometimes described as the modern-day leprosy, cancer is unquestionably the most feared disease in our culture. The fact that it is associated with death is probably a major reason for this. For cancer patients, that fear is often compounded by visions of a painful, lingering death that will drain family and friends emotionally and financially. Many patients are obsessed with these fears, and often hold them inside. Some find that when they do express their fear, family members avoid the feeling with some such statement as, "Stop talking like that! You're not going to die."

Of course, every one of us is going to die; the only question is when and how. This is not to say that someone with cancer isn't in a painful, anxiety-provoking position, but rather it is to mention once again that none of us knows how long we have. A certain amount of the anguish patients feel often comes from the fact that this is their first encounter with their own mortality. Those who can talk to their families about this often come to terms more easily with the uncertainty of their futures. One of my patients said this well in a recent group therapy session. "Yes, I have a potentially terminal disease, and I don't know how long I'm going to live. But who does? *Life is a terminal disease.*"

Once patients and their families get past their initial fear of the possibility of death, they will commonly begin to be afraid of the disease process itself. Most patients fear the effect that the disease will have on them. "Will I be in pain? Will I become emaciated? How will it affect my appearance? Will I end up semiconscious, out of control?" The family's fear tends to focus on the agonizing thought of watching the loved one suffer and being unable to do anything to help. Spouses have told me they were afraid they wouldn't be able to make it through such a situation. They imagined themselves lacking the sheer fortitude to stand by and be supportive when they were powerless to resolve the crisis.

The Legacy of Fear

While these fears are natural and normal, they are often exaggerated by the legacy of fear cancer carries with it today. Many still believe cancer is always incurable. Others are frightened by the occasional rumor that suggests that cancer may be caused by a virus. Such unfounded reports coupled with old superstitions have led some families to actually boil dishes after meals and to refrain from any physical contact with the patient. This is especially sad in view of the patient's increased need for the nourishment we get from being held and hugged and from generally receiving love through physical touch and intimacy.

Family members often carry another burden of fear. Once cancer is diagnosed within the family, everyone concerned is likely to begin tracing the family's cancer history. The illness is so common that it's a rare family that has not had a death from cancer some time in the past, and a large family may have had several. Those who are looking at medical history may gain perspective by considering how many family members have had other illnesses, such as heart disease. Some incidence of cancer in the family is not unusual at all, but too often family members become preoccupied with their own health and begin to worry incessantly about whether they, too, might have cancer.

Perhaps the major reason cancer arouses fear is that we do not yet fully understand it and cannot predict its course. Even a serious disease provokes less anxiety when it seems comprehensible and somewhat controllable. Heart disease, for instance, is a mechanical problem involving a muscle which is a pump, the workings of which we understand. Diabetes, which can also be life-threatening, is not fully understood, (we don't know quite why the diabetic's pancreas doesn't produce insulin) but we have ways to intervene and control it. Cancer, however, is less understood, less predictable, and harder to control. A patient in remission is always aware that the disease may lie dormant for long periods only to suddenly recur. Anything this mysterious naturally arouses feelings of insecurity; more than anything else, we want to fix it. Because we can't, we sometimes feel terribly frustrated. In some cases, unfortunately, family members are so bothered by their inability to fix the patient that they will avoid him. For others, the diagnosis of cancer makes it necessary to face for the first time one of the greatest human problems—we can't control everything in our environment. When this realization strikes home it is natural to feel an upsurge of fear and anxiety.

Because of the fear surrounding cancer, it was not until recently that patients began letting others know about their illness. One great help to public awareness was the openness of Betty Ford and Happy Rockefeller who courageously made public their cancer surgeries. Their frankness about what had been considered a very private, personal matter did much to bring other people out of the closet, too. Today, American Cancer Society public service announcements often show well-known people stating, "I had cancer and I beat it." All this has helped remove some of the fear from the idea of cancer. Certainly people with cancer need not feel as isolated as they once did now that so many public figures have talked about their own illnesses.

Nevertheless cancer's legacy of fear is still greater than it needs to be. We know that there are hundreds of forms of cancer, many of them with favorable survival rates. Many kinds of cancer are both less debilitating and less painful than other life-threatening illnesses. Modern research on pain has given us many ways to manage this aspect of the illness. In short, while cancer is certainly a serious disease and not to be taken lightly, its reputation as an awesome killer is really no longer accurate.

The Toll of Suppressing Fear

Nevertheless, it is natural for cancer patients and their families to feel some amount of fear. But real damage is done if they don't face it. The more an individual tries to avoid fear, the more his fear will grow. When he goes beyond avoidance and succeeds in denying his fear altogether, his anxiety balloons to such a point that his behavior may become irrational. The attempt to cover up a real and powerful feeling such as fear also leads to a sense of alienation from others.

Denying fear is also costly in terms of personal energy. The individual who is ceaselessly working to keep fear from surfacing is eventually drained and can hardly manage everyday activities. Moreover, the suppressed fear does not dissipate; unattended to, it remains chronic, constantly sapping one's energy. This can ultimately be a real danger to health since the chronic stress of suppressed fear creates a physiological upheaval, an upsurge of adrenalin that brings with it abnormal endocrine balances. While there is much to be learned about endocrine processes, we do know that when the endocrine system is disrupted it becomes increasingly difficult for the body to function in a healthy way. There is some evidence that this disruption is likely to make disease progress at a faster rate.

The hazard to physical and emotional health is increased by the fact that suppressed fear often interrupts one's normal sleeping pattern. The individual may find it harder and harder to fall asleep, or they may go to sleep with some ease but wake up suddenly in the middle of the night feeling scared. This loss of sleep should not be taken lightly. A person who fails to get his normal required amount of sleep for days or weeks on end will eventually suffer physical and emotional problems. The reason for this is primarily our need for adequate REM (rapid eye movement) sleep; REM sleep occurs in the last stage of the sleep cycle, and it is important for both the psychological and physical processes of the body. The initial symptoms of deprivation are crankiness and irritability. After many sleepless nights, the person can actually become psychotic. Anyone who is deprived of enough sleep will experience severe psychological disturbance. Some war movies that show prisoners of war who are tortured by sleep deprivation have depicted the symptoms. The theory behind this form of torture was that eventually the prisoner would break down psychologically, and it is true—any person who goes too long without adequate sleep will probably experience a breakdown.

In addition to poor sleeping habits, there are other signs that a patient or family member is suffering from denied fear. Usually he will have increased anger that is inappropriate to what has actually happened. He may become overly active, often working long hours. He may begin to display obsessional behavior or thinking on any number of different subjects. He may become quite withdrawn and emotionally unavailable to the rest of the family. All this is harmful to anyone, but it is particularly harmful to a patient who needs his resources and energy to combat his illness.

One antidote to all the problems caused by suppressed fear is to express the fear and gain support. Sometimes the frightened patient or family member is doing this, or trying to, only to be met by denial from the others: "Oh, don't worry! Everything's going to be fine." Certainly nobody knows whether someone with cancer is going to get well, but he will not benefit by being urged to suppress his fear.

Family members can be receptive to one another's expressions of fear. If the patient is not expressing his fear at all, the techniques in chapter 7, "Communicating Feelings," may be helpful. Physical touch also helps people move into their feelings. You might say to a patient, "This must be real scary for you," and hug him. You may find that this physical contact gives him courage, and with it, he may be better able to confront his fear.

Fear is a normal response to a life-threatening disease. Unfortunately, our culture encourages us to be *afraid of being afraid*. We are so conditioned to "think positively" that many people secretly believe that if they directly experience their fear and acknowledge it to someone, they will collapse into it and never get back out. Of course this is not true. Once fear is acknowledged and expressed, it dissipates. It helps to remember that fear is a natural response to uncertainty. We always fear the unknown, and many events in our lives have unknown outcomes, from entering college to starting a new business or getting married. Some amount of anxiety in these situations is normal and to be expected, and being afraid is not harmful. Cancer, a disease with an unknown outcome, naturally leads to some amount of fear in the patient and those who love him. This fear is not dangerous in itself. I have known patients who seemed consumed by their fear after the diagnosis, who acknowledged and expressed their feelings, and who are doing well today. The only danger fear holds for us is when we deny it.

Knowledge: Antidote to Fear

Once fear is expressed and acknowledged, an excellent antidote to the fear can be knowledge. The more a person knows, the less uncertain he will feel. The many cancer hotlines in communities across the country, which provide the patient with information about his specific form of cancer, are based in part on this idea. Other cancer organizations concentrate on giving people an opportunity to meet with other patients to trade information and feelings. Often such groups provide an especially important kind of knowledge and inspiration by featuring speakers who have recovered sufficiently to live healthy, rewarding lives. Patients who have a chance to be with other patients usually become less fearful. Often, they have never before known someone with cancer who didn't die.

Getting to know other people with cancer can have numerous positive benefits. Many patients have told me that despite the support of their families, they feel inexpressibly alone with their illness. It is an experience that they can ultimately only share with someone else who has, or has had, cancer. As Bob Gilley told his wife, BJ, "I know you love me, but you're out there, and I'm in here, in this body, with the cancer." A patient who feels depressed about the side effects of his therapy can be very comforted by hearing another patient say, "It was *awful* when I lost my hair," or, "Yeah, I really felt weak and down when I was on that drug." Patients who have recovered can also share their joy, and inspire the depressed patient who is wondering about his future. Members of Reach to Recovery make a point of looking and feeling their best when they visit women who are recovering from mastectomies. A patient often feels more hope-

ful after spending time with a healthy, vital woman full of life
who says, "I know how you feel. I was really scared after my
surgery." When this visitor leaves for her tennis game, the
patient gets a positive inspiration that no one else may be able
to give her. Equally meaningful is the discovery that she is not
alone in her feelings.

Knowledge about medical procedures is a specific and important antidote to fear. Many people are somewhat phobic about
treatment in general, perhaps because of a childhood experience.
Sometimes we are afraid of a specific procedure for reasons we
may not really understand. I had such an experience several
years ago when I was scheduled to be examined after a kidney
infection. The X-ray required the injection of a dye substance
that I knew very rarely caused an anaphylactic reaction with
dizziness, fainting, nausea, and irregular heartbeats. This reaction is rare, yet I got so terrified that I didn't sleep the night
before the examination. I insisted on seeing the doctor before
the test and asked him to tell me exactly what would happen
during that procedure. Then, because I'd been so frightened, I
broke down and cried.

"What's the matter?" he asked me. "You're so anxious about
this." Suddenly I knew what was behind my fear. Several years
before I had been working at a hospital on a cancer project
when a woman had a severe anaphylactic reaction to this test and
died. Now, that is very, very rare, and until then, I had no idea
that was the base of my fear.

The doctor was quite helpful. He went on to show me that
such a thing couldn't happen to me, explaining all the resuscita-
tion equipment in the room and telling me he would be right
beside me. "There's no way that can happen to you," he said.
"If I saw the slightest reaction start, here's what I'd do," and he
explained his emergency procedure. Once I had full knowledge
of this test that I'd been so afraid of, I was able to relax and go
through with it with no problems.

Very often fear of a medical procedure is caused by a
preconception, such as mine, that is not entirely accurate.
Knowledge goes a long way toward dispelling such fear. Some
patients, for instance, have heard terrible stories about chemotherapy. I have known people who were so frightened by the
time they got to the clinic that they fainted or become nause-

ated before treatment even began. Similarly, some people are very afraid of routine procedures such as having blood drawn or being fed intravenously. Often their fear is based on a childhood memory or on an inaccurate idea of what is going to happen. In all such cases, the best approach is to talk with the doctor in advance and get as much information as possible about the procedure you fear.

At the same time, it helps to explore such questions as: What exactly is it about medicine that frightens you? Is it the idea that you're not in charge? Is it that you don't trust doctors? Has someone in your family had a bad experience? Fear usually has a basis somewhere. One of my clients had lost a brother because a doctor treated him inappropriately; the patient's brother probably would not have died with the correct medication. After we talked about this, my client decided to discuss his fear with the doctor. He explained, "I've had a bad experience with doctors, and I need extra reassurance and support. My brother was given the wrong medication and died as a result. I need to know that you're not going to give me any drug without talking to me about it first." He found his doctor very willing to discuss treatment recommendations after that. In cases like this, it is the patient's knowledge and understanding of his own fear that make it possible to get the necessary help.

By assertively seeking out knowledge from their doctors, patients often find that they have been overly frightened by something that may not happen at all. Side effects from treatment are a good example. Many patients are afraid of the possible side effects of their therapy, and some believe that all patients experience the full range of side effects. In fact, this is far from true; ten people on the same drug can have ten entirely different reactions. Some get nauseous from their chemotherapy and some never do. In the same way, people have widely differing thresholds of pain. A patient who is worried about extreme side effects may be frightened over something that won't happen at all. Because of the prevalence of these concerns, I believe a patient may benefit from talking to his doctor in advance of the treatment. He should find out the possible side effects and ask what the doctor will be able to do to alleviate them.

Knowledge about our own bodies is a final important part of the antidote to fear. Patients who do well and recover constantly live with the fear of recurrance. Unfortunately, this is not an irrational fear. For such patients, everyday pains such as a tennis elbow, a backache, or a case of the flu trigger off thoughts of alarm: "Oh, that's cancer again." Those of us who work daily with cancer know this phenomenon first hand because we tend to do the same thing. Patients who find themselves dwelling on these fears do well to consult a physician. It may well be worth the trouble in order to be relieved of such anxious thoughts.

Overcoming Fear

When Franklin D. Roosevelt advised the nation during the Great Depression, "the only thing we have to fear is fear itself," his advice may have been appropriate for preventing panic in the economy, but I don't recommend that people with cancer follow it. To be afraid of fear is to deny it, and fear cannot be overcome until we recognize it. Once we face fear there are many ways to alleviate it or at least learn to live with it comfortably.

One of the oldest of modern techniques for dealing with fear is the process of desensitization. A person gets into a state of relaxation and then pictures the event he fears going as well as it possibly could. This differs from denial in that the patient is acknowledging the fear by visualizing it. Just doing this helps reduce anxiety. A patient might use this technique by imagining himself going in for treatment and in his visualization giving himself every possible kind of support: family beside him, the help and understanding of the medical staff, and so on. This visualization might include experiencing the treatment, making it as comfortable as can be imagined, and then going on with an image of being free of side effects.

Fear that their disease is getting worse causes some patients to do what you might call "visualizing in reverse." A patient whose neck begins to hurt may think, "What if my cancer is spreading?" Then he begins to visualize this, forming a negative image that can be terrifying. I suggest that a patient who finds himself doing this try to become aware of each incident, stop, and take thirty seconds to counteract the negative image. Although he does not know whether the sore area is cancer or a stiff neck, he can visualize his healthy white blood cells going to that location on a search-and-destroy mission. At the same time he can say to himself, "Okay, I'm afraid, and I have that picture in my mind. Now here's another possibility." Many of my patients say that this technique has helped them overcome their fears about their cancer returning. It can be used with equal effectiveness on other fears as well.

Fully developed imagery can also be used to overcome fear, and may, in the process, control side effects as well. If the immune system can be influenced by the mind, so may other body processes such as nausea. One of my patients who had been very nauseated by his oral medication used imagery very successfully to decrease this side effect. He began to visualize his medication going down his esophagus and into his stomach; in his stomach, he formed an image of a little circle he called "the nausea center." He visualized the chemotherapy going around this nausea center, so that he would not feel ill. As a result, he experienced much less nausea. Other patients have used imagery on other side effects. Some who are concerned about loss of energy visualize their chemotherapy avoiding their normal tissue. This is a good counter to the tendency to see chemotherapy, which acts as a poison, affecting all tissue it happens to come upon. In fact, some cellular biologists supports the theory that a normal cell is less likely to absorb the chemical treatment than a malignant cell.

There are limitless ways to use visualization in overcoming fear. Chapter 11, "Managing Stress," and chapter 19, "Dealing with Pain," include other examples. If the patient is using visualization to lessen his fears, the family can play a meaningful role by supporting his efforts and being willing to talk about his feelings.

For many people, religious or spiritual beliefs offer significant relief from fear. Certainly any life-threatening situation tends to give rise to the questions, What is the purpose of life? and Is there anything after death? These questions have been asked since the beginning of mankind. There are still no absolute answers today. But many people have a system of beliefs that resolves these questions. Because death involves so much uncertainty, people are often psychologically eased if they explore and develop beliefs around this issue. As with cancer, we can decide to hope for the best or expect the worst.

Dealing with the issue of death can add significant meaning to life. Some patients find solace in established religions they already belong to. Others, for the first time in their lives, want to arrive at some understanding of how the universe works, and what their role in it might be. They may be unconcerned with the questions of belief in God or in life after death, and ask instead, "Will the essence of me live on?" I know people who have come to great peace by accepting their own idea of immortality, the belief that they live on in the memories of people they have cared about. Whatever we believe in the face of death, it seems to add significant meaning to life to say, "It mattered that I was here, and something of me lives on." The belief that our lives have had meaning often seems to lessen the fear of dying.

The quality of daily life also has real impact on our ability to handle fear. A patient who is active and enjoying pleasurable things has less time to sit and brood about his condition, which could enhance his fear through negative images. In this respect, distracting oneself by focusing on the good things in life can be helpful; carried to extremes, it becomes denial. Usually the patient's body will let him know which he is doing. A patient who is in touch with his feelings may find that good, hard exercise helps him feel more empowered and in control. If, however, he is running to avoid his feelings, he will often be unable to run very far. In the same way, a patient who is worried about an upcoming treatment might choose to go to a movie and get his mind off it. This can be a good idea. But if what the patient is really doing is trying to evade and deny his feelings, he will simply sit in that movie and become more filled with anxiety and fear. A person can tell whether an activity is healthy or unhealthy by gauging how much peace and relief he receives from it. If fear is getting in the way of pleasure and involvement, going ahead and experiencing that fear should make it possible to enjoy the activity once again.

There are some people who are constantly paralyzed by fear about almost everything in their lives. One of my patients found her diagnosis of cancer doubly difficult to deal with because of a life-long fearfulness—but ironically her cancer spurred her on to overcome this very fear. She and her husband were planning a dream vacation to Hawaii, where she wanted very much to scuba dive. But she became worried about an ear problem she was having, even though the doctor assured her it would not be affected by scuba diving. As a person who was frequently anxious about any body pain, she was used to letting this anxiety stop her from doing things. But her attitude toward her fear had changed as she dealt with cancer. After much debate, she decided, "If I'm going to die from this disease—which I don't believe—I want to experience scuba diving first. The doctor says it's safe, and I'm doing everything I can for my ear. And dammit, I want to go ahead and experience things! If the worst happens, and I end up dying of cancer, at least I will have had this pleasure."

This patient freed herself from fear through several steps: The first is to be aware of the fear. The second is to express it and seek support from others. The third step is go on to gather any and all information that will help you gain understanding and control over it. Ask your doctor for his opinion. And the fourth, when you have done all these things, is to be willing to say, "Okay, that's enough. It's time to go on and enjoy some things about my life." If you have dealt with all your feelings, you are usually able at this point to go ahead and experience the activity.

When a patient is struggling with fear, family members often want to help by protecting him from anything they believe is anxiety-provoking. This can include certain newspaper and magazine articles about cancer, television programs on the subject that are billed as "heart-rending," and gloom-and-doom visitors. The family may feel very protective when the patient says, "Sally is so scared of cancer—every time she visits I get scared all over again. I'm a basket case by the time she leaves." Distressed family members sometimes react by cutting out offending articles, cleverly distracting the patient from the sad television movie about cancer, and seeing to it that Sally doesn't come by.

But all this can carry a real danger—it may undermine the patient's sense of strength. Imagine, for instance, what it feels like to come across that cut-out place in the paper. The patient thinks, "Oh no, my family really thinks I'm fragile. They don't think I can even stand to read what's in the paper. There must be something terrible going on that I don't know about." Such an experience can be both infantalizing and frightening.

The best way to help a patient cope with fear is to offer help and let the patient decide what he needs. If the patient says, "This article really scares me," the spouse can respond, "When I read things like that about people who die of cancer, I wonder what kind of impact it will have on you. Would you like me to do something so you won't have to see articles like this?" Such a question leaves the patient in control. This approach can be used for television shows as well. A husband can straightforwardly say to his wife, "I read the reviews on this TV movie, and it's about a young man who dies of cancer. Is this something you want to watch tonight?" Whatever his wife's decision, he can help by supporting her choice. In short, the family should take steps to protect the patient from situations that arouse fear only if the patient requests this kind of help.

One significant way family members can help is to make an effort to be physically present and emotionally supportive during anxiety-provoking events, such as visits to the doctor and appointments for treatment. The knowledge that someone who loves him is there helps the patient feel less anxious; in fact, this is one of the best ways I know of to help him through his fear of treatment. When a patient is agitated about an upcoming treatment or surgery, the family can also help by acknowledging his fear. "Of course you're afraid. I'll be with you. What can I do to help?" Sometimes it's helpful to ask, "What do you need for your fear?" since fear is often a signal that the patient needs something—perhaps more communication with the doctor, or more information about the surgery itself or merely to be held.

In summary, there are two basic ways family members can help the patient deal with fear. The first is to give support by encouraging the patient to express himself. The second is to ask how they can be helpful. If the patient's anxiety continues, a follow-up question sometimes helps: "Are you aware of what else you need—if not from me, from someone else?" Only the patient can effectively deal with his own fears, and this approach is one that keeps him in charge while giving love and support at the same time.

Fear is never easy to deal with since it reminds us of our vulnerability. We tend to meet uncertainty head-on by assuming the stance of being strong and invulnerable. Yet all of us, whether we have cancer or not, are vulnerable. This means that throughout our lives we will have to deal with fear. Only when we acknowledge and confront our fears are we in a position to act courageously and decisively to overcome them. Once we learn to accept our fears as natural, we can learn to live with them.

Chapter 13

Ambivalent Feelings

E ach of us is likely to have two opposite feelings about almost everything. As human beings we are, by nature, ambivalent and tend to experience conflicting feelings in every area of life. At times, we love our spouses, and at other times, we can't stand them. We are happy when our children get married, but in some ways we are also sad. Even though we may love our work, there are days when we feel so frustrated we want to quit. These opposing emotions around the same person or event are called *ambivalent feelings*.

Although ambivalence is a natural part of being human, it is not always easy to deal with. In the field of psychology, we sometimes define emotional health as the ability to recognize conflicting feelings and successfully resolve them. While this can be difficult, just being aware of the ambivalence is often a major part of the solution.

Split Ambivalence

An individual's ability to handle the conflict between opposing emotions is largely formed by his family. If his parents didn't resolve conflict well, he may not have learned how to deal with his own conflicting feelings. It is common for many people in our culture to have trouble resolving their ambivalent emotions. Some try to resolve internal conflicts by denying one side of the ambivalence altogether. As I have discussed, this denial can carry heavy consequences in terms of depression and anxiety. But it can also show up in destructive ways in a marital relationship.

Suppose, for example, that a woman who grew up in a family where conflict was not handled well still has difficulty as an adult. In her marriage, she may feel ambivalent about her emotional intimacy with her husband, wanting to be close, but also frightened about becoming too close. She may fear that she will lose herself if she becomes too close or will not be able to set limits in her relationship with him. So she is ambivalent: one part of her wants closeness, and the other part wants distance. Since she's uncomfortable dealing with two opposing feelings, she may deny one side of the feelings, in this case her need for distance. Now she is only aware of her need for intimacy, which she expresses to her husband: "I want more closeness in our marriage. I don't need distance."

The woman's husband may respond in a way that at first seems strange, but it is actually quite common: he may take on the denied feeling. In this example, he promptly decides, "I need more space, and I don't want all this intimacy." He is now denying *his* ambivalence and focusing on only one side of his feelings. It is as if they have "taken sides" in the matter, instead of acknowledging that both of them feel both of these feelings from time to time. When couples react like this, it is called *split ambivalence*.

Obviously, split ambivalence creates problems in the relationship. The woman, who is now carrying responsibility for the intimacy needs for both of them, may profess to want intimacy so much that her husband becomes annoyed and pulls even farther away. Since he is carrying all the distancing needs for both of them, he may be quite remote in the first place. But as he withdraws even farther, he invites her to chase after him in her effort to create intimacy. By the time a couple like this comes to therapy, they are locked in a struggle and blaming each other. In a session with this couple I might hear, "She wants to be too close," and "He wants too much distance."

The key to the problem is for both of them to unlock their denied feelings and acknowledge their ambivalence. Either one can begin this process—it only takes one. If the woman, for instance, can finally say, "Yes, I do want more intimacy, but I've always been afraid that if we got too close I'd lose myself," that would break the deadlock. She would then own both sides of the ambivalence, and the effect could be significant. As she expresses her need for distance, he may suddenly begin to act more intimate. It's as though he no longer has to do all the distancing for both of them.

Just as an individual must recognize and experience both sides of his feelings to resolve ambivalence, both partners in a relationship need to understand that it is natural to have conflicting feelings. Once they see that each of them has a set of opposing feelings, they generally are able to resolve them into some sort of comfort zone, most likely somewhere in the middle. In the example I've been using, the husband and wife would find a degree of intimacy and separation with which both felt satisfied and comfortable.

When a couple is dealing with a crisis like cancer, the numerous conflicting feelings can easily give rise to split ambivalence. A common example is what I call the *hopefulness-hopelessness.* split. This conflict rises out of the uncertainty that surrounds a life-threatening disease. It's very realistic for someone with cancer to have two feelings about the uncertainty of whether he will live or die. One minute he may feel very hopeful that he will recover, and the next minute he may feel equally hopeless and overwhelmed with visions of dying. This ambivalence is quite common and natural. The patient, though, may have difficulty dealing with his hopelessness and be afraid that if he really acknowledges it, he will collapse right into it and never recover. So he begins denying the part of him that is pessimistic and may continually say, "I'm going to get well; I'm going to get well!" But all the hopelessness he denies may be picked up by his wife, who reacts by being very pessimistic about his recovery. The patient may say to me very angrily, "She won't support me in my efforts to recover. I know she doesn't think I will get well. I think she wants me to die."

In reality, the patient is denying his hopelessness, and the wife is carrying the hopelessness for both of them. When I work with a patient like this, I encourage him to become more honest with himself about his feelings. In essence, I give him permission to experience both feelings. Eventually he may say, "I'm still very hopeful about recovering, but sometimes I wake up in the middle of the night thinking I'm not going to make it." Once he can say this to his wife, she can become much more supportive and hopeful. Recently I saw this happen with startling rapidity during a therapy hour. After the patient admitted his occasional pessimism, his wife said to him, "Maybe if we do everything we can, things will be okay. Let's both give this our best shot." I always marvel when I see how one spouse follows suit once the other has expressed his ambivalence.

Other Common Split Ambivalences

There are a host of ways couples can split their ambivalence. Some are particularly prevalent among cancer patients and their spouses. Like hopefulness-hopelessness, the *angry-nice guy* split is fairly common. This type of person has frequently grown up in a family where anger was not acceptable, and now he has a hard time expressing it. He may be locked in an unconscious belief that anger is terrible, and he thinks whenever he expresses it, people reject him for it. As an adult, he may continue to deny his own anger. His wife, on the other hand, acts his anger out. Many times I have seen a patient like this come into treatment with severe depression, the result of his suppressed anger; he may be accompanied by a wife who acts out anger in maladaptive, abnormal ways. Every time she does, the patient's belief is confirmed: "See how awful anger is? I'll never be angry like that."

This patient replaces his pent-up anger with resentment or depression and is likely to withdraw. When he does, he is inaccessible to his wife, and she often becomes more angry and intrusive in an effort to get through to him. Such a patient frequently denies at first that he has any anger. I will ask questions like, "What do you do with your anger when you start to feel it?" Once he begins to examine himself, he sees that his resentment or depression is a form of anger—it just isn't as direct as it might be. When such a patient begins to express anger, his wife may become less angry. Again, instead of the pendulum tilting wildly to one side or the other, it balances out somewhere in the middle.

Similarly, the *positive-negative* split is when one spouse is positive in his outlook and the other negative. This often has to do with the patient's efforts to recover. A husband may come into our Center saying, "I've read about the Simonton approach, and I'm 100 percent sure it will work, but my family thinks I'm nuts to believe I can help myself get well." In reality, I'm quite certain that almost every patient comes here with some second thoughts—feeling optimistic about what we do but not so sure it can really work. Just as people who are determined to deny their hopelessness, these patients sometimes decide to convince themselves, saying again and again, "Oh, I *know* this is going to work for me, I'm totally convinced." Since the patient has denied his opposing emotion, pessimism, the spouse may demonstrate that side of things: "You're foolish to believe in that."

This uncomfortable situation is often resolved when the patient comes to terms with his own negative thoughts and is willing to deal with his uncertainty. He may say, "This whole process has nothing to do with anything I have ever believed about the human body. On the other hand, at some level it makes sense. So I'm willing to try. I don't see how it can do any harm." Once he admits his mixed feelings, his wife is likely to admit hers, and become more positive and supportive of his efforts.

The positive-negative split can contribute to a patient's pessimism and depression. He may have days when he feels so depressed that he tells his wife, "I'm so down today, I don't even feel like getting out of bed." The wife, who has picked up the positive half of the split, then begins cheerleading. (See chapter 7.) "What do you mean, you don't feel like getting out of bed? You've got to think positive! Come on, get up." When she does this, the patient's depression may deepen, because his wife owns all the positive, happy feelings. Now he becomes even more passive and negative. He thinks, "I'll never be as positive as she is! What's wrong with me?" His negativism then continues to build until it is overwhelming.

Some couples split courage and fear with similar results. One acts too brave while the other expresses a tremendous amount of fear. The patient may come in trembling with anxiety, unable to sleep, and emotionally disturbed. Her husband will say, "I don't know what's wrong with her. Why is she so afraid? She ought to think positively—she's going to get better." In this instance, the husband is denying his own fear, while the wife is denying her courage. If I can get the husband to admit, "Yes, I'm hopeful and courageous—but sure, I'm scared," the wife will typically move in at once to say, "That's all right, dear. I know you're afraid, but I still think I can make it." Now that he has admitted his fear, she can admit her courage. Again, this change to more healthy emotional positions can be started by either spouse admitting his or her own ambivalence.

Aggressive-passive is another common split. The husband may be overworking, overdoing, and constantly tracking down information on cancer in an effort to fix things for his wife. Even though she is the one with cancer, she may be doing very little for herself. He is taking most of the responsibility for her health, and she takes little. She doesn't do her relaxation and visualizing; she doesn't eat well; she doesn't exercise; perhaps she drinks too much. The husband is always hounding her to do this and do that. As long as he takes responsibility for what she is supposed to do for herself, she will rarely take the responsibility. Unless he begins to back off and let her assume the responsibility, she may become more and more passive.

When one spouse has cancer, it is not uncommon for a *sick-healthy* split to occur. The patient says, "I'm the sick one," while the spouse asserts, "I'm the well one—and I don't know what's wrong with you. Why don't you get well?" In reality, the spouse is seldom perfectly well. With a couple like this, I often observe that the "healthy" spouse has some kind of physical problem, such as ulcers or high blood pressure, and may also have significant unresolved emotional conflicts. The truth is, they both have problems, although the split is usually translated, "He's the one with problems—I have no problems." The spouse's insistence that she is perfectly healthy may increase the patient's feeling of alienation. He berates himself: "How come I can't be healthy like her?" or "How come I have so many problems and she doesn't have any?" To encourage the patient to feel less isolated and worn out, his wife may admit, "He's the one with cancer, but sure, I have my problems, too."

Since every feeling has its opposite side, there are many, many ways to split ambivalence. Couples can split happiness-sadness or introvert-extrovert; the list goes on and on. A couple can also have several split ambivalences existing between them at one time. While these splits are clearly not desirable, they are common. None of us deals perfectly with our feelings. Split ambivalence exists in the best of families.

How to Detect Split Ambivalence

Almost all couples have some split ambivalences, but because they do not always surface, they may continue indefinitely. While they are not good for a couple's relationship, they can be even more harmful when one spouse has cancer since some splits can be especially unhealthy for the patient. For example, the patient may have low self-esteem and be a self-denying nice guy who does not express anger for fear of upsetting someone. He may also consistently deny his needs. "Oh, don't worry about me. I don't need anything." Since the patient is so selfless and has so little self-esteem, the spouse may be habitually insensitive and unresponsive to him. The patient does have a need to be nurtured, but the spouse doesn't detect it and offers little affection or closeness. So the result of the split is that one of the patient's deep needs is not being met. As chapter 16, "Intimacy and Affection," discusses, we need affection to build and maintain optimum health.

A couple like this, however, doesn't quite realize that the split is taking place. How *do* people see that they are splitting ambivalent feelings? One way is to look for any wide differences between members of the family. Is one person always very happy and another very sad? Is one pessimistic and another always optimistic? Is one member always angry, and given to losing his temper while another is generally agreeable and gentle and rarely gets mad? Such significant extremes are often good signs of split ambivalence.

Another good clue is the language people use. The frequent use of such extreme terms as *absolutely, never, always,* and *positively* can be a tip that the speaker is denying his emotions. People don't *always* feel anything, and it is rare for a person to *never* experience a feeling. Some patients, for instance, harp on how optimistic they *always* are; in the same breath they tell me their spouse *always* has a black cloud over his head. In addition to the absolute terms they use, such patients also display a great need to have me know how optimistic they are, another sign that there they may be denying their ambivalence.

We can detect our own ambivalence in yet another way, by asking ourselves questions about our feelings. A person who is never angry may ask, "Are there some feelings here that I am denying?" Someone who never feels scared might ask, "Why am I waking up in the middle of the night? Am I having scary thoughts?" In other words, is fear being denied? A very optimistic spouse can ask himself, "Do I ever have fleeting thoughts that my wife may die? When I do, how do I react? Do I stuff them down by getting very busy at my work?" I have found that people who ask themselves this kind of soul-searching question do develop an awareness of how they're feeling. They also begin to take a good look at the other side—how their spouse is feeling.

Split ambivalence is important because, as I have emphasized throughout this book, denial of feelings leads to depression, which potentially decreases the body's resistance to disease. But splits can be recognized, and once they are, couples can begin to solve the deadlocks in their relationships. They can then become closer and more supportive of one another.

Chapter 14

Helping Versus Rescuing

For the record, I know your intentions are good—*you want to help* the patient. If you didn't, you wouldn't be reading this book! But helping a patient with a life-threatening disease is something many of us have little prior experience with nor can we depend on simply doing what comes naturally. Some ways to help are more effective than others, and common sense does not always lead to the best results, no matter how good our intentions. Helping someone with cancer is no simple matter. You need to know *how* to help.

There is a distinct difference between helping and rescuing. Rescuing behavior starts with the view that the patient is a victim—and a victim is hopeless and helpless. A victim has no influence over the situation he is in. Because we cannot entirely control the course of cancer, many people assume the patient has no control or influence over his destiny, but this is not necessarily true. Although we can't control everything in our lives, we can be active participants and influence what happens to us. Rescuing, however, treats the patient as though they had no influence over themselves; and a patient with no sense of influence feels helpless. This helplessness can significantly increase fear, anxiety, and depression. A person who is feeling like a victim often becomes obsessed with self-pity, and thinks,

"What's the use? There's nothing I can do about it. Life has tricked me." It is common to hear a person who believes he is a victim sigh that something or somebody "did this to me." Because they feel powerless, victims are often resentful, toward the doctor, the universe, or for that matter, God. The patient who feels this helplessness and lack of control over his own life has great difficulty summoning up a sense of fight and may even lose his will to live.

Victims and rescuers have learned these attitudes in part from the cultural concept of cancer as a disease that creeps up on you in the night and completely controls you. In addition, we traditionally treat people who are sick as if they were suddenly children. When one member of the family is in bed with the flu, the others will be very careful to be quiet so he can rest. They may serve him his meals in bed, including the legendary bowl of chicken soup. The spouse may be exceedingly solicitous: "Can I get you anything, dear?" and "Oh, no, don't get out of bed, I'll get it for you." So even a patient with a minor illness is often treated as if he were helpless; in other words, he is rescued. In our culture, this attitude is so prevalent that it's very difficult not to rescue someone who is ill—let alone someone who has cancer. We have been conditioned to believe that sick people are victims. When a person has a long-term, chronic illness, it becomes important to reverse this attitude.

It's important to note, however, that any patient is likely to feel like a victim *at times,* which is certainly understandable. Likewise, the family may see him that way—sometimes. A patient does at times feel helpless, hopeless, and depressed; the important thing to remember is that there's a big difference between feeling like a victim occasionally and feeling that way most of the time. When a patient frequently sees himself as a victim, that becomes a matter of real concern. Family members can help such a patient by learning not to rescue him.

Why People Rescue

Undoubtedly, it's very difficult to watch a loved one deal with cancer. Many family members feel so helpless that they have great trouble dealing with it. They want to "fix" the situation but cannot, and so they are plagued with a sense of inadequacy and feelings of helplessness. Some try to avoid these feelings by rescuing the poor, pitiful victim. They do everything they can think of to help and fix the patient, and in this way these support people are able to avoid their own feelings of helplessness. Unfortunately, all this rescuing is not necessarily helpful since it casts the patient in the role of victim.

The patient who is rescued is robbed of his responsibility and sometimes of his ability to respond and participate. The rescuer's behavior often invites a split in ambivalent feelings so that the patient stays stuck in his hopelessness. This is not at all what the rescuer wants to happen, of course, but it is simply the outcome of the rescuer's attempts to be responsible for the patient. For instance, a wife may feel that she is responsible for her husband's moods now that he has cancer. So when she comes home after work and finds him sitting in a darkened living room, obviously depressed, her first thought is, "Oh my, the poor thing feels bad. Let me see if I can cheer him up." She turns on lights, gives him a big smile, and says, "How would you like to go to a movie and dinner tonight?" Or she may begin telling him a long, funny story about her day. At once she has begun trying to fix the patient by diverting him from the feelings he is clearly having. This, unfortunately, may tend to drive him more deeply into his depression since she has "taken over" the positive, cheerful feelings. Rescuing often involves the rescuer taking the opposite polarity in this way. If the patient is frightened, the rescuer tries to minimize the fear. A husband whose wife is scared after a poor prognosis might say, "Well, everyone's gotta go sometime. I don't see why you think you're any different than anyone else." If the patient is angry with God over her illness, the rescuer begins to argue against anger: "It won't do you any good to be mad at Him. Being mad is only going to make things worse." Whereas empathy helps us express and dissipate our feelings, this kind of polarity only tends to make matters worse.

Infantalizing the patient is a form of rescuing that is quite common in families where there is cancer. Family members see the patient as a victim who must rely on others—just as an infant does. As a result, they assume a somewhat parental relationship with the patient and become overly protective, controlling, and critical. Overprotecting may take place, for example, in regard to the patient's medication. At exactly the time when the patient is supposed to take it, the spouse barges in and says, "It's 9:00, dear, time for your pills." This invites the patient to feel like an infant and to become passive about his treatment. The spouse, on his part, is burdened with the responsibility and must fret about the time and whether the patient has taken his medication.

Ultimately, a person who assumes this kind of responsibility for a patient over a long period of time will often become increasingly resentful and may eventually turn on the patient. Suddenly he is tired of playing parent to this great big infant; an adult who sees another adult in the capacity of a child for too long gets to feeling overburdened by responsibility. When he does, the rescuer may flip sides and assume the role of persecutor. Now, instead of trying to "fix" the victim in nurturing, parental ways, the rescuer may become very critical. As persecutor, he says, "Why don't you take your pills? I can't understand what's wrong with you! It's such a simple thing to do." If he finds the patient in a darkened living room, feeling sad, he snaps, "Look at this place—it's like a morgue!" and then flicks on all the lights abruptly. The rescuer may have been in the habit of coming home every evening and asking his wife, "Did you do your three visualizations today?" When he is in the role of persecutor, and she says, "Well, I only got in two today," he begins to berate her. His behavior often stems from his frustration at his own sense of inadequacy.

A family member's feeling of inadequacy can lead to another extreme reaction, abandonment. In our culture, most of us are taught to believe that if we deeply love somebody, we must show our love by demonstrating how much we can do for him. As a result, a husband who can't make his sick wife well often believes that he is a bad husband. He will attempt to avoid this painful feeling of failure, sometimes by blaming the patient and sometimes by avoiding or abandoning her. This does not necessarily mean he picks up and moves out of the house. One husband may resume an old habit of drinking heavily. Another may spend countless hours at the office, buried in his work. A wife may suddenly become involved in a dozen different charita-

ble activities—anything to occupy her time and keep her away
from home and her sick husband. Spouses who do this might
still live at home but have abandoned their mates emotionally.

Doctors and Hospitals— Coming to the Rescue

As I discussed in chapter 6, "Dealing with the Doctor,"
doctors have traditionally assumed a directive role. Doctor-
patient relationships in the past have been similar to those
between parent and child or teacher and student. The doctor
simply told the patient what to do. Although doctors don't
write prescriptions in Latin today, there are still remnants of
the old role. Patients are sometimes treated as if they were
children. In turn, many patients see their doctors as parents,
rather than paid consultants. I believe it is important for a
patient to maintain his autonomy as much as possible, including in his relationship with his doctor.

The hospital environment may invite the patient to feel infantile and passive and to assume the role of a victim. The sterile,
impersonal atmosphere of some large hospitals can create the
illusion that the patient has no choice in anything and must
comply with all the institution rules and regulations. After all,
many patients feel that in a hospital they have nothing to say
about when they go to sleep and get up each morning. Nor do
they have a choice in when they eat. Some patients feel further
victimized in being governed by other people's time schedules.
The medical staff may determine without the patient's input
when he is to be examined, have blood drawn, be bathed, and
so on.

Because the hospital setting can lead a patient to feel passive
which often leads to depression, I believe it is very important
for the patient to make every effort to maintain his autonomy.
One way he can do so is to seek information, so that he knows
his own schedule, for instance. A patient might ask the nurse,
"When are my medications being brought around?" "What
time are meals?" "When is the bloodwork done?" A patient
can also assert the importance of his own needs. For instance, if
the laboratory people come to do blood tests while the patient's

pastor is visiting, the patient can say, "Listen, my pastor is here, and it's very important that I talk to him. Would you please come back later?" Or if the patient and his family are involved in an important discussion and the nurse comes to take his temperature, the patient can ask her to return later. Some hospitals have environments that don't encourage patients to make such a request. The nursing staff may be somewhat surprised and even a little upset when a patient asserts himself in this way. But we're now finding that the more assertive patient is the one who does better. I believe this is because he doesn't feel victimized in the hospital. He doesn't see himself as helpless, being moved around at the whim of the institution. Instead, he sees the system and its schedule as a tool—a collection of services that can be worked with and is there to help him. A patient with this frame of reference feels comfortable asserting himself by asking the hospital staff to consider his needs.

I have seen many patients, who wanted to maintain their autonomy during their hospital stay, make their rooms more personal. One, for instance, always brought her own sheets and pillowcases, with brightly colored flowers on them. Other patients have made arrangements with the doctor to allow family members to bring in special foods. One woman put photographs of her family around her room. Bob Gilley also used photographs when he was hospitalized—blown-up pictures of himself when he was in good health, which gave him a visual reminder of what it was like for him to be healthy.

While bringing your own linens and decorating the walls of your hospital room can be very helpful, patients do not always have this luxury. Even those in private and semi-private rooms may find that their hospital has regulations that must be respected. This is particularly true in crowded wards. Still, even a patient in a ward that has no wall space available for the family photographs can have a family album or at the very least some wallet-sized snapshots to remind him of happier times.

Some patients benefit from maintaining important outside activities as much as possible. One patient makes arrangements for her personal masseuse to come in and give her regular massages when she's confined to the hospital. Others, who are committed to regular exercise, make a point of taking walks up and down the hospital corridors every day. One woman had the habit of having a chat with a neighbor over coffee every morning. Although the neighbor could not visit every day, they kept up this ritual by talking on the telephone at the same time each morning. Some patients have turned their hospital rooms into mini-offices to do some paperwork and make business telephone calls from their beds.

In many cases, patients who stay involved with some of their normal activities while hospitalized do better than those who lie around as passive victims. However, there's an important distinction between being victimized and being nurtured and cared for. A hospital patient who is feeling sick may not want to take responsibility for everything or to keep up normal activities—and if that's the way he feels, he needn't try to. All of us at times need to relax and be pampered and let someone else temporarily take over. When a hospital fulfills this need, it's definitely a benefit for the patient. In fact, he may want to let others know that he wants them to take care of him for now. He might ask his wife, "Listen, I'm feeling really crummy. Would you please talk to the nurses for me?" He might tell the doctor, "I feel awful. I don't want any calls from my office. I don't want to do anything while I'm in the hospital except lie here, rest, take my medicine, and get better. Can you arrange for my phone calls to be put through only between the hours of 11:00 and 3:00?" A patient who asks for the vulnerable part of himself to be recognized in these ways is still assuming responsibility for his own needs by the fact of making the request. In this way he remains in charge and maintains his autonomy. This is quite different from being infantalized by institutional settings because he has *asked* to be nurtured and taken care of.

How to Help—Not Rescue

Let me pose four questions that can indicate whether you are rescuing someone—perhaps without even realizing it. (1) Have you decided that you know what's going on with the patient, instead of letting *him* define it? (2) Do you think you know how to get the patient out of his feelings, so you're telling him what to do, rather than offering support and letting him decide what he needs? (3) Do you believe you know the absolute right way, and you're so certain you're right that you're forcing your way on the other person? (4) When you examine your motivations, do you find that you're dealing with the patient in the way you are in order to avoid your own feelings? (This may be the case if you find you are often angry with the patient. Anger is much easier for many people to deal with than helplessness, fear, or sadness.)

I list these four points because so often well-intentioned family members, in their efforts to help, are instead rescuing, and their behavior is actually harmful, not helpful. Family members who believe they are sometimes rescuing can begin positive change by examining their own feelings and needs. Often, rescuers do not take care of their needs, putting all their energy instead into caring for the patient. After weeks of self-neglect, they finally become so needy that they may become angry. One of the best ways they can avoid rescuing is to begin focusing on their own needs and to ask for their needs to be met, too.

Support people sometimes hesitate to ask the patient for help. This is unfortunate because the patient needs to feel useful and wanted too. No matter how debilitated a patient may be, there are usually some ways in which he can be helpful. His wife might say, "Honey, I could really use a hug. I'm feeling down today." While visiting his wife's hospital room, a man might say, "Lynn, I've had a rotten day at the office! Can you listen for a few minutes? Are you feeling good enough to hear about my day?" Let me stress that such requests can be good for the patient. One factor that often contributes to a patient's infantalization is that he feels guilty because he is not contributing to the family. As a result, he tends to withdraw little by little, not asking for what he needs, which invites more rescuing from the family. It becomes a vicious circle. One way to break it is for family members to begin to ask for things from the patient. When family members begin to focus on their own needs and stop rescuing behavior, the patient is given the opportunity to initiate and ask for what *he* needs. This kind of assertive action requires him to be responsible for himself; it makes him feel that he is needed, so in turn, he can ask others to respond to his needs.

A person with cancer can be so concerned about how his illness is hurting his loved ones that he becomes guilt ridden. He may express this in a number of ways. "I'm not worth all the trouble and sadness I'm causing you." Or, more directly, "I'm really upset about how tough all this is for you. I feel so bad about how miserable this cancer has made your life." The patient who makes this kind of remark is forgetting that the risk of loving someone involves bad times as well as good. Both the patient and the family need to remember that when we love another person, there is no guarantee that either of us will always be healthy, physically or emotionally. If a patient does express guilt, the support person can reassure him. "Yes, it is tough right now. But I've been sick in the past, too. Do you remember how you cared for me when I had that slipped disc three years ago? Well, I want you to know that you're worth it to me, too, honey."

In some cases, the patient may assume that dealing with his illness is more difficult for the family than it really is. It may be reassuring for the spouse to say, "It's inconvenient, and it's a major difficulty—but I'm not the one who's lying there with cancer. It's not as hard on me as you imagine. The kids and I are taking pretty good care of ourselves. We'll manage."

Family members sometimes inadvertently rescue a patient by assuming that he cannot continue his normal activities. A spouse can help—rather than rescue—by letting the patient be the one to say, "No, I just don't feel up to doing that," rather than speaking for him, "Oh, my husband won't be able to attend that meeting," or "John won't be playing golf this season, so don't bother calling him." Too often, as soon as the family learns the diagnosis they begin to limit the patient's activities, assuming he can't do anything now. This tends to infantalize the patient by increasing his feelings of helplessness. Let him make his own choices about what he can and cannot do. In all probability, he is capable of doing more than the family thinks.

It can also be tempting to rescue the patient when he is depressed. Perhaps he has been suppressing his fear for several days, growing more passive and depressed each day. The support person may desperately want to help his loved one out of the depression and sometimes becomes frightened, too. If this fear becomes anger directed at the patient, then the support person may be rescuing. A more helpful approach is to express your perception that the patient is passive. It may be appropriate to say, "Gee, you seem passive and depressed, and I get awfully scared when you stay that way for a long time." After this, it's best to say nothing further. You have stated your feelings, and that in itself is helpful.

A depressed person can also be helped by being supported in his feelings. When you empathize with someone, you begin by joining him. For instance, a patient may be staring glumly out the window, and his wife can sit down next to him, take his hand, and say softly, "It's been a tough day, hasn't it?" She is joining the patient and acknowledging that he's having a bad time right now, and this gives him an opportunity to open up and talk about his feelings. "You know, I went to the doctor today, and I'm just not making the progress I want to. I get so angry at not being able to do better!" His wife can support these feelings by listening and replying that she understands how tough it must be for him. This empathy encourages the patient to share his frustration and pent-up feelings. If his wife listens and gives support long enough, the patient will usually begin to come out of these feelings.

There will be times when a spouse may share feelings with the patient about his depression, join him and support his feelings, and yet the patient stays stuck in these difficult feelings for several days. Certainly it is very hard to see someone you love feeling depressed and down, and a spouse may become quite concerned and want to make suggestions. Again, it is important to respect the patient's autonomy. Rather than making a decision to go ahead and help the patient in some way, the spouse can *ask* what she can do. "Is there something I can do to help you?" This allows the patient to decide whether he wants to be helped, and if so, what kind of help he wants. This keeps him in control of his problem, and the fact that *he* is in charge allows him independence.

The patient's decision, at this point, may be that he doesn't want any help—and his right to refuse help needs to be respected. Admittedly, it's very difficult to stand by and do nothing for a loved one who is obviously feeling emotional pain, but the support person must be careful to avoid the temptation to jump right in at this point and rescue the patient. There's a natural desire to try to fix things for a depressed patient, attempting to talk him out of his feelings, loading him with a lot of information he hasn't asked for, and telling him what he needs to do to feel better. Support people may desperately want to do this kind of rescuing, but it is not often helpful since it may discount the patient. If, after enough time has lapsed, the family member feels he must do something, he can again share his own feelings with the patient. "My perception is that you have been down for a long time. I'm really concerned about you." It can be difficult at this point to refrain from telling the patient what to do, but it is still more helpful than rescuing.

It may be that the support person has some information he believes might help the patient handle his feelings. Instead of forcing this on the patient, he can ask whether the patient wants to hear it or not. "I have some information that may have something to do with what's going on. It may or may not be helpful to you. Would you like to hear it?" By approaching the patient in this way, the support person is *asking* for permission to give support or feedback. The patient has a right to refuse this support and say, "No. I don't want to hear it." Even if he refuses, becomes angry, and walks off in a huff, the offer to share information has been registered. Frequently, a patient who has abruptly rejected an offer of feedback will come back some time later and say, "I've been thinking about it, and I do want your feedback. What was it you wanted to tell me about?"

In conclusion, I believe it's important for every support person to understand the difference between helping and rescuing someone with cancer. Certainly it is natural to want very much to help. But if that desire leads to rescuing, no matter how well-intentioned, it may not be helpful. Instead, it can defeat the patient's efforts to work toward recovery. Family members who can instead support the patient and respect his autonomy will play an essential and very positive role.

Chapter 15

Overcoming Depression

D epression is closely associated with cancer, and there are several good reasons for this. First, as I've discussed, personality profiles of people before they develop cancer indicate that they tend to bottle up their feelings, and holding in such emotions as anger, sadness, and fear can lead to depression. So a person with cancer may have been depressed even before the diagnosis. The diagnosis of cancer is also likely to trigger depression in both the patient and his family. For the patient, both the disease and the side effects of treatment usually cause fatigue and emotional stress that can also contribute to depression. It must also be noted that when people are physically ill, there may be physiological and chemical reactions that cause depression. Certainly the very nature of cancer, with its ups and downs, its uncertainty, and the possibility of death, will create some periods of depression.

Many studies in recent years have linked cancer with depression. R.W. Bartrop of New South Wales, Australia, has done a particularly interesting study. The hypothesis was that depression resulting from suppressed grief can actually be harmful to a person's health. Bartrop focused on widows and widowers. One year following the death of their spouses, these people have a higher incidence of cancer and of almost every

other major disease than the general population. What he wanted
to establish was the physiological link that would explain this
data. He did this through immune competence studies on a
group of people whose spouses had recently died. He per-
formed blood studies on them immediately after the death, and
then followed up periodically with more blood tests. He found
that the immune activity of these widows and widowers was
significantly lower than that of control subjects who had not
experienced a death in the family during the previous two years.
It is important to note, however, that the loss itself did not
lower the immune activity; rather, the investigators felt that the
depression, brought on by suppressing the grief that surrounds
the loss of a spouse, was the trigger. While there are several
factors that can lead to depression, denial of feelings is one of
the most common and should be considered as a possible major
factor.

Recognizing Depression

It may come as a surprise that much of the time depression is
not recognized by either the patient or the family members.
Yet, since depression has so much potential of interfering with
immune activity—let alone the quality of life—it is very important to recognize it. Furthermore, people have difficulty dealing
with depression when they are not really aware of its presence.

Many people experience some mild depression from time to
time as a result of pent-up feelings. This is a consequence of
centuries and centuries of learning to override our instincts and
natural drives in order to live in civilization. For instance, in
modern civilization it is not appropriate to follow the urge to
hit somebody over the head when you get angry with him. We
control this urge, and many other spontaneous reactions every
day, out of necessity. The problem comes when we also bottle
up and restrict the accompanying emotions. We can become so
good at this that we are not even aware of denying the feeling.

Denying feelings over some event can result in short-term,
acute depression. We all experience this now and then. For
instance, a salesman may spend his day making three important
presentations to clients and get three rejections. He goes home

depressed and upset. But the next day he bounces back up and says, "Well, darn it, I'll just go out there and try again." Eventually he gets a sale, and his depression goes away.

Acute depression is routine, and everyone suffers it from time to time. Chronic depression, however, is not resolved overnight but lingers on and may build. This long-term depression is the form that can be harmful to the person with cancer and family members. The patient who is depressed may not be aware of it himself, for several reasons. One is that in our culture many people consider depression taboo. Not only are these people frightened of being depressed but they are also afraid of what others may think of them, so much so that they may deny their feelings. They are also concerned about the effect their depression might have on their families. A family may not know how to express their feelings to one another about depression, and so withdraw. When an individual denies his depression to the extent that he is not even aware of it, the depression is very hard to resolve. This denied depression is often the most serious kind, for it continually saps the person's physical and emotional energy.

People who deny their depression are likely to lose perspective about themselves, so that it may be a support person who detects the problem. With this in mind, let me point out some common symptoms that may indicate that a person is depressed, perhaps without his knowledge. (1) The person will display a pessimistic, hopeless attitude towards events, saying such things as "Oh, what's the use?" (2) He may lose his future orientation, as though the cloud hanging over him prevents him from seeing into the future. This can show up in an inability to make plans for the next summer's vacation or to become interested in a daughter's wedding set for the next year. Feeling overwhelmed by daily events, the person cannot deal with long-term plans. (3) He may seem to cut off emotional awareness, so that he expresses little feeling. In cancer patients, this can result from cutting off awareness of their anxiety about the possibility of death. (4) The person has what is known professionally as a "flat affect." He displays very little in the way of emotional ups and downs and comes across as emotionally flat. His appearance is "blah," gray, even numb, with no sparkle in his eyes and not much expression or color in his face. His activity level is significantly decreased, and he seems to move very slowly and to be tired a great deal of the time. (5) His sleeping habits have changed. He may be sleeping a great deal more than usual, as much as ten, twelve, or fourteen hours a day, or he may be waking up in the middle of the night and unable to fall back to sleep. (6) The person may show a decrease in sexual interest.

These symptoms are typical of chronic depression. There is, however, a form of depression with another cluster of symptoms that may be important for family members to be able to identify. This is called an agitated depression. Whereas a typically depressed patient is lethargic, a person with agitated depression hides his feelings through overactivity. In order to avoid facing his depression, he makes sure he is busy all the time. Characteristically, he is in almost constant motion, always doing something, and making sure he has people around him. He rarely allows himself to slow down. He may not appear depressed, but instead may seem overly cheerful and optimistic. Such a patient may be denying his depression—a behavior that is potentially hazardous. But the denial is so deep that if someone says to him, "You seem depressed to me," his reaction will be to say, "Who me? You've got to be kidding!"

Patients with agitated or chronic depression may deny their feelings, which presents the real danger of the ongoing depression diminishing the effectiveness of their immune systems. This physical threat is coupled with the possibility of alienation within the family since the depressed person is withdrawn and emotionally uncommunicative. Often it is a support person who is the one to identify the depression, rather than the person who is depressed.

Dealing with Depression

If you suspect depression in the patient, you might suggest he give you feedback. This is more effective than defining his depression for him. If the patient is unaware that he is denying his feelings, and someone tells him, "You look depressed to me," he may only deny his feelings further and reject the statement. Instead, as a support person you can put your own feelings in perspective. The support person might say something like, "You don't seem to me to be yourself." He can give the patient the opportunity to express his feelings, "I'm concerned about you, John. Is there something going on? Do you want to talk about it?" These statements reflect what the support person has observed, rather than telling the patient how he feels. On the other hand, a statement like, "I think you're depressed," can be perceived as intrusive and is likely to have the effect of deepening the patient's depression.

The important thing to remember is to allow the patient to identify his depression for himself. When he does, he is taking the first step out of the role of victim. The healing process begins not when the support person makes the discovery but when the patient does. The support person can only encourage discovery through questioning, "John, I'm concerned—you seem tired and lethargic. Is there anything you want to talk about? What are you feeling?" The essence of this kind of communication is that it *asks* the patient about his feelings rather than tells him.

In all likelihood, even if the patient is depressed, he may at first respond, "Oh no, nothing, I'm fine." If he does, respect his definition of himself. He may shrug off the question because he doesn't feel entitled to let other people know how he's feeling. If he is denying his depression, for whatever reason, he may need time to think about your question and become aware of how he's feeling. By not pushing for an answer, you encourage him to think about it. Bear in mind that even if he didn't respond immediately, that doesn't mean your message didn't register. Just the fact that you let him know your concern and desire to help gives the patient an opportunity to identify his feelings.

It is also possible that the patient *will* respond, sometimes very emphatically: "I just feel lousy! Like I want to toss in the towel and forget about it!" A family member can feel so uncomfortable and frightened hearing this that his first reaction is to try to cheerlead the patient. "Oh, well, come on, let's think positive," or "Things really aren't that bad, you know." These attempts to cheer the patient up really tell him, "Don't feel your feelings." They imply that it's wrong to feel depressed, and he may react by denying his depression that much more.

When the patient does respond by pouring out his sadness and depression, it is more helpful to empathize. "I'm sorry you're so depressed—and I can understand it." You can also support the patient's statement of feelings: "I'm glad to hear you say that because I've been concerned about you." This kind of response acknowledges and accepts the patient's feelings without infantalizing him through cheerleading. The family member can also offer help in a way that lets the patient maintain his autonomy, by asking, "Is there anything I can do?" If he says there isn't, you may want to reply with, "Okay, but if you think of something, I want you to know I'm available."

There is always a possibility that the patient can't think of anything, but the family member has in mind some ways he would like to help. This is a touchy area. There is a very thin line here between helping and rescuing—moving in and defining the patient's needs. It may be better to let the patient struggle to figure out what he needs, and what you can do for him. If he can't, you may want to give him some options. "I am available to hold you." or "If you ever need me to take care of the kids, I'd be glad to."

A patient with agitated depression may respond to a somewhat different approach. Since this person is always on the go, the support person might say, "John, I'm concerned about what happens when you slow down. And what happens when you're alone?" In all likelihood, this individual is seldom alone since he is more likely to encounter his feelings in solitude. Sooner or later, however, he will be alone; no one can stay busy and involved with other people all the time. When he is, the support person's question may begin to take on meaning and help the patient define for himself how he feels.

Giving the patient an opportunity to acknowledge his depression, then, is one good way to offer support. Another is to express *your* feelings to him; in many instances, this is the best support of all, since it may encourage the patient to feel needed and useful. It also includes him in the family, which is obviously very important. By not sharing both the good and the bad events with patients, family members can inadvertently exclude and alienate them from the family. Many people find it difficult to share their problems with someone who is ill. "Oh, I can't burden my husband with the fact that I'm so upset about my job," a caring wife will say. "He's already overwhelmed with his own depression about his cancer." In fact, sharing is not likely to add to her husband's burden; on the contrary he will feel needed. It would be very helpful for her to say, "Gee, honey, I really feel down. I'm not doing very well at work right now. I'm feeling hopeless and upset because I'd so much like to do more for you, and sometimes I feel I'm just no good to anyone." This is *sharing*, and it invites the patient to help somebody he loves. In turn, he is likely to share his own feelings.

There are times when family members hesitate to share bad news with a patient because they are not sure he has the emotional energy to handle it. Again, it may be better to leave that decision up to the patient. You might ask, "I'm feeling kind of sad and down—do you feel up to listening right now?" This gives the patient the opportunity to say, "No, I'm really feeling sick and in pain. I don't want to hear anything depressing." If this is his response, fine. There is no harm in asking. What may be harmful is the decision family members sometimes make to always be optimistic and cheerful around the patient. This behavior creates an unreal atmosphere that only increases the patient's feeling of alienation. He may begin to think that he's the only person in the family who has these feelings; he's different—so something must be wrong with him.

Nonverbal Help for Depression

So far I have concentrated on ways to help a depressed patient through verbal communication. There are also several nonverbal ways to deal with depression. One is physical exercise. When a person becomes depressed, his exercise program is doubly important. Family members can be supportive by participating with the patient—if he requests it. For instance, he might say, "I'm really depressed today, and I don't feel like walking, but I know if I do, I'll feel better. Will you come with me for a walk?" Many patients habitually use walking as an antidote to depression. Marge Deacon says, "I think exercise is one of the finest treatments for depression there is. When I feel low, I get out of it by taking a two mile walk. After the first half mile,

I've got a lot of oxygen in me, and I've taken a good, long look at the trees and flowers, and listened to the birds, and I feel a lot better. By the time I've finished the second mile, I'm out of my depression."

Another excellent antidepressant can be physical touch. Many people withdraw from touch when they are depressed, and one of the best remedies for depression is to do the opposite and seek out physical contact. Some patients go to a family member or friend and simply ask to be held. Even if patients do not initiate it, family members can offer physical affection. There's something very comforting about being held that seems to communicate something words often cannot express. Moreover, depression is relieved when pent-up feelings are expressed, and a person who is being physically held is more likely to experience his feelings. In some cases, he may even begin to cry while in the other person's arms. The following chapter, "Intimacy and Affection," discusses this subject in more detail.

There are many small, thoughtful expressions of love that can help a person feel needed. Just bringing home a rose to a depressed patient might improve his spirits. "I saw this down in the garden, and I thought about you, dear." Or, "I couldn't wait to get home from work today so I could give you a great big hug." Playing soft music can be comforting. The possibilities are only limited by one's imagination. But a word of caution is in order. While thoughtful, loving acts are nurturing and reinforcing, creating a cheerful atmosphere in order to "snap him out of it" may not be. Playing cheerful, upbeat music to a gloomy patient, having a big party, or suggesting he watch a silly movie on television may be a way of discounting the depressed person's feelings. It's very important to support the patient in facing his depression. Trying to cheer him up only helps him avoid his feelings.

Some medications cause or contribute to depression. While side effects vary, some patients do become depressed when their chemotherapy includes certain medications. Then, too, a patient who is taking too much medication may become depressed. When there is a possibility that the patient's depression is a result of treatment, the patient and family should be sure to discuss it with the doctor. Unless they do, the doctor may not be aware of the severity of the depression. When the quality of a patient's life is being seriously eroded by medication-related depression, doctors are likely to adjust the medication schedule. Individual tolerances for depression vary, of course. But if the patient has been depressed for a long period of time it may feel intolerable to him and may significantly effect the quality of his life. If this is the case, it may be time to go for outside help. Sometimes everyone in the family is so disturbed by the illness that the family becomes overwhelmed with a sense of helplessness. When this happens, it's unlikely that they will be able to overcome it without professional counseling since every member is so close to the situation.

Too often, people fear depression so much they won't even acknowledge its existence. It is as if they believe that acknowledging it will only make it get worse. Actually, the opposite is true. By experiencing your own depression, acknowledging it to someone else, and having your feelings accepted, you begin to move out of it. It is not true, although some people seem to believe it is, that if you concede to depression you might collapse into it forever and die. By accepting that we are depressed, we gain the strength to overcome it. Moreover, depression and some feelings of hopelessness are normal and to be expected during an illness. So it is a matter of degree. Depression that is too severe, or lasts for too long a period of time, can seriously erode the quality of living and should not remain unattended. When a patient acknowledges his feelings and gets the support of his family, the depression is likely to diminish significantly.

Chapter 16

Intimacy and Affection

E ach of us, no matter what our state of health, has a need to be loved and nurtured. When we are ill, and most vulnerable, this need is frequently even greater. In fact, intimacy and affection can play a significant role in healing; for this reason, I wholeheartedly prescribe large doses of both for my patients.

Recent studies have demonstrated the role affection and love play in regaining health. At the University of California at San Francisco, researchers found that heart patients who had pets at home did better than those who did not. Another study divided hospital patients recuperating from heart attacks into three groups. The patients in the first group were given plants in their rooms to care for. Those in the second group also received plants, but did not care for them directly; their only responsibility was to inform the nurse when the plant needed care. Patients in the third group were not given plants. Those in the first group required the least hospitalization and medication; group two did less well; and group three did poorest.

These studies and others in this area seem to indicate that a patient with something or someone to care for has a greater sense of purpose in life, and purpose, I believe, is related to the will to live. If a plant or pet can give a patient a sense of purpose, then think how much more the will to live can be strengthened by meaningful relationships with other people—by intimacy and affection.

While giving love is important, each of us also needs to receive it. This was dramatically shown some years ago in studies of infants in foundling homes. Orphans who were physically held and loved thrived. But those who had little or no cuddling and touch fared far worse, both physically and emotionally. These findings confirm the importance of affection to survival itself.

As a culture, we have seen a significant rise in chronic degenerative disease during the past hundred years or so. This increase corresponds with changes that have led to the loss of an important source of affection—the extended family. At one time, people were likely to be born, grow up, and die within a radius of only a few miles, and throughout their lives they were surrounded by a broad and intimate support system of family and friends who had always known them. These were people they could go to in times of trouble, or who would come to them, offering help, people they could let their hair down with; people they could lean on. In today's urbanized and mobile culture, by contrast, many of us live hundreds of thousands of miles from where we were born, and few of us have adequately replaced the extended family. Our increased alienation and isolation undoubtedly takes its toll and there is evidence that it is related to the higher incidence of disease.

The lack of intimacy in modern urban life is striking. Imagine your great-grandparents walking down the streets of their small communities. They were likely to be greeted by a relative, the clergyman, an old friend from childhood, and other people they had known all their lives. Because these relationships were so deep-rooted, greetings might be accompanied with warm, genuine smiles, handshakes, and hugs. We know today that the general sense of affection and security imparted by these support systems has a positive effect on health. Today's lifestyle is often so fast-paced that we are too busy to recognize the lack of intimacy we may experience in our environment. Nevertheless, it is very real, and it means most of us have needs for affection and intimacy that are not met by an extended family as they once were. But there are ways to resolve this problem. One is to develop a support system, as discussed in chapter 5. Another is to build upon the love and affection you already have within your family and among your friends.

Touching and Holding

The importance of touch has been demonstrated in an experiment with rabbits. One group of rabbits was handled and cuddled by a graduate student; the other was not. The rabbits that were given loving touch showed little evidence of coronary disease; those that were not showed a significant incidence. Touch conveys a kind of love which we, as human beings, may also need to help our healing process.

Much of this book has concentrated on communicating and expressing feelings verbally. Certainly, verbal expression is important. Nonverbal communication, however, is sometimes more effective and moving. I have found this to be true many times when I've gone to visit one of my patients in the hospital. Sometimes I have walked in to find the patient emotionally constricted, attempting to keep the family members around his bed from knowing how much he was hurting. I have often sat down by the bed and just held the patient's hand, perhaps stroking it gently, and sometimes not saying a word. On occasion, some of my "toughest" patients have broken down and cried. The caring expressed by touch burst the dam, and they were able to get some relief from their pent-up feelings.

The same patients may not be very responsive to verbal communication. They clam up and withdraw when a loved one tries to talk with them about feelings. A patient may, for example, be unable to deal with his fear of dying, and equally unable to talk about it, until his wife or lover puts her arms around him and holds him tightly. Then, suddenly, he may begin crying and telling her how frightened he is. Sometimes we can confront painful feelings more easily when we are being given actual physical support by someone we love.

In some ways, holding another person is the best and most uncontaminated way to express love for them. Holding has a special warmth and sincerity that conveys your feeling directly and without censorship to the other person. While not everybody is good with words, and words often fail to really say what we feel, a warm hug gives a clear message. Even when we express ourselves accurately, words may not be as moving as touch. "I like you" is very different from a big, warm embrace. It's too bad our culture doesn't permit us to touch one another more often; most of us could do with more of this special warmth and support.

A person who is ill has an increased need to be held and loved. In fact, it is sometimes appropriate to compare a seriously ill patient to a small child in terms of this need because both feel vulnerable and helpless. Each, in some ways, is frightened because he cannot control what will happen to him. And each needs a good deal of nurturing. To some extent, all of us share this need, although we tend to deny it. There is within us a kind of little, infantile part of us that needs understanding, nurturing, and acceptance for who we are rather than what we do every day in the world. Ideally, a mother gives this unconditional love to her child, and when she does, it allows him to feel safe in the world and to develop a healthy self-esteem. It would be wonderful if each of us would be loved like this—simply because we existed. For a patient under severe stress, this need for unconditional acceptance is increased. Particularly for the patient who doesn't look attractive or feel well, physical affection is one of the best ways to communicate acceptance and love. It can do wonders in providing nourishment to a patient at a time when he's not doing his best.

Not every patient, however, will accept physical affection at first. When a patient rejects touch, it is important to respect his wishes. He may have good reasons for feeling this way. Being touched is so intimate that it is important to respect other people's right to refuse it and to maintain their psychological boundaries where they choose. For some, touch may be difficult because of its association with bad experiences in childhood, such as being abused. Others may be feeling unwell or in pain and find that being held does not feel good to them.

Some people turn down affection because of low self-esteem; they feel they aren't entitled to be loved. Some people learned in childhood that they had to perform in order to deserve love. Since their parents' acceptance was conditional, these people have grown up believing that they must earn love. Any member of the family—patient, spouse, or child—can hold such a belief. When someone, such as the patient, does reject touch, he needs to be offered support and assurance that he is loved and needed anyway. His loved one might tell him, "I think I understand that you don't want to be held right now, but I still want you to know that I love you and care about you. I want to hold you, and express my deep feelings toward you no matter how badly you may feel. You don't have to earn my love." For many people, accepting this unconditional love takes time, but ultimately they may come to trust and accept the affection being offered to them.

Certainly there will be times when the support person wishes to be held—after all, every one of us has a need for nurturing and affection. A family member who is feeling this way should, by all means, let the patient know that. A spouse might say to the patient, "I would really like a hug." When a support person makes this kind of request, it may help the patient feel needed, which can do wonders for his self-esteem. Remember that any patient's self-esteem can be damaged by the feelings of weakness and vulnerability surrounding an illness.

Just as verbal communication can be unclear, touch can sometimes give the wrong message. It's important for a support person to know his own feelings when he is nurturing the patient and to be aware of what he may be conveying at the time. If the support person is feeling angry, for instance, because the patient is sad, that anger is liable to come across subtly in the actual hugging. I suggest such a person first deal with his angry response to sadness and *then* give comfort. Another possible response to sadness is to move in with physical affection as a way of blocking the patient's feelings or of denying them nonverbally. If a patient is crying, it is best to beware of the kind of patting on the back that tends to be patronizing. It can convey the message, "Don't worry, I'll make it all better." While the patient may need physical affection, he does not need to be infantalized and made to feel like a helpless victim.

Support persons sometimes ask me to tell them the best way to hold a patient. My answer is always that there is no one right way and that it is up to the patient to define what feels good. Some people love to be hugged, while others prefer a simple kiss on the cheek, and still others feel most nurtured when their hair is stroked. What feels comforting to us as adults usually has to do with our warm memories of physical affection as children. It's best to remember that what you prefer may not be what the patient likes. Two people may both like back rubs, but one likes to have his back stroked lightly while the other likes a good, strong rubdown. So you might ask the patient what he finds most comforting through occasional questions, such as, "How does this feel?" and "Does this feel good?"

While I have talked primarily about the patient's need for touch, his loved ones also need to be held and physically comforted. All members of the family, including the patient, will do best if they have a support system of several people who can provide physical affection. It may be risky to rely on only one or two people for these needs because that can mean there are times when no one at all is available. Good friends can hold you, hug you, give a back rub or simply hold your hand. This kind of physical affection is still easier for women friends in our society than for men; sadly, our cultural homophobia doesn't permit men to share their feelings or to hold one another as freely as it allows women to. But men, too, need this kind of nourishment—from other men, as well as from women.

Intimacy, Affection, and the Single Person

People with cancer who live alone need nurturing too, of course. They may be less likely to receive it, however, unless they assertively reach out to friends. Single people need to stay in touch with their need for physical affection and look to their support groups for this nourishment. Certainly some friends enjoy giving hugs; others are comfortable holding the patient or holding hands. Still others like to give backrubs now and then.

Another source of physical contact that I recommend is a physical therapist or massage therapist. These professionals offer their services through such places as the local YMCA, health clubs, and beauty salons. Some even make house calls. Therapy of this type can give real relief from depression, anxiety and pain. The medical profession recognizes the importance of being touched, and for years nurses gave backrubs to hospital patients each evening. This sort of nurturing was known to help many patients relax and sleep more comfortably. It did wonders to aid the healing process, and it's too bad that nurses are kept so busy now that they seldom have time to give this kind of "medicine." It *is* good medicine, and those who live alone often find that massage is a real boost in their efforts toward recovery.

Children are another good source of affection for those who live alone. A child extends to a loving adult an unconditional acceptance and affection that is very special and nourishing. Children, too, need to be touched and are usually much more comfortable with holding than many adults. When you hold a child, both you and the child will experience warm feelings—so it's a two-way street. Many single people have married relatives or friends with children who would enjoy this kind of relationship. For those who don't, there are some fine community organizations, such as Big Brothers of America and Big Sisters of America, that are based on the idea that there are children and adults who need each other's love. Older patients can become involved in services that "rent" grandmas or grandpas to sit with children.

Sexual Intimacy

In our culture, one of the most common ways we meet our touching and holding needs as adults is through sexual intimacy. There is probably no relationship more intimate than one between two people in love. Many couples, however, interrupt or change their sexual activity when one of them becomes ill with cancer. Often, this decrease in intimate touch is not made necessary by the disease but is a response to the stress, anxiety and depression one or both partners begins to experience.

It is helpful, when this happens, to remember that the need to be touched and held is not the same as the need for sexual fulfillment. This is an important distinction since either partner may be temporarily so overwhelmed that he or she cannot function sexually. If so, it is important for the couple to continue holding one another and feeling physically close without pressure to perform sexually. The couple can maintain physical closeness and intimacy, as long as they are both aware of the sexual limitations either may have at the moment for physical or emotional reasons. This can be a delicate problem because it may be that one partner is now feeling sexually unfulfilled and frustrated. This can be either the patient or the spouse who feels the stress and uncertainty surrounding the illness.

It is often helpful for couples to frankly discuss their sexual needs, but open communication becomes more important when a couple is dealing with a life-threatening illness. Both now have a greater need for the reassurance of touch and physical intimacy, and a change in sexual desire need not be allowed to frustrate that need. The patient can express a desire for touch, while being clear about sexual limitations, by saying something like, "I'm really feeling bad, and probably can't relate sexually, but I'd sure like to be held." This tells the spouse what the patient can and cannot do.

It can happen that embracing and cuddling will arouse one partner while the other is unable to perform sexually. If it does, they may want to talk about ways the aroused partner can be satisfied. One way is through sexual contact short of actual intercourse, if the less aroused person is comfortable with that. Another way is for the couple to agree that the partner who is feeling sexually aroused has permission to masturbate as a way to achieve satisfaction. Often couples complain that masturbation is unsatisfying because it does not involve holding. If this is the case, a couple might want to embrace and cuddle afterwards. There are many creative ways a couple can satisfy disparate needs, so long as they communicate and share their desires and limitations. It is very important that one partner be able to say, "I still need more sexual contact," and the other feel free to reply, "I don't feel good, and I'm not able to have sex now, but what else can we do to satisfy you?" If a couple's imagination doesn't provide enough options in this regard, the library and the local bookstore will have many good books on human sexuality that can open up possibilities. Rather than have one or both partners frustrated, the couple can also consult a sex therapist.

If the patient's sexual functioning is very much reduced, a

talk with the doctor is a good idea. Sometimes such inability is caused medically, and the physician may be able to manipulate the drugs accordingly. But unless the patient communicates with the doctor on this issue, the doctor will have no way of knowing a problem even exists.

I will conclude by saying that I have devoted an entire chapter to intimacy and physical affection because I firmly believe a nurturing touch is one of the best medicines for a person who feels down and depressed. Even when the patient is feeling weak, a support person can give the warmth and acceptance of touch and simply hold and stroke the patient, which requires no energy on the patient's part. To some extent, touch will nearly always alleviate depression. There is nothing quite like being held to boost one's self-esteem.

Chapter 17

The Side Benefits

A t first, most people are amazed at the idea that having cancer can have any benefits at all. Certainly the difficulties of the disease are much more apparent, and most of this book focuses on how to effectively handle the problems associated with cancer. But a life-threatening illness may also change a family in ways that are positive, fill some unmet needs for the patient, and provide a new perspective on life for everyone concerned. These positive changes are the side benefits of the disease.

These benefits can be very meaningful. Again and again, patients have told me, "I know this may sound really strange, but I'm glad I went through that experience with cancer." They go on to talk about how much better the quality of life is for them now because through their illness they learned to live better and fuller lives.

Anyone who becomes sick in our culture is likely to receive certain "automatic" benefits. Unfortunately, we treat people who are ill much better than we treat those who are healthy. Of course, when people are sick they need that nourishment, and it's wonderful that they get it. But no one should have to become ill to receive love and attention. In effect, we often reward illness and punish health. We have the highest expectations of the strong, healthy person and tend to place enormous responsibility on him. He is taught to overachieve and to never fail at any cost. He is told not to be selfish and to take care of other people's needs before his own. Nobody ever thinks the strong, healthy person needs to be stroked. Unlike someone who is ill, he doesn't seem to need it.

We are indoctrinated at a very young age with the idea that there are certain benefits available only to someone who is sick. One case in point is getting excused from school. The school child soon learns that the only excuse for staying home from school is a demonstrable illness, one with an obvious symptom like a fever or a terrible sounding cough. The child knows he will not be excused, however, on the grounds that he is terrified of his teacher, or worried about the fight his parents had the night before, or sad because his dog was recently hit by a car and killed. No matter what our problems, many of us are in the same predicament—only sickness is a valid excuse for not performing according to our rigid cultural values.

When a person is sick, he is likely to be rewarded and nourished in many ways, receiving the kind of treatment we all would benefit from on an everyday basis. Large doses of love, consideration, and attention improve the quality of life for anyone who gets them, sick or well. But we tend to reserve such treatment for the person who is ill, particularly if he has a life-threatening disease such as cancer.

Common Side Benefits

While there are obvious reasons why we don't *want* to become sick, illness can bring numerous benefits, or positive gains. It is important to recognize these side benefits so that the patient, and often the entire family, can continue to realize them and incorporate them in daily life after health is regained.

Serious illness is often accompanied by an internal permission for the patient to express his feelings and ask for his needs to be met. This is likely to promote more open communication within the family and creates a healing atmosphere. For some patients, this internal permission to express themselves is very significant. Many men have never before felt they could express certain of their emotions or ask for certain needs to be met. A husband, for instance, may believe it would be a sign of weakness to say he felt overworked, overstressed, and insecure about his job. During illness, however, he may allow himself to have these feelings and to discuss them with his family and friends. Likewise, a woman may directly ask for her husband's attention and affection when she is ill, something she rarely felt she could do until then.

Another very important side benefit of serious illness is our sudden realization that none of us can take our own lives or those of our loved ones for granted. A diagnosis of cancer tends to bring us an awareness of our vulnerability and finiteness. The patient and those around him are likely to stop postponing their recognition of one another and begin expressing their love. A wife who loves her husband very much may realize how long it's been since she told him so and how important it is to do that. So the uncertainty of illness may lead us to see how deep and valuable our love for others is.

Recognizing our mortality has other implications, too. So many of us conduct our lives as though we were going to live forever and are often driven by our basic cultural belief that a person must work hard in order to receive any pleasure. Unfortunately, there is rarely an end to that hard work, and the pleasure, for many, never comes. Once people realize that one day they will die, they begin to think about this and often decide, "I'm entitled to live the time I have left as fully as I possibly can." This does not mean they stop working, but they may stop postponing gratification and begin to value life on a day-to-day basis. Suddenly they think, "Wait a minute—I'm not going to live forever! So what are the things I've always wanted and been putting off? If I keep putting them off, I'll never get to do them." With this realization, the patient begins to unconditionally experience more of the joys of the here and now—the scent of flowers, the vibrancy of colors, the things happening around him that he never paid attention to in the past. Family members as well as patients often make this decision to begin enjoying each day, to re-evaluate their priorities, and to discover the pleasures they've been putting off.

Earl Deacon is one of many of my patients who has realized this benefit from battling cancer. Earl told me, "My cancer made me ask myself, 'What do I really want to do with the time I have left?' The realization that my life might be shortened led me to change in some major ways. I used to be so wrapped up in my work that my head was constantly spinning with all kinds of business deals and problems and frustrations. Now I try to avoid deadlines. The whole quality of my life has improved as a result of having had cancer. Whatever I'm doing—driving my car, traveling—I have an awareness of nature around me. I have a deep respect for all life now; I still fish, but I no longer hunt. I enjoy just being with nature. As they say, I take time to stop and smell the flowers."

Many other patients have expressed similar sentiments. One woman who had been a fanatic housekeeper told me that her life no longer depended on whether her house was in perfect order and all her floors scrubbed clean. She added, "After I'm gone, what am I going to leave behind in people's memory that's really important? Maybe I don't want my children to remember how clean the kitchen floor always was. It's going to be a lot more important to them that I sat down to talk with them and was with them. What they're going to remember is how we related to one another."

Patients and family members alike often feel entitled to say "no" to others for the first time in their lives when they learn they have cancer. One patient's husband had been working sixty-hour weeks for many years until his wife's illness. He told his boss, "My wife is sick, and I've got to spend more time with her and my kids." He had never before been able to stand up and object to working overtime. When he did, his employer was understanding and accepted the fact that he would have to expect less from his employee.

The ability to say "no" is a positive gain many patients prize. One told me, "I was never able to turn down a request to serve on a committee until I got sick. Then I learned to say, 'I'm sorry, but I'm not interested.'" Others have found this extended to changes in their social lives. One patient never turned down an invitation to a dinner party until his priorities changed after his diagnosis. "Then I was invited to one party," he told me, "where there were going to be people I just don't care to be around. I decided I wasn't interested in going. In the past, I don't think I ever turned down an invitation of that kind. But now that I'm ill, I feel I have a right to."

Until their diagnosis, many of my patients had defined themselves in terms of their material accomplishments. When they began to examine their values, they became aware that many of their actions had been based on what other people would think of them. They also began to see that their desire to satisfy other people's expectations often led them to discount their own physical and emotional limitations. Many of these people decided there were other things in life more important than their careers or the size of their bank accounts. Very often they began to spend more time with their mates, children, and grandchildren. They came to believe that building warmth and closeness with others was more important than building a large estate.

Often the most important discoveries someone with cancer makes have to do with his feelings toward his family—and their feelings toward him. Some people are amazed to find that the people they love value them for who they are, not for what they do and how much they produce. A patient who is sick and in pain may believe he is at his worst; he may look and feel bad and be unable to do much for others. A patient in this condition may be surprised to find that others still care for him. Being liked and loved no matter what, just for yourself, can be a great source of comfort—and can put a patient in touch with what is really important in his life.

Bob Gilley, who had always been on the go building his thriving insurance business, found that his diagnosis of cancer radically changed his priorities. He and his wife, BJ, began to live according to a new ideal: "Be here now." When Bob began to worry out loud about something that had happened the day before or some business appointment scheduled for the next day, she would softly remind him: "Be here now."

Bob recounts, "I started to pay more attention to little things, little moments. I might walk in after work, and my thirteen-year-old son, Sean, couldn't wait to tell me how he was doing on the wrestling team. I've been able to watch him change and become much more extroverted—and it's very joyful for me to see his progress. There are other things with the children, special times. I remember one night lying in bed reading *The Velveteen Rab-*

bit to my ten-year-old daughter, Erin. Moments like that are precious; you can't buy them, and no one can give them to you. They're just there for you."

In 1982, I was invited to speak on the same platform with Bob at the annual Million Dollar Roundtable convention in Atlanta. Bob spoke on the quality of life. He told the audience that most of us don't stop to smell the roses because we spend all our time either thinking about what we should have done yesterday or worrying about what we should do tomorrow. "We're not in the here and now," he emphasized, "and I'm often a good example of that. Today BJ and I were taking our morning walk when I realized a mockingbird was singing. And I wondered, 'Where has my mind been?' I'd been preoccupied with a deal I've been working on, and I'd allowed myself to just tune out on what life is all about."

Bob also told the large crowd of insurance agents about a change in his perspective on minor problems. "I no longer let trivial things bother me. When somebody hassles me, or a client tells me he's going to start doing business with another agent, or someone says he doesn't care for me, I feel comfortable saying, 'Well, that's your opinion.' I don't take things like that personally anymore. Those are things that used to hurt my feelings but not now."

Like Bob, so many patients have told me little things don't bother them in the same way. This often represents a real change in attitude. One patient said, "I used to get uptight about the simplest things—like having to sit and wait for a traffic light to turn green. I'd get more and more impatient. And if another driver would do something like pull in front of me suddenly without signaling, I'd get so upset it would ruin my day. Well, I just don't let insignificant things like that bother me now—once in a while they get to me, I'm only human, but not often. I'm a different person compared to the way I used to be."

For many patients, an important gain from cancer is the strengthening of their marriages. Much of this has to do with the fact that when we realize how finite we are, we appreciate each other more. And, as I discussed in chapter 7, "Communicating Feelings," a life-threatening crisis can lead family members to communicate more openly with one another. Some

couples are impelled by the news of cancer to see family therapists and to begin to work on problems that may have existed
for many years. This often happens so that the patient can be
supported in his efforts to change in healing ways. Tom McNamara says, "We've had lots of counseling since Pat's diagnosis,
so that expense has raised the ante in our marriage quite a bit!"
Although Tom jokes about it, he and Pat agree that their commitment to work together to fight Pat's disease has made their
marriage stronger and more satisfying for both.

Pat McNamara adds that as she and Tom learned to communicate more openly, other family members have benefited. "I
know that both our married children have more open communication in their marriages than they would have if they hadn't
had parents who were doing this kind of thing." Marge and
Earl Deacon also feel their grown children have gained through
the example of their growing relationship. "Our psychotherapy
opened up all these worlds of self-improvement for us," Marge
says, "and our children and their spouses have made the jour-
ney with us."

As you can see, a patient and his family can experience a
whole host of positive gains, both tangible and intangible. So
far I've concentrated on the intangible gains that have to do
with changes in philosophy, in one's feelings, and in relationships.
Some of the more tangible gains concern new and better habits
in such areas as nutrition, sleep, and exercise. Other gains
involve personal adjustment. A single patient I worked with
learned how to be closer to his friends and build his support
system as well as how to adapt to his aloneness. Many spouses
have told me how they learned to share household duties.
Business people very often become better time managers as they
change priorities or adapt to a somewhat reduced energy level.
Both patients and spouses have told me that they have been
able to use what they learned about visualization to diminish
other health problems. Marge Deacon was told by her doctors
that because of her high blood pressure she would be on
medication the rest of her life. But by using visualization regularly,
she succeeded in lowering her blood pressure and has not had
to take medication for three years.

Some families gain by doing things they had postponed for
years and years. One couple finally built their dream house,

and another fulfilled a lifelong desire by taking a cruise around the world. And, while the patient is the one who is generally more concerned about exercise and a healthy diet, other family members usually become aware of their own health needs and develop new habits, too. It's as if everyone, not just the patient, takes the diagnosis as a warning signal and begins to change and grow. Often, a major gain for all members of the family is a heightened awareness of the effects of stress. Once they have an awareness, they begin to make adjustments in their lives to reduce stress, thereby creating a more healthy environment for the entire family.

Maintaining the Side Benefits on a Permanent Basis

A family can respond to the diagnosis of cancer by significantly improving the quality of life for both the patient and the family members. This is not to minimize the pain, fear, and distress that accompany a life-threatening disease, but rather it is to suggest that there are two sides to everything and that nothing in life has to be totally negative. Even illness usually brings some gains that can be maintained. Perhaps it's time to take another inventory and review some of the benefits your family may have reaped. Ask yourself such questions as: Do we now communicate more openly than we did before we learned about the cancer? Have we learned to pull together and work as a team? Do we now permit more autonomy for individual members? Do we express our feelings more freely? Are we more affectionate and expressive of our love for one another? Do we appreciate one another more? Do we ask more for our needs to be met? Do we put less emphasis on achievement now? Do we pay attention to the small things that once went unnoticed?

These questions can help the family reexamine how they have changed and what side benefits they have gained since the diagnosis of cancer. Many of my patients conclude that since the illness became a major influence, they have begun to think and do things differently—and in the process have realized some positive gains.

Once individuals are aware of what they have gained, the important question is: What can the family do to keep these gains? *Will* the family keep them when the patient begins to recover, or will members go back to behaving in the same old ways? This is very significant because, as I mentioned earlier, in our culture we tend to reward the sick and punish the healthy. The patient who begins to get well is in danger of being "punished" by the fact that both he and his family will now go back to their old ways. If the patient formerly had emotional needs that were neglected until the illness, the loss of the illness can mean the loss of those new emotional benefits. So it may be very important for the patient to ask, "What will adequately replace the benefits I got during the illness?"

A typical benefit that can be lost is the internal permission to feel and experience feelings that the culture allows someone who is ill. Often, an individual is so caught up in the race to achieve that he doesn't take time to know what he's feeling—let alone express himself. For instance, he may be so involved in desk work that he doesn't even realize that the muscles at the back of his neck are getting tight. If he'd slow down, he'd probably feel the discomfort, and perhaps even ask someone to rub his neck—but he doesn't slow down. When the same person is sick, however, the illness slows him down to the point where he has time to be aware of how he feels. He also has permission to express his feelings and to ask for what he needs, such as a good neckrub. He enjoys a general permission to be more assertive. If somebody in the family does something that really irritates him, he can say, "Hey, I don't like that—that feels bad," and the family will respect his wishes. So while he is ill, the patient may stop suppressing his feelings and, consequently, experience less anxiety and depression. This freedom can, I believe, have both psychological and physiological benefits.

Sometimes patients stray from the gains they've made quite dramatically as they get well—and so can family members. Once he recovers, it is not as easy for the patient to treat himself in the same manner nor will others treat him as well. One of my patients, for example, had a marriage that had been very difficult until she became ill. Then, suddenly, she and her husband were able to communicate with one another and generally got along very well for the first time in many years. Finally one day she got a good report from her doctor—she was in remission. That same night, she and her husband had a big argument, just like the old days. It was as if they had stored up all their disagreements for the year of her illness, and now that she was well, the marital happiness they had gained was gone. While this is a dramatic example, it is often true that the patient and family assume their old lifestyle when the patient recovers health and in the process lose what they've gained.

Sometimes, a patient who is cognizant of the possibility of losing the side benefits will experience anxiety, depression, and even a new, bizarre physical symptom after he has been given the good news that he is better. While he may be very happy about recovering, internally he is afraid of losing what he has gained. The sudden emotional discomfort patients sometimes experience when they receive good news about their health can be a helpful clue that may benefit them in the long run. It may mean that they need to think about how much of their secondary gains will no longer exist when good health is restored. I then suggest that they ask themselves some questions about this. "When I think about being well again, what do I imagine will change? Will I begin to work at a breakneck pace again? Will I still feel subject to the same old pressures at work? Will I still be able to say 'no' when I feel like it?"

Some people experience physical pains that signal that they are neglecting themselves in some way after being given a clean bill of health. One of my patients, a physician, had been diagnosed with cancer of the colon. After he regained his health, he went back to his office, and in no time he was carrying his old, heavy workload. Very soon he began having internal pains. Wisely, he asked himself, "What am I doing? What's responsible for this pain?" Knowing that it was not a medical problem, he soon traced it to working too much. He gave himself permission to work on a reduced schedule—and his pain went away. It had been a mild warning signal, and it tipped him off to the need to pace himself. Often, the body will let an individual know in this way what his limitations are.

If family members are no longer supportive after the patient begins to get well, this is another signal; they may have been neglecting themselves. As I have emphasized, family members who deny their own needs to take care of the patient can become very resentful and worn-out. When the patient finally gets well, they are likely to abruptly withdraw the affection they have been giving. This is why it's so important that family members not overtax themselves during the illness. If they do, they may not be available to the patient after he recovers. During the illness, the family, too, will receive benefits, such as support from friends; likewise, family members may need to examine what they have gained and decide how to maintain these benefits.

Patients and their families may want to identify the side benefits they realize from the disease. Then, as the patient begins to get well, they can start thinking about how they can keep these gains. If it is used creatively, the experience of cancer can be a powerful teacher. Not only do patients and families typically gain some important side benefits during the illness, but *they can keep these benefits thereafter*. It is the patients who learned how to do this who have said to me, "If I had to have cancer all over again, I would."

Chapter 18

When the Patient
is a Child

Parents who have children with cancer suffer terrible emotional pain. It is certainly one of the most difficult of human experiences. The initial role of a parent is to provide care and nurturing to a helpless and vulnerable infant. When the child is ill, that memory of infant dependency makes us want all the more to protect him. These protective feelings are also aroused by our cultural conditioning to take care of the young and the sick as well as those we love. A child with cancer fits all three categories: he is young, sick, and very much loved. And so caring for the patient who is a child is a very delicate matter—parents want desperately to do what's best for their child but are often not sure what that is.

While I realize that parents of children with cancer may yearn for some solid guidelines on exactly how to treat a child of a certain age, it isn't possible to make hard and fast rules. Each child has different needs. Certainly a five-year-old should be treated differently than a ten-year-old, and a twelve-year-old has different needs than a fifteen-year-old. But even children of the same age have widely varying levels of maturity, so in the end parents must judge the needs of their children as individuals. This makes parenting a demanding task under any circumstances, but when a child is seriously ill, parents are called upon to give still more devotion and energy.

The Child's Autonomy

Although I have emphasized the cancer patient's need for autonomy throughout this book, I know that some adults will be surprised to hear that it is also a major consideration when the patient is a child. This does not mean a four-year-old should be permitted to make treatment decisions, but many people err in the other direction and do not give children the opportunity to participate in decisions they *can* handle. Every child, whatever his age, can be actively involved in making some of his own choices. A mother can give a small child a choice by saying, "Yes, honey, you're going to the hospital for treatment. Why don't you decide what you want to bring with you?" This lets the child decide what will give him the most comfort in the hospital. A child might choose a favorite doll or toy, a certain pair of pajamas, or a special blanket. Parents can also let even a small child make decisions about visitors. "Tell Daddy and me whether you want us to be with you. Both of us together, or would you rather have just one of us at a time?" So, depending on the child's level of maturity and past experience with making decisions, parents can encourage his autonomy in certain areas.

I believe this is very important. When people—including children—are allowed to participate in their illness, they are often less passive, less depressed, and less frightened. Children, additionally, tend to be less rebellious. All this means that the child is better able to harness his energy toward recovery. If we infantalize a child, which we naturally tend to do, he can have feelings similar to those of an adult patient who is infantalized. He can become helpless and depressed.

Children can be made to feel particularly vulnerable in ways that adults seldom can. Children are dependent for their very survival on adults, and there are usually many areas in a child's life over which he has little control. When adult authority figures arbitrarily make decisions for him, what can a child do?

Run away from home? While some children do resort to that, the majority feel too dependent on their parents, which just increases their vulnerability. Even if what the parents say runs counter to the child's belief about what is right for him, the child knows he can't survive without his parents. For the child who has cancer, this vulnerability is greatly compounded.

Often the child's treatment is in the hands of doctors and parents, authority figures who are responsible for making decisions the child cannot deal with yet. A young patient in this situation may feel much more secure when these authorities encourage him to communicate his feelings and wishes. If the child feels heard, understood, and responded to, he will be better able to trust the adults he must rely on. The fact that they permit him to communicate his wishes and feelings, listen, and respond to what he says, tells him that they *really* care about his welfare. It's easy to imagine how reassuring this is. Moreover, children are so often told "you can't because you're too young," that the opportunity to participate in some decisions about an illness can be an exciting experience. Here, at least, the child is being treated as an adult, and he is likely to relish this opportunity.

One special and important kind of "adult treatment" is for parents to be open with the child about their feelings. The extent to which this is possible depends on the child's maturity, but children are good at sensing when parents are trying to hide their emotions. A sick child is likely to put the worst possible interpretation on this concealment. I have found that children can usually handle their parents' grief better than adults think they can, and children feel more comfortable when they know what's going on. For a child to see his father, the authority figure who never cries, weeping, can be very frightening. It's generally better when father explains "I'm crying because I love you, and you're sick, and I can't protect you from it. I want you to know how frustrating this is to me." I have found a child can usually handle this. Not only does it tell him just what's going on, but it also encourages him to express his feelings, too.

This is not to say that parents should share all their painful feelings with a sick child. They may need to work through their feelings about the diagnosis, for instance, before confronting the child with it. Parents may have undeserved guilt feelings or feel panic about the possibility of the child dying. These are emotions they should gain some personal understanding of before telling the child. Naturally, too much delay adds to the child's apprehensiveness, which is also an important consideration. But parents who face a difficult task, such as telling the child that an amputation is necessary or that death is almost certain, may need to work out their own feelings so they can be supportive.

I believe it is extremely important to be honest with children. If things are bad, a parent can say so. Even when it looks as though the child may die, the child has a need and a right to discuss that openly. On this point, I would caution that rarely are things certain, and I am deeply concerned when I see parents tell a child he or she is going to die. Instead, parents can say, "Things look bad, and you may die—but nobody knows for certain." It's very important for the child to be able to talk with his parents about death and know they will listen. How does the child feel about dying? Is he ready? If he anticipates dying, there may be some things the child needs help in dealing with.

A child who has been able to communicate with adults during the course of his illness will be better able to talk about any crisis that may occur. One way to develop this communication is to encourage the child to ask the doctor questions. Pamela and Bob Mang believed asking the doctor questions would help Jessica gain a sense of control over her illness. Whenever Jessica approached one of her parents with a question, they answered as well as they could, and then added, "But this is something you need to ask the doctor about." Jessica got in the habit of adding questions to a list she took with her each time she saw the doctor. She became comfortable with asking for information.

Pamela tells just how effective this was in teaching Jessica to communicate with her doctors. "I'll never forget, when she was in the hospital for her surgery, how she cornered the doctor when she saw him go by the recreation room. Jessica was in a wheelchair, and she wheeled up to him and said, 'Doctor, I have some questions.' He stopped casually and smiled at her, and then she started to fire away at him. 'Is it okay?' 'Is the tumor like you expected it to be?' 'Is it going to hurt?' 'Now that I've had this kind of cancer, does it mean I'm more likely to get other kinds of cancer when I'm old?'

"The room was full of parents and children," Pamela continues, "and everybody just stopped and listened to Jessica rattling off her questions. The whole thing stunned the doctor, so he finally wheeled her out in the hallway, and knelt beside her to talk. For nearly half an hour, Jessica had his complete, undivided attention. He answered her questions, one by one, until she was satisfied. I don't think he was used to this from children, because at one point he looked at me and sighed, 'My word!' But he stayed with her and answered everything. It was really neat."

Pamela and Bob encouraged their daughter's participation because, as Pamela says, "I profoundly believe no one operates well unless he's involved in the decision-making process in his own life. We fool ourselves if we expect to make decisions for other people and have them buy in. Bob and I have always felt this way. If we want our children to be responsible, how can we withhold their right to take responsibility by making their own choices? It was Jessica's body, not mine or Bob's—so she was an equal partner in the decision making."

Parents who have this attitude find many ways to allow their children to take responsibility and maintain autonomy. The issue is often something small, but giving a child choice in small things is important, too, and leads to autonomy in a larger sense. In this vein, I am reminded of a story a colleague told me about a mutual friend of ours and her five-year-old daughter.

My colleague was having coffee with our friend at her house when the friend's little girl came in. She was dressed in a beautiful dress and was waiting until it was time to leave for a birthday party. She was holding a Fudgesicle she had taken out of the freezer, and asked my friend, "Mommy, can I have this?"

"Well, Susan, you can have it if you want to." Her mother began by giving her a choice. Then she continued, telling Susan the potential outcome. "What I want you to know is that you have no more clean party dresses. And if you get the Fudgesicle on your dress, you'll have to go to the party dirty, because I won't have time to launder your dress." She paused to see whether Susan understood, and concluded, "So you decide. You can have it, but those are the consequences."

Susan stood in deep thought for several seconds, and then she said firmly, "I want the Fudgesicle."

Her mother said that was fine. So Susan took it, and went out to play while they finished their coffee. A few minutes later she came back, pointed to one single stain on her dress, and said, "See? That's all I did." She was proud of herself; she had made her decision, and she had no trouble accepting the outcome. She went off to the party happily.

The little story is an excellent example of how a parent can allow a child to choose, explain the possible consequences, and then allow the child to deal with the consequences. Naturally, we wouldn't allow children to make choices that entail the risk of some real harm, such as the decision to ride their tricycles in a heavily trafficked street, and perhaps get run over. But the minor consequence Susan risked—going to a party in a dirty dress—is something a child can handle. When children are permitted to deal with their own feelings, it makes them stronger in their capacity to face emotional decisions.

A Young Patient's Special Qualities

Although sick children seem very vulnerable, they also have an outlook on life that can be a real asset as they work toward recovery. For one thing, children seldom have the negative adult belief system that sees cancer as synonymous with death. To most children, cancer is a disease that makes you sick; and when people get sick, they go on to get well. Since most children rarely have direct experience with a serious illness, they tend to see illness as temporary. When Jessica Mang was first told of her diagnosis, osteogenic sarcoma, or cancer of the bone, her reaction was far different than that an adult might have. She says, "I knew something was wrong, but I thought it was something easy like a broken leg that would heal pretty soon. I knew what cancer was, but I always thought it was something only grownups got." While Jessica cried when she learned an amputation was recommended, she did not go into a period of panic. Like so many children, she simply did not carry around the load of pessimistic beliefs so common among adults in our society.

While many adults have an expectation that they will someday die, a typical child believes he will someday grow up and be an adult. Children rarely know other children who have died and associate dying with the elderly. They *expect* to be big people before they die, and so they view illness as a hurdle to be overcome in the growing up process. If they have had minor illnesses in the past, they have recovered with amazing resilience, which confirms their attitude that illness is a temporary setback. While an adult too often expects the worst with cancer, a child normally expects to regain good health.

A child's optimism can be changed, however, by adults who convey their own fear of cancer. Children are very intuitive and susceptible to other people's beliefs. They are likely to look to authority figures, particularly their parents, to see what this experience is going to be like. This makes it important for parents to be aware of their own feelings. If they are fearful and sad, they need to talk it out with one another. It is crucial, I think, for parents to also discuss their fears with the doctor and establish what fears are irrational and what are realistic. Once we are in touch with such feelings, we are far better able to keep from communicating unnecessary pessimism to the child. At the same time, it is important not to deny fears, for the child may sense that something is wrong. Frequently I see children who, because their parents are so distraught, believe they are dying—when in fact, the prognosis is favorable. It is unfortunate to see a child's natural optimism undermined in this way since that optimism is a real asset in moving toward recovery.

Children have another asset in working toward health: a talent for imagery. When we teach them how to visualize their immune systems fighting off cancer, they usually do very well. I believe this is often because they have no preconceived notions to get in the way. If someone tells them the mind can influence the body, they believe it. As a result, they may accept the value of imagery more readily than some adults.

Overreacting to a Child's Illness

While all parents want to do what's best for their children, it is easy to react to a diagnosis of cancer in ways that can harm the child. Some parents become terrified about the child's future and remain frightened. They will take a recovered child out of school and rush him to the hospital when he has merely come down with a bad cold. I have seen others, who had a child in remission, call in a priest when the child was only in bed with the flu. It is easy to imagine what kind of message this behavior conveys to a child. Worse, I have seen more than one family celebrate Christmas in July. It is impossible to imagine a way to more clearly tell the child of your total pessimism for his future.

A good rule of thumb when a child has cancer is to *treat the child as normally as possible.* If parents overreact to the prognosis by deciding their child is going to die, that child will almost undoubtedly detect this belief. If everyone around him acts like he's going to die, he may begin to believe it, too. This is an area where it's vital for parents to be able to tolerate uncertainty. My suggestion for families is to remember that nobody really knows what will happen. When parents conclude a child is dying, they often begin to behave very differently toward him, in ways that may not be healthy. I have known parents who took their child out of school, even though he was capable of attending and happy to do so. It's as though they were saying, "Well, he's dying, so there's no use trying to teach him anything or prepare him for the future."

One way parents may express their pessimism about the child's future is to stop disciplining him. They no longer punish the child nor expect him to be as responsible as he once was. In other words, they overgratify the child, who may begin thinking, "I must be very fragile if they're treating me like this. There must really be something wrong with me." Overgratified children, who don't have limits set on their behavior and who are not required to be responsible for the consequences, are usually destined to have deep emotional problems. One or two years later, when such a child has recovered, imagine the disciplinary problems that will arise. Meanwhile, he has formed a belief system to the effect that, "When I'm sick, I'm not held accountable." This can be risky because it invites the child to unconsciously see being sick as a way to avoid being held accountable for his behavior.

Because of this, I encourage families to continue to discipline the child and let him know he still has certain responsibilities, such as cleaning his room, doing the dishes, and so on. In short, he should feel he is a contributing member of the family—just like the other children. Pamela and Bob Mang handled this very sensitively. While Jessica was still on crutches after her amputation, she was just as responsible for clearing her plate off the dinner table as every other member of the family. "When she was feeling really lousy," Pam explains, "we'd say, 'You don't have to do it right now. But you have to do it when you're feeling better.' Bob and I knew that easing up on her wouldn't be good for her or any of us." Treating a sick child normally in this fashion can be difficult, as so much of parenting is. What is best for the child is not necessarily the easiest route for parents to take, but, as the Mangs' experience illustrates, maintaining discipline shows the child you believe in his future, which adds immeasurably to his own belief in his recovery as well as the security and quality of his daily life.

Other Children in the Family

When parents learn their child has cancer, it is natural to focus attention on him, but often parents do so to such an extent that they begin to neglect their healthy children. There is a real temptation to do this since the sick child's disease demands so much of their thought and time. It is very important not to ignore the other children, however, for this can have serious consequences. When other children in the family suddenly stop receiving their share of time and attention from the parents, they can react by resenting their sibling who is ill. They may also begin trying to get the attention they crave through destructive behavior. They might develop sudden problems in school work or begin getting in scraps with other children, for instance. When this kind of trouble develops, it is often a mechanism designed to attract the attention of their parents to their needs. Signals like this deserve consideration, for such behavioral problems are stressful to the entire family, including the child with cancer. Finally, the child who is neglected on behalf of the cancer patient may eventually begin to think that only by being sick can he, too, receive love and care.

Families that avoid such problems are often those that decide, once they are past the initial shock of the diagnosis, to give top priority to the overall health of the entire family. This means parents recognize the needs of the other children in this scary time and concentrate on giving every child the attention he needs. Finding enough time to devote to the family as a whole does take effort and planning. Some parents I have worked with have told me, "The time just isn't there!" Certainly a father who is devoting his time to working all day and then visiting a sick child in the hospital every evening is likely to be exhausted. But parents who undertake to manage their time effectively do find ways to be with their other children, too.

One helpful technique is for the father and mother to split their time and take turns visiting the hospital so that one parent is at home with the rest of the family. It may also be important for each parent to spend some amount of individual time with each child. Such one-to-one activities as going out for dinner, taking a walk, or playing a game of tennis can be very meaningful to both parent and child. Doing things as a family also contributes to a sense of family unity. These activities don't have to be elaborate events. Simple rituals are equally effective. One family I know schedules every Wednesday night for a special family dinner, with the children planning the menu. Another family plays Frisbee in the backyard every Saturday morning. The type of activity isn't as important as the family continuing to do things as a unit—as well as maintaining healthy one-to-one relationships with one another. The patient's brothers and sisters are especially vulnerable during this time and have a real need for the parents' attention. An emphasis on maintaining the health of the entire family provides the kind of healing atmosphere that benefits not only the patient but also everyone else.

The Young Patient and His Peer Group

Every child, sick or well, is remarkably influenced by his peers. Children deal constantly with pressure to conform to the group and the threat of rejection if they don't. Observe how rigidly children often comply with their group's dress codes and other standards. They see the same movies, listen to the same records, have the same movie and sports heroes, and use the same words and expressions. To a large extent, a child's behavior may be dictated by his desire to be accepted by his peers. If there is one thing difficult for children, especially preteens and teenagers, it's being different. This being the case, imagine how a child with cancer feels about losing his hair. Just facing other children who know he has cancer can be very difficult. Children can be cruel and may subject a sick child to merciless teasing. Others, influenced by their parents' belief system that cancer means death, may withdraw from the patient altogether.

These peer pressures can be so difficult that it's crucial for the child's family to understand what he may be experiencing and to be able to talk with him about it. They may need to hear him complain and cry. As painful as this can be, they can listen and encourage him to express his feelings. Children have such a strong need to work through their emotions about peer rejection that many hospitals have set up groups where children with cancer can talk to each other about their experiences. In some, a therapist meets with several children on a regular basis for group therapy. Groups of this kind can give children enormous comfort because here they can learn that others have had the same difficulties they have. Often these peer groups work wonders.

For the child who is able to deal with peer pressure, the experience of cancer can actually be a positive growth experience. The ultimate task of growing up is for a child to become comfortable with himself. Typically this means a period of rebelling against his parents and overconforming to his peer group. A child who has, for instance, lost his hair because of chemotherapy, may learn that he can be different and still be accepted. It is difficult for a young person to face being so unusual, but with special support from the family, he can learn and grow through this experience.

Good parenting is fundamentally the same, whether a child is ill or healthy. While all parents want to do what's best for their children, they must ask themselves what is really best. Is it good parenting to take care of, make decisions for, and try to control the child? Or is it, instead, better to encourage autonomy? I believe a child does best when his parents permit him to know who he is and how he feels and help him see what his choices are and understand the potential consequences of those choices. Children also need unconditional acceptance and love from their parents. In sickness or health, a child needs to know that his parents always care about him and that their love and support is available.

For a child with cancer, good parenting also means providing good medical care and helping the child communicate with his doctors, as I've discussed. In addition, concerned parents can be an important source of information for the child's doctors. A doctor may not always be in a position to observe subtle changes in the child that might result from the disease process or from the medication. Nobody can know the individual child as well as the parents. Parents can spot a change in eating habits, an unusual sleeping pattern, or a variation in normal study and play activities. Such information can be relayed to the doctor and sometimes results in a significant change in treatment.

Cancer in the family is a highly sensitive, emotional experience. When the patient is a child, the difficulties are intensified. The sick child as well as the children in the family need good parenting now more than ever. Parents will need all the resources available to them to help their children face this painful crisis.

Chapter 19

Dealing with Pain

Many people equate cancer with pain. But, while pain is a major concern for the patient and his family, often their fear is out of proportion to what actually happens. There are many kinds of cancer, and the related discomfort can range from moderate to acute, but the pain is rarely as severe as many people expect it to be.

Why people react as they do to pain is not clearly understood, nor do we know precisely what causes it. Much depends on the individual. Two people may have apparently identical tumors in the same locations, but one will experience excruciating pain while the other will have virtually none. We do know that pain is both psychological and physiological, which complicates matters. The individual's physical condition, mind, and emotions are interdependent with the pain he feels. Many people see pain as purely physical in origin, but pain that is related to the mind and emotions can be just as severe. Regardless of its source, all pain is real.

How Pain Fluctuates

There is really no such thing as constant pain because the level of pain will always fluctuate. When I work with patients who are troubled by pain, one of the first things I ask them to do is monitor it—when do they experience it and when don't they? I suggest they keep a simple chart for a week to record when their pain is highest each day and when it is lowest, what activity they were involved in at each of those two times, how they were thinking and feeling, and who they were with. It is soon apparent that the pain they thought was continual actually does vary. To give a simplistic example, most patients feel much more pain while scrubbing the kitchen floor than they do while enjoying an absorbing movie.

Some time ago I saw striking evidence of how pleasurable activity can diminish pain. I was working with a group of patients in a residential treatment program. One of them, a physician who had advanced lymphoma, was in so much pain that at times he could hardly walk. During his stay, another patient asked him if he would like to go fishing. An avid fisherman, the patient could hardly resist the temptation, even though it would mean walking a quarter of a mile to the stream. Despite the fact that he was hardly able to walk from one room of the house to another, he decided to see how far he could go. He cautioned his friend, "I won't make it all the way down there—I'll just walk part way with you."

They set out, and the patient found the prospect of fishing so enticing that he kept walking just a little farther, until he walked the entire way to the stream. What's more, he fished for nearly two hours before he walked back. I asked him how he felt during this expedition and he said, "My word, I was in no pain at all!" Even though he was a doctor and knew how much pain could fluctuate for patients, he was amazed at what had happened to him.

The next day we encouraged him to take more of the same kind of "therapy." Knowing he had been a fine tennis player, we invited him to join us for mixed doubles. He had not hit a tennis ball in the two years since his diagnosis, but he finally agreed to try. For the most part we simply hit the ball to him so that he wouldn't have to run or stretch a great deal to return it, and after about thirty minutes of this he decided he'd had enough exercise for the day. "How are you feeling right now?" I asked him. He replied that during the entire game he had not experienced any pain. Moreover, he remained pain-free for the next two days.

This patient had always enjoyed pleasurable exercise, but since his diagnosis, he had denied himself such activity because of his pain. Like many, many people, he found that his pain was in fact diminished by involvement in something he enjoyed. Norman Cousins, in *The Anatomy of An Illness—As Perceived by the Patient*, writes about how he reduced his own severe pain by doing things he enjoyed. He found that funny movies had a wonderful effect on him; the more he laughed, the longer his pain-free periods were. Many patients I have known found they felt much better whenever they were involved in something they especially liked. Just why this happens remains a mystery.

Listening to Pain

Our bodies, I believe, are excellent biofeedback devices that signal our mind when something is healthy or unhealthy for us. In a sense, pain is a message. Disease itself can be similarly viewed as a symptom of something that is going wrong in one's life. Often, when someone begins to enjoy life more fully, increasing the quality of his daily life, he gains in health, and his disease begins to diminish. This may mean that elements of the disease, such as the symptom of pain, will also decrease when we are involved in something that is pleasurable for us as individuals.

The value of this way of understanding pain is that we can then use pain as a sort of guide. A patient who has been going along and doing well and then suddenly has a day with a lot of pain may be receiving a message to look at what he's thinking and feeling that day. What is different in his life? Why is his body giving him this feedback? Is something going in the wrong direction today? In a similar fashion, athletes have long been accustomed to what they call "listening to your body." They affirm that their bodies let them know whether they're overtrained or undertrained and whether they're doing something unhealthy. In the same way, pain is a feedback device we can "listen to" to find out what we need. Once we have heard the message, we should respect what it has to say to us.

One of my patients learned to listen to her body during her chemotherapy treatment in which she was experiencing violent side effects. Once every six weeks she would take her treatment in the morning at a local clinic and then head back to her office and attempt to work—until she became severely ill. She would drag herself home and invariably end up sick in bed for three days. This happened during the entire eighteen months she was on this particular treatment.

During a long discussion, she and I talked about what was happening inside her body after each treatment. I suggested, "This may be the heat of the battle between your cancer and the adryomiacin. When you're out there driving yourself as hard as you possibly can, trying to live your normal, hectic lifestyle, you may be draining your body of energy that is vital to the healing process. If you had a high temperature, you'd certainly go to bed to allow your body to heal, wouldn't you? Well, your symptoms after treatment might be giving you the same message: go home and stay in bed for three days. Perhaps those side effects are actually a benefit. So think about the wisdom of your body."

She decided this made sense. When she took her next treatment she deliberately took all the benefits of her side effects and prepared for three days in bed. She told her family, "Okay, my chemotherapy is coming up, and I'll be in bed for a few days, so let's get ready for that." Family members were all assigned different household chores, and her friends agreed to prepare meals for the three-day period—her favorite meals. She called other friends and asked for their support. "Would you come over and read to me?" Or, "Would you come over and give me one of your wonderful backrubs?" She also stacked up her favorite books by the bedside, and generally prepared to pamper herself for three days. On the day of treatment, she didn't drive herself as usual but asked her husband to drive her to her physician's office. Afterward, they went straight home and she went to bed. She experienced only a fraction of the terrible side effects she previously had!

What this patient had done was give her body everything it normally asked for after her chemotherapy, but she didn't wait until the symptoms were crying out for her attention. It worked so well that she felt she had this licked after a few treatments and decided to take off only a day and a half, instead of three. After all, she was feeling almost normal after a day and a half. But her side effects returned when she went back to work. "Well," she told me, "I guess my body wants three days in bed!" I agreed. As her experience demonstrates, when our body signals us, we might as well learn to respect what it has to say. Otherwise, as in this woman's case, the symptoms may just persist in trying to get our attention.

The Conversion Reaction

Sometimes, when an individual denies feelings because he believes they would be too painful to deal with, this denied hurt is converted into physical pain. As the emotional problem increases, the very real pain in the person's body increases, but when he lets himself feel the emotion, the pain may diminish or disappear altogether. The physical aches and pains, in such cases, are a signal from the body that there are suppressed feelings that must be admitted to consciousness. Sometimes this happens dramatically. I have known patients who were denying their grief over a serious loss, the death of a child or spouse, and were experiencing severe physical pain. As soon as these patients broke down and cried and expressed their emotional pain, the physical pain began to subside.

Denied feelings can be converted into other symptoms, too. One of my patients, an active professional woman, began having extreme nausea and a greatly lowered energy level as side effects of her chemotherapy. The medication she was on, however, was one that very seldom warrants such a strong reaction. I wondered what these side effects might be trying to tell her and asked, "Are you doing anything differently in your life since you started this chemotherapy?"

She began telling me how once the chemotherapy began, she had restricted herself by cutting out almost all the activities she had once enjoyed. Although she was a physician, she had begun telling herself, "I'm on chemotherapy, so I shouldn't swim or hike." Even though she knew it was not really rational, she had begun denying herself all the physical recreation that had been so meaningful to her. We talked about what was behind this, and soon she realized, "I'm treating myself exactly the way my mother did when I was a child. If I was ill, she would restrict all my activities." This led her to examine many feelings about her relationship with her mother.

When I saw her the next week she told me, "I never cry, but last week I cried nearly every day. I realized I was grieving about my feelings for my mother." Until now, she had not really faced these painful emotions. Now she did, and the result was that her nausea was gone, and her former energy had returned. While this may seem amazing, it is just one of many cases I have seen where the body stopped hurting when the patient released his pent-up feelings.

In some ways, pain can be an ally because it is a feedback device that tells us we need something. I suggest patients ask their pain, "Why are you here? What am I not attending to?" This can put them in touch with feelings that are blocked, and/or things in their lives that are not going well. For each patient, the message will be somewhat different. Some people, like the woman I mentioned before, have to learn to stop driving themselves so hard and to take steps to slow down. Others need to deal with suppressed feelings and to permit themselves to have pleasurable activity.

Your Medical Treatment is Your Ally

In many cases, patients have no pain at all until they begin their treatment. If they experience significant side effects, such patients often complain, "I was feeling great until the doctor put me on chemotherapy. They're killing me to make me get better!" Unfortunately, if a patient sees his treatment as an enemy, he's apt to have more side effects.

When a patient's side effects are unusually severe, it may be because he doesn't have enough information or hasn't participated in the decisions regarding his treatment program. The patient who is being handled in a directive manner may begin to resist the doctor's treatment without being aware of it because he feels out of control—run over. If this is the way a patient feels, it may be helpful for a family member to accompany him to the doctor's office. With the patient's permission, the family member can ask questions and remind the patient of questions he wanted to ask. The two can then discuss the treatment program after they leave the doctor's office. Once a patient has enough information about the treatment, he is often able to understand the reason for it and is more comfortable with it, which can result in fewer side effects. It is easier to bear discomfort when we believe the results will be worth it. A good analogy is getting a tooth drilled by a dentist; although we know it will be painful, we also know this pain is more tolerable than the toothache we will ultimately have if we don't undergo the dentist's treatment. Because we understand this, we willingly endure the unpleasant drilling.

Side effects of treatment can also be diminished when the patient actively participates in the treatment by using visualization. This is a very good time to use visualization since chemotherapy is administered at the time new cancer cells are growing and are most susceptible to medication. While he receives the treatment, a patient can focus on imagery, visualizing the cancer cells being destroyed by the chemotherapy.

Medical treatment for pain is another ally, and one that should certainly be explored when psychological strategies are not giving the patient enough relief. If pain is a symptom, it is wise to first examine the possible underlying issues before masking the pain with medication—some of which can leave the patient feeling drugged and groggy. So I suggest that patients first explore their feelings, add pleasurable activities to their lives, and so on, before turning to medication.

Pain medication, however, is always an option, and significant pain should be alleviated. Acute pain can depress a patient and diminish his will to live. When people are tormented by pain, the most important thing is to get the pain stopped. I suggest that patients and their families keep good lines of communication open with the doctor, so that he is aware of the patient's level of pain. Again, the ability to communicate with a doctor—particularly one who cares about the patient—makes an important difference.

Three Techniques for Managing Pain

Although we can't pinpoint how large a role any patient's emotions play in his pain, it is known that the mind and emotions are significant factors. For instance, some patients will become nauseated *on the way* to chemotherapy; their anticipation of the treatment causes them to develop symptoms that should not begin until the medication is in their bodies. In the same way, a patient's fear of the pain that may accompany cancer may stimulate actual pain. We know that pain can have a significant psychological aspect, and for that reason, I suggest trying three mental techniques that sometimes help manage pain and, for some patients, relieve it altogether.

Conversing with Pain. Dr. David Bresler, of the University of California Los Angeles Medical School Pain Clinic, has had a great deal of success with patients by teaching them to visualize their pain as an imaginary creature. The patient gets into a state of deep relaxation and converses with the creature, asking it such questions as, Why are you here? What's the message you can offer me? Is there something I'm not paying attention to? Am I not taking care of myself emotionally, or am I neglecting my body? This technique, which may seem somewhat humorous at first, actually enables you to create a symbol of your inner self and to talk with that self on a deeper level of consciousness, which is otherwise hard to tap. Similar techniques are used in other ways. Dr. Art Ulene, in his book, *Feeling Fine*, recommends a "creature-advisor" that allows a person to call on the symbolic, intuitive functioning of the right hemisphere of the brain. (Most of us function more from the left hemisphere, or rational thinking side.) Through conversing with creature-advisors, people are sometimes able to get in touch with their own creative solutions, just as cancer patients who converse with their pain creatures can get in touch with their own deep needs.

Visualizing Pain. Some techniques for relieving pain encourage the person to distract himself from his discomfort. Visualizing pain asks the patient to do the opposite. This technique focuses attention right in the middle of the pain. In a semitrance, the patient creates an image of his pain, visualizing its color, shape, size, texture, odor, and even taste. He repeats the process, imagining again the size, shape, etc. He will often gradually see the pain becoming smaller and smaller until it goes from the size of a basketball to the size of a baseball, then a golf ball, then a marble, and finally is gone. As the imaginary ball reduces in size, the real pain frequently does too.

The patient can also describe his image of the pain to a support person, who in turn can help the patient by asking questions. "Tell me the color. How big is the ball? What is the texture?" As the patient talks, he will sometimes talk himself right out of the pain. Often a patient will be surprised at how effective this is and suddenly announce, "You know what? The pain is gone!"

Visualizing Pleasure to Replace Pain. Just as enjoyable activities often reduce pain, visualizing pleasant scenes can have the same effect. This exercise, like the others, is done when the patient has fully relaxed. Much as in daily relaxation, the patient visualizes something that gives him great pleasure. He focuses on that image. Earl Deacon uses this technique with outstanding results. Five years after his diagnosis of cancer, Earl had a serious jeep accident that virtually demolished four vertebrae, and left him with "excruciating, indescribable pain." Since he lost four inches of height, his internal organs had to readjust, and he had tremendous pain with every movement.

One way Earl works with his pain is through visualizing. He puts on soft classical music and relaxes, imagining that he is "lying next to a beautiful clear stream that runs through my Colorado ranch. There's a flower in the tundra country of Colorado called the Alpine Forget-Me-Not, and I see that growing here and there. Let me tell you, that flower's so lovely that once you see it, you'll never forget it. I've gotten to the point where I completely relax just by mentioning that wildflower. So I visualize that, and once I'm relaxed I've found that it's best for me to *go* with the pain. I used to get angry with my pain but that made it worse, so now I say to my body, 'Okay, do something for me, whatever it is.' It works—the pain really diminishes when I do this."

Earl has another way of visualizing pleasure, which he does in what he calls "almost a hypnotic state, part meditation and part visualization." He explains, "In this, I see the beta endorphins helping my pain. Beta endorphins are manufactured by the brain, and are actually a natural pain-killer. They seem to have the same chemistry as morphine. I visualize these coming from my brain and alleviating the pain in my back, where my vertebrae have moved against my nerve endings because of the accident."

For Earl, this is an excellent visualization, in part because his scientific background makes it natural for him to think in these terms. Visualizing pleasure can be done in as many ways as there are individuals. Jessica Mang learned to do it under the guidance of a therapist who taught her in five sessions how to reduce her pain during treatment. The twelve-year-old explains, "My parents took me to see him. First he'd talk with me about cancer, and then he'd count to twenty and I'd listen very carefully to each number and breathe very slowly. Then he had me start imagining things. On my third visit he said, 'Today I'm going to give you this magic carpet. Where do you want to fly?'

"I said, 'I'd like to visit my great-grandmother.'

"He said, 'Okay, you're going to get on your magic carpet and fly right down to your great-grandmother so you can hold her.' So I would visualize that. At the end of my final visit, he said, 'Jessica, I'm going to give you a present. You can have the magic carpet and use it whenever you want.'

"So later, when I'd have my chemotherapy treatments, my mom would make up stories, and we'd use the carpet the way he taught me. When we did that, I never even felt the IV."

Like Jessica's parents, family members can participate with patients—children or adults—in visualizing pleasure. In fact, when a patient is experiencing acute pain, it is sometimes helpful to have somebody "talk him through" the exercise. Very often the family member's voice and support are important ingredients in diminishing the pain. And when the patient is able to verbalize the pain and express his feelings about it to someone, that can also be helpful. Conversely, it is generally not helpful for support people to deny the patient's pain with something like, "Oh, just don't think about it." The technique of visualizing pleasure does focus the patient's attention away from his pain, but this should not be seen as a suggestion that he deny it. Instead, he is acknowledging it and then taking action to diminish it.

A Blitz Attack on Pain

Recently I was a consultant on a research project at a major pain management center. This center works with patients whose chronic pain has not been alleviated by medical treatment. Some, for instance, have suffered major back injuries, like Earl Deacon, and must find ways to manage the resulting pain for which there is no lasting cure. I observed with great interest the results of this study.

A patient's hospital stay in the pain center ranged from two to four weeks, and during this time he was exposed to a multimodality approach. He could choose from over two dozen treatments: daily psychological therapy, physical therapy, biofeedback, group therapy, hypnosis, massage, etc. The center's studies confirmed my own observation that the more kinds of treatment a patient participates in, the more his pain decreases. What was even more intriguing, however, was that the center divided treatment into two types, "hands-on" and "hands-off." Hands-on treatment was when a staff member actually touched and physically cared for a patient; an example is massage. Hands-off treatment would be exercise the patient did for himself. The more hands-on treatment the patient elected, the greater the decrease in his pain—and in his depression, as well. This is information family members can take advantage of in offering support to the patient. Being touched, cuddled, massaged, stroked, or otherwise physically touched and nurtured by family members can reduce the patient's pain.

As I hope this chapter illustrates, pain can be managed and, for many patients, greatly reduced. In addition to medical options, there is a wide variety of ways a patient can diminish his pain; family members can participate in many of these. By all means, every patient who is troubled by pain should work actively to find those strategies that do the most for him. Pain is too often seen as an inevitable accompaniment to cancer, when in fact it can be greatly diminished. Contrary to popular belief, cancer should not necessarily be synonymous with pain.

Chapter 20

Recurrence and Death

Throughout this book I have suggested that a patient and his family approach the uncertainty of cancer with optimism and hope. Nevertheless, because the course of this disease *is* uncertain, people often do best when they are prepared for any eventuality. What happens if there is a recurrence or a whole series of ups and downs? What if the patient dies?

A pervasive belief in our society holds that cancer may have an up and down pattern, and a patient may battle the disease with some success, but in the end, the biological process wins out and death occurs. This is not an accurate picture of the disease nor does it have a straight uphill or straight downhill course, as some people believe. Even those patients who go on to get well may find it a rocky road. It's not uncommon for a patient to go into remission only to later have a recurrence, and then eventually recover. So, contrary to what many people think, recurrence of the disease does not mean that death is inevitable.

I bring up the subject of recurrence so that a patient and his family will not ignore it as a possibility and be ill-prepared to cope should it happen. So often, patients who have decided to work toward recovery expect this to be a straight uphill course. In my early days at the Cancer Counseling and Research

Center, I used to ask, at the end of a new patient session, "How many of you expect to go home and get well, to experience steady upward progress?" Without hesitation, the majority of patients would raise their hands. I knew that some of them might be setting themselves up to feel like failures if that expectation did not come true, so I would caution them that few of our major accomplishments in life are achieved that straightforwardly. In working toward any significant goal, an up-and-down course is quite likely, and patients and their families may want to be prepared to deal with setbacks should they occur.

With this in mind, I like to ask my patients to imagine their response to a major setback. "Let's assume you go home and you're getting better, but then your disease flares up. This time the pain is greater, and there's sizable growth, so it's evident that you've either had a recurrence, or at least you're not remissing as you would like. What meaning are you going to assign to this event?"

Some patients answer, "That nothing I've been doing has worked for me." Some will elaborate: "The process doesn't work, and I've failed. The whole thing has been a failure. I'd give up." And there are patients who give up when they have a recurrence. They lose faith in their doctors, their therapist, their medical treatment, their visualization—in everything.

Responding to Recurrence

Generally, patients are more frightened when they have a recurrence than they were at the time of the original diagnosis. Often this reaction is based on a false belief system about cancer: "Well, once it spreads to here, it's all over." Contributing to the reaction for many is bitter disappointment. Since the diagnosis, the patient and family have taken some degree of responsibility for their health, have done their best—*but the disease came back*. In our culture, we tend to want control, and if we can't have it, we feel hopeless and give up. When a patient has a recurrence of his disease, he is likely to feel, "I tried. What's the use? I have no control over this." They are devastated by the fact that even though they worked at it, even though they grappled with the disease psychologically and in other ways, they *still* lack control. What they fail to realize is that although they don't have total control, they may have some influence. This ambiguity is part of the human predicament. We have some influence over our destiny, but our fate is not entirely in our hands.

A period of shock following a diagnosis of recurrence is typical and normal for any patient. During this period of shock, which usually lasts two to eight weeks, a patient may not sleep well and may feel anxious, depressed, and generally very disturbed emotionally. His moods will fluctuate, and he may have considerable difficulty functioning, with little interest in work. In general, this is a time of confusion, turmoil, and despair. A patient who has been exercising, doing imagery, watching his diet, and so on may stop all these things. His self-esteem may drop, and he may become terribly frustrated with himself because he can't seem to keep on doing things as he did before the recurrence.

It is important for a patient in this shock period to realize that these are normal reactions, that this is a time of confusion, and that his expectations of himself must not be too high. As time passes, it will be easier to return to normal activities, the patient's mood-swings will level out, and he will begin to feel once again that his feet are on the ground. The adjustment will be easier if the patient and family make a point of staying close to their support system and not withdraw from people. Many tests will also be done, and treatment should be reevaluated when all the medical data is in. Now the patient faces the question, "Where do I go from here? Do I want to continue working towards recovery, or is it time now to go towards death?"

The natural temptation when recurrence is diagnosed is to immediately begin asking, "What does this mean about whether I live or die? Am I going to die?" But I strongly caution against a premature decision about death during the first days of shock and confusion. Usually medical data is not complete for two to six weeks, and until it is, I suggest the patient try not to make a decision about his destiny. During a crisis there is too much emotional pain to resolve anything of major consequence, and the patient usually feels dismal and hopeless just now: "I've worked so hard and been through so much, and now this! I just can't go through all that again!" In a few weeks, the patient will begin to feel better and stronger, and his decision will not be so colored by despair. This initial reaction of hopelessness is similar to what we feel when we lose a loved one to death. We may think at first that we will never again want to risk such pain by loving anyone, but in time we overcome our sorrow and start living once more. So, although patients are tempted to solve the ambiguity of their future by deciding to accept death, the first weeks after a diagnosis of recurrence is not a time when they are apt to use good judgement.

Supporting the Patient After Recurrence

The family can be very helpful to the patient during this time by understanding that his feelings of hopelessness, guilt, anger, and fear are normal. They can then support the expression of these feelings and not try to talk the patient out of them. As I discussed in chapter 7, the patient will do better, and his feelings will dissipate faster, if he is allowed to go ahead and cry. Just holding him can be more therapeutic than anything family members can say. These feelings *are* transitory and will begin to change—if the patient is given time and loving support.

Often a family member tries to help by telling the patient, "Hey, we licked it once, and we can lick it again!" This cheerleading is likely to produce exactly the opposite result from what you want. When a support person moves in with a "fix-it" strategy, the patient is invited to deny his feelings. He may obligingly do this and hide his hopelessness to protect his family. In the process, he may become more depressed and hopeless and may lean towards deciding to die. The most supportive thing family members can do is to allow the patient to fall apart after his recurrence and to express all his difficult feelings. It may take some time, but this will eventually clear his feelings, and a kind of natural, spontaneous optimism will return. Denial, by way of contrast, produces a whistling-in-the-dark, talking-yourself-into-it attitude. So, as always when a patient is depressed, it may be most helpful to simply show empathy by holding him and by saying something like, "I

understand that you're feeling hopeless. It must feel really awful to put in all that energy and then have this happen."

Family members, too, feel a natural anxiety at this time.
Sometimes they try to resolve this by pushing the doctor for a
firm statement as to the patient's future. "Tell us what's going
to happen. How long does he have to live?" At best, any doctor
can give no more than an educated guess; nobody has an
answer to such a question. But a doctor may say that, in his
opinion, the patient will die. Some families who have heard
that prognosis from the doctor may then not support the patient's
decision to work for recovery. I have had family members come
to me and say, "He's just had a recurrence, and the doctors say
he'll probably die, and he won't accept it! Make him accept it."
I am generally unwilling to do that. What a family member
sometimes forgets is that it is easier for them to accept the fact
that the patient may be dying than it is for him. The person
who is actually facing death is experiencing what is probably
the most anxiety-provoking event of his life, and his coping
mechanisms are being pushed to their limits. Not everyone can
accept the fact that he is dying. Some patients respond by
regressing emotionally and by using many defense mechanisms
to defend against the knowledge. When anxiety pushes a patient into that response, I don't believe his defenses should be
crashed through—even though that might be more comfortable
for those around him. It is best to respect the patient's emotional needs as he faces this critical experience.

I suggest to both patients and families that they delay important decision-making until all pertinent medical information is
gathered, and the patient has begun to come out of the period
of shock. So often when families panic, they try to settle their
anxiety by making external decisions prematurely. It is much
better to *deal with anxiety as anxiety*. During this time, family
members, too, are vulnerable and needy, and the recurrence has
undoubtedly severely shaken them. Rather than try to settle
anxiety by imposing certainty on the patient's future, family
members do well to reach out to their extended family for
support—to outside people who are a little further removed
from the crisis. In addition to emotional support, close friends
can be especially helpful during these weeks with such things as

running errands and preparing meals. This gives the family time to get over their shock and helps conserve their energy to deal with their own feelings and to be with the patient.

The Message of the Recurrence

When the shock period ends, the patient will begin to really examine his decision for the future: "Do I want to go back and work towards health, or do I want to accept death and begin preparing for it?" Those who decide to work for recovery can find significant meaning in the recurrence of the disease by asking themselves what their body might be telling them. Just as pain can be a message, so can disease, including recurrence of cancer. I suggest such patients ask themselves, "What is the meaning of my recurrence? Can I learn something from this about emotions I might have been denying? Did I lose some important secondary gains when I got well? Is my body giving me a message I can put to good use in my overall scheme of recovery?"

Many of my patients have learned through a recurrence experience that they had not been taking care of themselves as they needed to. With this knowledge, they became more attentive to their needs and ultimately recovered. These were patients who found that during the period before their recurrence they had lost the gains they had made and in some ways returned to the same lifestyle they believed had contributed to their illness initially. The recurrence was a strong reminder from their body that they had stopped taking care of themselves and were once again living stressful lives. These patients used the message of their recurrence to save their lives—by regrouping and once again working to get well and stay well.

To Live or Die

For many patients, the decision of whether to make a new commitment to regain health or to begin accepting death is one that takes a good deal of time. Such a decision naturally creates ambivalence, which may last for days, weeks, or several months.

The ambivalence is natural, however, for it means the patient sees himself as having choices; if he did not, he would feel more hopeless and helpless. It can be very hard for family members to tolerate this time of uncertainty, but it can be important to do so, to permit the patient to keep his autonomy, and to refrain from attempting to control his thinking. Families sometimes do this unknowingly with such statements as, "I think you should face the fact that you are dying," or, on the other hand, "I don't even want you to think about dying. Everything's going to be all right." The patient needs, instead, permission to explore both choices—including the possibility of death—so that he can feel in charge of it. A supportive family member can help the patient by saying, "Look, I'm with you no matter how serious things are, whether you want to return toward working for good health or go toward death."

Sometimes family members are afraid the patient has decided to die when he is only exploring the possibility of death and taking a look at his fears. He may be asking, "What happens in the process of dying? What will it be like?" He may be afraid of the physical pain and deterioration and want to discuss that; if so, family members may talk with him and try to keep from leaping to the conclusion that his mind is already made up. He may, instead, simply be trying to assess whether he can tolerate the process of death. This might lead him to ask, "What will I do if I have a lot of pain while I'm dying?" Family members tend to react by saying, "Oh no, you've decided to die," but such a reaction can only make him reluctant to share his thoughts about either alternative and hinder his ability to resolve his feelings. It is often more supportive if the family can confirm the patient's ambivalence directly: "Look, we're up against uncertainty again."

Direct information can be reassuring and helpful to a patient who is confronting a decision about death after a recurrence. He may be very concerned about pain. If so, he can ask the doctor, "What do you do about pain control when somebody's dying?" The doctor, in turn, can give reassurance by discussing the medications that are available to keep the patient in comfort. Some patients feel much better discussing their wishes beforehand with the doctor in the event they should die. One patient may say, "I'd rather tolerate some pain and be kept conscious.

Please see to it that I'm conscious as long as possible, so I know what's going on." Another will ask for any measure that will reduce pain, "I don't care whether I'm conscious or not, I just don't want severe pain. I'd rather be knocked out." This kind of information-gathering and planning gives the patient a sense of being in charge of his life. That feeling of control gives the freedom to make a choice either way. It's important for family members to remember that a patient who is talking about these things has not necessarily decided to die. In fact, the control he gains from this exploration may be what he needs to decide to work toward health.

The idea that thinking about death can help a patient affirm life may seem strange, but it does happen. Normally, as the patient explores questions about pain, fear, and incapacity, his anxiety significantly decreases. Once he feels some understanding of the process, he begins to relax, and often begins to think, "Okay, I can see that I can handle dying if I have to." This confidence frequently gives him the renewed energy to move back toward living. He has seen that he can handle the worst that could happen; now he is free to move between both possibilities. A patient is immeasurably aided in this process by family members who respect his autonomy and let him know they won't reach a decision before he does. In other words, they will stay one step behind him so that he is in charge.

I also want to emphasize that nobody is so exquisitely in touch with his body, or has such total control over it, that he can entirely determine the outcome of a life-threatening disease. We can, however, take responsibility and participate significantly in the process of dying. And the more permission a patient has to talk openly about the possibility of death, the more comfortable the death process can be for everyone.

The Quality of Death

Marge and Earl Deacon, both having had cancer, have often said that the disease has given them an awareness and acceptance of death. Marge recalls how, last winter, she and Earl watched the death of an aged deer. "We had laid out hay around our house in the Colorado mountains, and a herd of deer came to get shelter from a bad ice storm. When the weather cleared, the herd took off up the mountainside, except for one, who was obviously old. She went down to the valley, instead, laid down beside a tree, and died. She died with dignity. We thought it was very beautiful."

We all want a serene death. Cancer, unlike many other causes of death, usually gives ample time to prepare, and preparation can be very comforting. People prepare in a variety of ways. Some plan their funeral and burial arrangements; others prepare their wills and put their estates in order. Some sign a document known as the living will, which gives permission to the doctor to discontinue life-support systems when there no longer appears to be any hope of survival. A patient can do any or all of these things without having decided to die.

Sometimes a patient also wants to explore the facilities and services in his community that would help him die in comfort. His doctor, therapist, or a social worker can direct him to the various options. Many communities now have at least one hospice, which is designed to ease dying as much as possible. This can be a good choice when the family isn't physically able to give the patient the necessary care. Many patients also consider dying at home. Certainly, the family's feelings about this are important. Some find the idea too frightening or burdensome. If so, it is wise to consider whether that choice might result in the illness of an overstressed family member.

The patient's ability to die with dignity is very important. Dignity comes from the participation and autonomy of the patient, his ability to make choices about his own death. The family can help by avoiding anything that is incompatible with his wishes or causes him discomfort. Even seemingly small things can be of great importance at this time. One of my patients, an elderly woman, hired a wonderfully sensitive, thoughtful nurse to care for her at home since she could no longer do many things for herself. My patient was a woman with a great need for privacy and had a sense of discretion about her own body. But when she was totally bedridden, it became necessary for the nurse to give her sponge baths in bed. Although the patient said nothing, the nurse was astute and soon saw that the baths made the elderly woman quite uneasy.

So the nurse asked her, "Is something emotionally uncomfortable for you?" In this way, she gave her patient permission to talk about it. The nurse learned that the woman was deeply embarrassed by these baths. Now that she knew this, the nurse washed only certain parts of the woman, and then left the room so her patient could finish bathing herself. While this may seem like a small thing, it was one of the ways the nurse helped her patient maintain her sense of dignity.

For many patients, dying is greatly eased by the knowledge that loved ones will survive and be cared for when they're gone. This can involve financial questions, such as how the children's education will be provided for, and it can also focus on more personal, emotional questions. Sometimes a patient feels torn and guilty about deserting his family through dying. A spouse may unwittingly add to this feeling. A wife might, for example, tell her husband, "I love you so much, I can't imagine living without you." Too many people have the impression that this is what love means. In our culture we tend to think of love symbiotically—when you love someone, you merge with them and give up your own autonomy so that you really can't get along without them. But for a dying patient it may be a relief to know that his spouse can survive and continue her own life afterward even though she will miss him. It can be very helpful for a couple to talk about this and about how the surviving partner will manage. Open communication on this subject of how the family's life will go on if the patient dies of his disease can greatly relieve the patient.

A family that can help a cancer patient approach death in the ways I've talked about in this chapter is doing a great deal to ease the process of dying. What else can the family do? First and foremost, the physical presence of loved ones is one of the greatest comforts anyone can provide. Just knowing he is not alone is wonderfully supportive to the patient. Second, it is very meaningful for the patient to know that his family does love him—and will miss him. This knowledge helps reduce what may be the greatest anxiety a dying person faces, the fear that he may stop existing altogether. No matter how strong a patient's religious faith may be, there can be no guarantee of conscious experience after death. If a patient knows that he will be remembered, then he can feel that he will not be completely annihilated: "Part of me will be left in the memories of people who have loved me. And part of me will exist in what I have contributed to this world." I have known people who are dying who felt tremendous peace knowing they had loved and been loved.

The time will come for every one of us to face the last day of our life. For patients and families dealing with recurrence or death, the awareness of mortality is vastly heightened. It can lead us to ask, "If this were the last day of my life, how would I want to live it?" And for each of us, this question can open a new perspective on living. The realization that each of us must ultimately die makes time more precious. If each of us would approach each day, each week, each month, as if it were our last, then no matter what the state of our health might be, the quality of our lives could be immensely richer.

---------- *Chapter 21* ----------

In Pursuit of the
Healing Family

Throughout my work with cancer patients and their families, many family members have expressed in their desire to help a sense of frustration: "If only I could *do* something—anything. I'd be willing to trade places with him if I could." None of us, of course, can exchange health with another person, but each of us can do many things to help a loved one who has cancer. My purpose in writing *The Healing Family* has been to inform support people of the ways they can help the cancer patient and of how they can play a significant role in determining the outcome of his disease.

For many readers, the approaches and concepts in this book may represent a whole new way of understanding the roles of the family and patient in this crisis. It takes flexibility and deep concern to examine our beliefs, and I congratulate you for having read this book—examining alternatives is, in itself, a courageous step to take. It is difficult to reevaluate our attitudes toward helping a loved one who is seriously ill—especially when we have always believed that the usual approach was the best.

This book presents suggestions for ways to interacting in the family and responding to the patient that run counter to many of the common, everyday practices in our culture. Some of these values—such as the free, open expression of feelings—are not supported to a very great degree in our society, and that can make them very difficult to accept. For example, I have stressed that the patient's ability to express emotions is a significant influence in the healing process, but our tradition teaches men not to express fear or anxiety and, above all, not to cry. This sort of thing has conditioned us to believe that expressing certain feelings is a weakness. On the contrary, the suppression of feelings can actually be unhealthy. Nevertheless, it takes effort to overcome these attitudes that are so strongly embedded in the culture.

Another example is the work ethic. I believe our culture overemphasizes achievement at the expense of personal satisfaction, leading many people to drive themselves constantly. Men, in particular, are often encouraged to overwork themselves and neglect their families in the belief that this is in everyone's best interest. Men and women alike may place themselves under severe pressure to accomplish something and to define their worth only on the basis of what they achieve. I have emphasized that both patient and family members need to ask for support and nurturing during this crisis, but this cultural ethic leads many people to feel they must always be "strong" and giving, never needy. For so many families and patients, learning to stop driving themselves and accept nurturing is a difficult task and a major challenge.

Nobody need feel guilty for having reacted to the crisis of cancer in ways that may not always be helpful to the patient. The best-intentioned family members can unintentionally inflict pain because they are handling the illness in the only way they know how. For instance, I have stressed the importance of encouraging the patient's autonomy and not rescuing him. Most people rescue only in the hope of giving comfort; they have no idea that this often adds to the patient's helplessness and vulnerability and erodes his will to live.

Similarly, family members are often distressed to realize that their well meant cheerleading is not useful to the patient. They tell me they have responded with "pep talks" as a matter of course to anyone in trouble. Many people do this. If a friend loses his job of twenty years, they tell him, "Cheer up! Things aren't so bad—there are lots of other jobs." If someone's underinsured house burns down, they try to help by saying, "Hey, at least nobody was killed! Be thankful. You can always buy another house." And, of course, so many people do the same with a cancer patient. Perhaps his disease has metastasized; concerned family members tell him, "Don't worry about it—it's okay. Everything's going to be all right." In this book, I have pointed out that it may be more helpful when loved ones show empathy for a patient's feelings.

It is important to remember, in examining yourself and your family, that the ways you have responded to people in the past may not have been the most healthy and constructive. You were only following cultural guidelines. Behaviors like these are based on beliefs that have been handed down in our culture from one generation to the next. Certainly our schools and universities, until recently, have not taught us new and healthier ways of looking at illness; for that matter, our institutions of learning have rarely addressed the issues of human relationships in depth. Instead, we learn our attitudes from our parents, who learned from their parents, and so on. Generation after generation has blindly accepted the cultural view of serious illness. No one is to blame for initially accepting this attitude.

The concepts of *The Healing Family* are based on new findings in the field of family therapy as well as on my work at the Center. Family therapy itself is a new area of study and has only begun to make real progress during the past fifteen years or so. As more knowledge surfaces in this area so does a new awareness of the need for more healthy family models, such as I have presented here. But this model is just that—an ideal. No family is perfect, and no reader can hold his family against the model given here and find that his family interacts in perfectly healthy ways in every area. Every family, like every individual, has shortcomings and room for improvement. I caution you not to be downhearted about your family's problems or your unintentional errors in the past. Instead, congratulate yourself for having already begun to change by reading this book and by thinking about the ideas presented here. Then, look to the future. With this new knowledge, you can begin to avoid the old mistakes. As you do, your children can learn new ways of acting and thus break the pattern that has existed for so many generations. Every family that begins now to change to healthier ways of interacting brings hope for the future. These new and better ways are a legacy that can be handed down and multiplied in each generation. Change takes time but rest assured that your efforts are not in vain.

With the crisis of cancer in your family, change may already be happening, perhaps unnoticed. Crisis can begin a process of change that would not have occurred otherwise. But change takes time, and cancer is a formidable adversary. There may be some discouraging times ahead when it seems terribly difficult to apply the concepts in this book; you may begin to doubt whether they can work at all. It will be during these periods when you may most need to consider new patterns of relating.

Becoming a healing family is no easy task. No matter how devotedly you work at change, it does not happen overnight. But it is a realistic and attainable goal, and the ultimate reward can be better health and a richer quality of life for the patient and the entire family.

I extend my very best wishes to you and your loved ones in your commitment to become a healing family.

Bibliography

Abse, D.W., Wilkins, M.M., Kirschner, G., Weston, D.L., Brown, R.S., and Buxton, W.D. Self-frustration, night-time smoking, and lung cancer. *Psychosomatic Medicine*, 1972, *34*, 395.

Abse, D.W., Wilkins, M.M., VandeCastle, R.L., Buxton, W.D., Demars, J.P., Brown, R.S., and Kirschner, L.G. Personality and behavioral characteristics of lung cancer patients. *Journal of Psychosomatic Research*, 1974, *18*, 101–13.

Achterberg, J., and Lawliss, G.F. *Imagery of Cancer*. Champaign, Ill.: Institute for Personality and Ability Testing, 1978.

Achterberg, J., Lawliss, G.F., Simonton, O.C., and Simonton, S. "Psychological factors and blood chemistries as disease outcome predictors for cancer patients." *Multivariate Clinical Experimental Research*, December 1977.

Achterberg, J., Simonton, O.C., and Matthews-Simonton, S. *Stress, Psychological Factors, and Cancer*, Fort Worth, TX: New Medicine Press, 1976.

Ackerman, N.W. *The Psychodynamics of Family Life*. New York: Basic Books, 1958.

Ackerman, N.W. *Treating the Troubled Family*. New York: Basic Books, 1966.

Ader, R., and Cohen, N. Behaviorally conditioned immunosuppression. *Psychosomatic Medicine*, 1975, *37*, 333–40.

Amkraut, A.A., Solomon, G.F., Kasper, P., and Purdue, A. Stress and hormonal intervention in the graft-versus-host response. In B.P. Jankovic and K.

Isakovic (Eds.), *Micro-environmental aspects of immunity.* New York: Plenum Publishing Corporation, 1973, 667–74.

Andervont, H.B. Influence of environment on mammary cancer in mice. *National Cancer Institute,* 1944, 4, 579–81.

Bacon, C.L., Rennecker, R.; and Cutler, M. A psychosomatic survey of cancer of the breast. *Psychosomatic Medicine,* 1952, 14, 453–60.

Bahnson, C.B. Basic epistemological considerations regarding psychosomatic processes and their application to current psychophysiological cancer research. Paper presented at the First International Congress of Higher Nervous Activity, Milan, 1968.

Bahnson, C.B. The psychological aspects of cancer. Paper presented at the American Cancer Society's Thirteenth Science Writer's Seminar, 1971.

Bahnson, C.B. Psychophysiological complementarity in malignancies: Past work and future vistas. Paper presented at the Second Conference on Psychophysiological Aspects of Cancer, New York, May 1968.

Bahnson, C.B. Second Conference on Psychophysiological Aspects of Cancer. *Annals of the New York Academy of Sciences,* 1969, 164, 307–634.

Bahnson, C.B., and Bahnson, M.B. Cancer as an alternative to psychosis: A theoretical model of somatic and psychologic regression. In D.M. Kissen and L.L. LeShan (Eds.), *Psychosomatic aspects of neoplastic disease.* Philadelphia: J.B. Lippincott Company, 1964, 184–202.

Bahnson, C.B., and Bahnson, M.B. Denial and repression of primitive impulses and of disturbing emotions in patients with malignant neoplasms. In D.M. Kissen and L.L. LeShan (Eds.), *Psychosomatic aspects of neoplastic disease.* Philadelphia: J.B. Lippincott Company, 1964, 42–62.

Bahnson, C.B., and Bahnson, M.B. Role of ego defenses: Denial and repression in the etiology of malignant neoplasm. *Annals of the New York Academy of Sciences,* 1966, 125, 827–45.

Bahnson, M.B., and Bahnson, C.B. Ego defenses in cancer patients. *Annals of the New York Academy of Sciences,* 1969, 164, 546–99.

Behavioral factors associated with the etiology of physical disease. Bahnson, C.B. (Ed.), *American Journal of Public Health,* 1974, 64, 1034–55.

Baker, L. and Barcai, A. Psychosomatic aspects of diabetes mellitus. In O.W. Hill (Ed.), *Modern Trends in Psychosomatic Medicine,* Vol. 2. London: Butterworths, 1970.

Baker, L., Minuchin, S., Milman, L., Liebman, R., and Todd, T. Psychosomatic aspects of juvenile diabetes mellitus: A progress report. In *Modern Problems in Pediatrics.* Vol. 12. Basel: Karger, 1975.

Baker, L., Minuchin, S., and Rosman, B. The use of beta-adrenergic blockade in the treatment of psychosomatic aspects of juvenile diabetes mellitus. In A. Snart (Ed.), *Advances in Beta-Adrenergic Blocking Therapy.* Vol. 5. Princeton: Excerpta Medica, 1974.

Bathrop, R.W. Depressed lymphocyte function after bereavement. *Lancet,* April 16, 1977, 834–36.

Beavers, W.H. *Psychotherapy and Growth: A Family Systems Perspective.* New York: Brunner/Mazel, 1977.

Beecher, H.K. The powerful placebo. *JAMA,* 1955, *159,* 1602–1606.

Bennette, G. Psychic and cellular aspects of isolation and identity impairment in cancer: A dialectic of alienation. *Annals of the New York Academy of Sciences,* 1969, *164,* 352–64.

Benson, H. *The Relaxation Response.* New York: William Morrow and Company, 1975.

Benson, H. Your innate asset for combating stress. *Harvard Business Review,* 1974, *52,* 49–60.

Benson, H., and Epstein, M.D. The placebo effect: A neglected asset in the care of patients. *JAMA,* 1975, *12,* 1225–26.

Berenson, D. Alcohol and the family system. In: P.J. Guerin (Ed.), *Family Therapy: Theory and Practice,* New York: Gardner Press, 1976b.

Berenson, D. A family approach to alcoholism. *Psychiatric Opinion,* 1976a, *13,* 33–38.

Berger, H., Honig, P., and Liebman, R. Recurrent abdominal pain: gaining control of the symptom. *American Journal of Disorders of Childhood,* 1977, *131,* 1340–1344.

Bittner, J.J. Differences observed in tumor incidence of albino strain of mice following change in diet. *American Journal of Cancer,* 1935, *25,* 791–96.

Blumberg, E.M. Results of psychological testing of cancer patients. In J.A. Gengerelli, and F.J. Kirkner (Eds.), *Psychological Variables in Human Cancer.* Berkeley and Los Angeles: University of California Press, 1954, 30–61.

Blumberg, E.M.; West, P.M.; and Ellis, F.W. MMPI findings in human cancer. *Basic Reading on the MMPI in Psychology and Medicine.* Minneapolis: Minnesota University Press, 1956, 452–60.

Blumberg, E.M.; West, P.M.; and Ellis, F.W. A possible relationship between psychological factors and human cancer. *Psychosomatic Medicine*, 1954, 16(4), 276–86.

Booth, G. General and organic specific object relationships in cancer. *Annals of the New York Academy of Sciences*, 1969, 164, 568–77.

Boszormenyi-Nagy, I., and Spark, G. *Invisible Loyalties*. New York: Harper and Row, 1973.

Bowen, M. *Family Therapy in Clinical Practice*. New York: Jason Aronson, 1978.

Bowen, M. Intrafamily dynamics in emotional illness. In: A. D'Agostino (Ed.), *Family, Church, and Community*. New York: P.J. Kennedy and Sons, 1965(b).

Bowen, M. Toward the differentiation of self in one's family of origin. In: F. Andres, and J. Lorio (Eds.), *Georgetown Family Symposia*, Vol. 1 (1971–72). Washington, D.C.: Department of Psychiatry, Georgetown University Medical Center, 1974.

Brown, B. *New Mind, New Body*. New York: Harper and Row, 1975.

Brown, F. The relationship between cancer and personality. *Annals of the New York Academy of Sciences*, 1966, 125, 865–73.

Brown, J.H., Varsamis, M.B., Toews, J., and Shane, M. Psychiatry and oncology: A review. *Canadian Psychiatric Association Journal*, 1974, 19(2), 219–22.

Bulkley, L.D. Relation of diet to cancer. *Med. Ed.*, 1914, 86, 699–702.

Burnet, F.M. The concept of immunological surveillance. *Prog. Exp. Tumor Research*, 1979, 13, 1027.

Burrows, J. *A practical essay on cancer*. London, 1783.

Butler, B. The use of hypnosis in the case of cancer patients. *Cancer*, 1954, 7, 1.

Cannon, W.B. *Bodily changes in pain, hunger, fear, and rage* (2nd ed.). New York: Appleton-Century, 1934.

Capra, Fritjof. *The Tao of Physics*. Boulder: Shambhala, 1975.

Carlson, Rick J. *The End of Medicine*. New York: John Wiley and Sons, 1975.

Castaneda, C. *Tales of Power*. New York: Simon and Schuster, 1975.

Chesser, E.S., and Anderson, J.L. Treatment of breast cancer: Doctor/patient communication and psychosocial implication. *Proceedings of the Royal Society of Medicine*, 1975, 68(12), 793–95.

Cobb, B. A social-psychological study of the cancer patient. *Cancer*, 1954, 1–14.

Coppen, A.J., and Metcalf, M. Cancer and extraversion. In: D.M. Kissen, and L.L. LeShan (Eds.), *Psychosomatic aspects of neoplastic disease*, Philadelphia: J.B. Lippincott Company, 1964, 30–34.

Cousins, Norman. *Anatomy of an Illness as Perceived by the Patient: Reflections on Healing and Regeneration.* New York: W.W. Norton and Company, Inc., 1979.

Cousins, N. "The mysterious placebo: How mind helps medicine work." *Saturday Review*, October 1, 1977, 8–12.

Cousins, N. "What I learned from 3,000 doctors." *Saturday Review*, February 18, 1978, 12–16.

Crile, G., Jr. *What Every Woman Should Know about the Breast Cancer Controversy.* New York: Macmillan, 1973.

Cullen, J.W., Fox, B.H., and Isom, R.N. (Eds.). *Cancer: The behavioral dimensions.* New York: Raven Press, 1976.

Cutler, E. *Diet on cancer.* Albany Medical Annals, 1887.

Cutler, M. The nature of the cancer process in relation to a possible psychosomatic influence. In J.A. Gengerelli, and F.J. Kirkner (Eds.), *Psychological variables in human cancer.* Berkeley and Los Angeles: University of California Press, 1954, 1–16.

De Chardin, Teilhard. *The Phenomenon of Man.* New York: Harper and Row, 1959.

Doloman, G.F. Emotions, stress, the central nervous system, and immunity. *Ann. N.Y. Acad. Sci.*, 1969, 164(2), 335–43.

Dorn, H.F. Cancer and the marital status. *Human Biology*, 1943, 15, 73–79.

Dossey, Larry. *Space, Time and Medicine.* Boulder: Shambhala, 1982.

Ellerbroek, W.C. Hypotheses toward a unified field theory of human behavior with clinical application to acne vulgaris. *Perspectives in Biology and Medicine*, Winter 1973, 240–62.

Evans, E. *A Psychological Study of Cancer.* New York: Dodd, Mead and Company, 1926.

Everson, T.C., and Cole, W.H. *Spontaneous Regression of Cancer.* Philadelphia, 1966.

Ewing, J. Animal experimentations and cancer. Defense of Research Pamphlet 4, American Medical Association, Chicago, 1911.

Faraday, Ann. *The Dream Game.* New York: Harper and Row, 1974.

Faraday, Ann. *Dream Power.* New York: Coward, McCann, 1972.

Farquhar, J.W. *The American Way of Life Need Not Be Hazardous to Your Health.* New York: Norton, 1978.

Feder, S.L. Psychological considerations in the care of patients with cancer. *Annals of the New York Academy of Sciences,* 1966, *125,* 1020–27.

Ferguson, Marilyn. *The Brain Revolution: The Frontiers of Mind Research.* New York: Taplinger, 1973.

Fisher, S., and Cleveland, S.E. Relationship of body image to site of cancer. *Psychosomatic Medicine,* 1956, *18*(4), 304–309.

Fox, B.H. Psychosocial epidemiology of cancer. In: J.W. Cullen, B. L. Fox, and R.N. Isom (Eds.), *Cancer: The behavior of dimensions.* New York: Raven Press, 1976.

Fox, B.II., and Howell, M.A. Cancer risk among psychiatric patients. *International Journal of Epidemiology,* 1974, *3,* 207–208.

Frank, J.D. The faith that heals. *The Johns Hopkins Medical Journal.* 1975, *137,* 127–131.

Friedman, M., and Rosenman, R. *Type A Behavior and Your Heart.* New York: Alfred A. Knopf, 1974.

Garfield, Charles. *The Psychosocial Care of the Dying Patient.* New York: McGraw-Hill, 1978.

Garfield, Patricia. *Creative Dreaming.* New York: Simon and Schuster, 1975.

Gendron, D. *Enquiries into Nature, Knowledge, and Cure of Cancers.* London, 1701.

Gengerelli, J.A., and Kirkner, F.J. (Eds.). *Psychological Variables in Human Cancer.* Berkeley and Los Angeles: University of California Press, 1954.

242   THE HEALING FAMILY

Glade, P.R., Zalvidar, N.M., Mayer, L., and Cahill, L.J. The role of cellular immunity in neoplasia. *Pediatric Research*, 1976, *10*, 517–22.

Glasser, R. *The Body Is the Hero*. New York: Random House, 1976.

Goldfarb, O., Driesen, J., and Cole, D. Psychophysiologic aspects of malignancy. *American Journal of Psychiatry*, 1967, *123* (12), 1545–1551.

Green, E., and Green, A. *Beyond Biofeedback*. New York: Delacorte, 1977.

Green. H.N. An immunological concept of cancer: A preliminary report. *British Medical Journal*, 1954, 2, 1374.

Greene, W.A., Jr. Psychological factors and reticuloendothelial disease: I. Preliminary observations on a group of males with lymphomas and leukemia. *Psychosomatic Medicine*, 1954, *16*, 220–30.

Greene, W.A., Jr. The psychosocial setting of the development of leukemia and lymphoma. *Annals of the New York Academy of Sciences*, 1966, *125*, 794–801.

Greene, W.A., Jr., and Miller, G. Psychological factors and reticuloendothelial disease: IV. Observation on a group of children and adolescents with leukemia: An interpretation of disease development in terms of the mother-child unit. *Psychosomatic Medicine*, 1958, *20*, 124–44.

Greene, W.A., Jr.; Young, L., and Swisher, S.M. Psychological factors and reticuloendothelial disease: II. Observations on a group of women with lymphomas and leukemia. *Psychosomatic Medicine*, 1956, *18*, 284–303.

Grinker, R.R. Psychosomatic aspects of the cancer problem. *Annals of the New York Academy of Sciences*, 1966, *125*, 876–82.

Grissom, J.J., Weiner, B.J., and Weiner, E.A. Psychological substrate of cancer. *Psychologie Medicale*, 1976, *8*(6), 879–90.

Grof, Stanislav, Halifax Joan. *The Human Encounter with Death*. New York: E.P. Dutton, 1977.

Grossarth-Maticek, R. Cancer and family structure. *Familiendynamik*, 1976, *21*(4), 294–318.

Gurman, Alan S. and David P. Kniskern, (Eds.). *Handbook of Family Therapy*. New York: Brunner/Mazel, 1981.

Hagnell, O. The premorbid personality of persons who develop cancer in a total population investigated in 1947 and 1957. *Annals of the New York Academy of Sciences*, 1966, *125*, 846–855.

Haley, Jay. *Strategies of Psychotherapy*. New York: Grune and Stratton, 1963.

Haley, Jay. *Uncommon Therapy*. New York: Norton, 1973.

Hall, H.R., Lango, S., and Dixon, R.H. Hypnosis and the immune system: The effects on T- and B-cell function. Presented at the Society for Clinical and Experimental Hypnosis, 33rd annual Workshop and Scientific Meeting, Portland, Oregon, October 1981.

Harrower, M., Thomas, C.B., and Altman, A. Human figure drawings in a prospective study of six disorders: Hypertension, coronary heart disease, malignant tumor, suicide, mental illness, and emotional disturbance. *Journal of Nervous Mental Disorders*, 1975, *161*, 191–99.

Hedge, A.R. Hypnosis in cancer. *British Journal of Hypnotism*, 1960, *12*, 2–5.

Henderson, J.G. Denial and repression as factors in the delay of patients with cancer presenting themselves to the physician. *Annals of the New York Academy of Sciences*, 1966, *125*, 856–64.

Holland, J.C. *Psychological aspects of cancer*. In: J.F. Holland, and E. Frei III (Eds.), Cancer medicine. Philadelphia: Lea and Febiger, 1973.

Holmes, T.H., and Masuda, M. Life change and illness susceptibility. Paper presented as part of Symposium on Separation and Depression: Clinical and Research Aspects, Chicago, December 1970.

Holmes, T.H., and Rahe, R.H. The social readjustment rating scale. *Journal of Psychosomatic Research*, 1967, *11*, 213–18.

Horney, K. *Neurosis and Human Growth*. New York: Norton, 1950.

Jung, C.G. *Memories, Dreams, Reflections*. A. Jaffe (Ed.). New York: Pantheon, 1961.

Kavetsky, R.E., Turkevich, N.M., Akimova, R.H., Khayetsky, I.K., and Matveichuf, Y.D. Induced carcinogenesis under various influences on the hypothalamus. *Annals of the New York Academy of Sciences*, 1969, *164*, 517–19.

Keleman, Stanley. *Living Your Dying*. New York: Random House/Bookworks, 1974.

Keleman, Stanley. *Your Body Speaks its Mind*. New York: Simon and Schuster, 1975.

Kidd, J.G. Does the host react against his own cancer cells? *Cancer Research*, 1961, *21*, 1170.

Kissen, D.M. Lung cancer, inhalation and personality. In: D.M. Kissen, and L. LeShan (Eds.), *Psychosomatic aspects of neoplastic disease.* Philadelphia: J.B. Lippincott, 1963, 3–11.

Kissen, D.M. Personality characteristics in males conducive to lung cancer. *British Journal of Medical Psychology,* 1963, 36, 27.

Kissen, D.M. Psychosocial factors, personality, and lung cancer in men aged 55–64. *British Journal of Medical Psychology,* 1967, 40, 29.

Kissen, D.M. Relationship between lung cancer, cigarette smoking, inhalation and personality and psychological factors in lung cancers. *British Journal of Medical Psychology,* 1964, 37, 203–16.

Kissen, D.M. The significance of personality in lung cancer in men. *Annals of the New York Academy of Sciences,* 1966, 125, 933–45.

Kissen, D.M., Brown, R.I.F., and Kissen, M.A. A further report on personality and psychological factors in lung cancer. *Annals of the New York Academy of Sciences,* 1969, 164, 535–45.

Kissen, D., and Eysenck, H.J. Personality in male lung cancer patients. *Journal of Psychosomatic Research,* 1962, 6, 123–127.

Kissen, D.M., and Rao, L.G.S. "Steroid excretion patterns and personality in lung cancer." *Annals of the New York Academy of Sciences,* 1969, 164, 476–479.

Klpofer, B. "Psychological variables in human cancer." *Journal of Projective Techniques,* 1957, 23, 331–340.

Kowal, S.J. Emotions as a cause of cancer: Eighteenth and nineteenth century contributions. *Psychoanalytic Review,* 1955, 42, 217–27.

Kübler-Ross, Elizabeth. *Death the Final Stage of Growth.* New York: Prentice-Hall, 1975.

Kübler-Ross, Elizabeth. *On Death and Dying.* New York: Macmillan, 1968.

Kushner, Harold S. *When Bad Things Happen to Good People.* New York: Schocken Books, 1981.

LaBarba, R.C. Experimental and environmental factors in cancer. *Psychosomatic Medicine,* 1970, 32, 259.

LaBaw, A.L., Holton, C., Tewell, K., and Eccles, D. The use of self-hypnosis by children with cancer. *The American Journal of Clinical Hypnosis,* 1975, 17(4), 233–38.

LeShan, Lawrence. *How to Meditate.* New York: Bantam Books, 1975.

LeShan, Lawrence. *You Can Fight for Your Life.* New York: M. Evans and Co. 1977.

LeShan, L. *The Medium, the Mystic, and the Physicist.* New York: Viking, 1974.

LeShan, L.L. A basic psychological orientation apparently associated with malignant disease. *The Psychiatric Quarterly,* 1961, 35, 314.

LeShan, L.L. An emotional life history pattern associated with neoplastic disease. *Annals of the New York Academy of Sciences,* 1966, 125, 780–93.

LeShan, L.L. Psychological states as factors in the development of malignant disease: A critical review. *Journal of the National Cancer Institute,* 1959, 22, 1–18.

LeShan, L.L. A psychosomatic hypothesis concerning the etiology of Hodgkin's disease. *Psychologic Report,* 1957, 3, 365–75.

LeShan, L., and Gassman, M. "Some observations on psychotherapy with patients with neoplastic disease." *American Journal of Psychotherapy,* 1958, 12, 723–734.

LeShan, L.L., and Worthington, R.E. Loss of cathexes as a common psychodynamic characteristic of cancer patients: An attempt at statistical validation of a clinical hypothesis. *Psychologic Report,* 1956, 2, 183–93.

LeShan, L.L., and Worthington, R.E. Personality as a factor in the pathogenesis of cancer: A review of the literature. *British Journal of Medical Psychology,* 1956, 29, 49–56.

LeShan, L.L., and Worthington, R.E. Some psychologic correlatives of neoplastic disease: Preliminary report. *Journal of Clinical and Experimental Psychopathology,* 1955, 16, 281–88.

LeShan, L.L., and Worthington, R.E. Some recurrent life history patterns observed in patients with malignant disease. *Journal of Nervous Mental Disorders,* 1956, 124, 460–65.

Levinson, D. *The Seasons of a Man's Life.* New York: Alfred A. Knopf, 1978.

Lewis, J.M., Beavers, W.R., Gossett, J.T., and Phillips, V.A. "The family system and physical illness." In: *No Single thread, psychological health in family systems.* New York: Brunner/Mazel, 1976.

MacGregor, R., Ritchie, A.M., Serrano, A.C., Schuster, F.P., McDanald, E.D., and Goolishian, H.A. *Multiple Impact Therapy with Families.* New York: McGraw-Hill, 1964.

Marcial, V.A. Socioeconomic aspects of the incidence of cancer in Puerto Rico. *Annals of the New York Academy of Sciences*, 1960, *84*, 981.

Margolis, J., and West, D. Spontaneous regression of malignant disease: Report of three cases. *Journal of the American Geriatrics Society*, 1967, *15*, 251–53.

Marmorston, J. Urinary hormone metabolite levels in patients with cancer of the breast, prostate, and lung. *Annals of the New York Academy of Sciences*, 1966, *125*, 959–73.

Marmorston, J., Geller, P.J., and Weiner, J.M. Pretreatment urinary hormone pattern and survival in patients with breast cancer, prostate cancer, or lung cancer. *Annals of the New York Academy of Sciences*, 1969, *164*, 483–93.

Maslow, Abraham. *Toward a Psychology of Being*. New York: Van Nostrand Reinhold, 1968.

Mason, J.W. Psychological stress and endocrine function. In E.J. Sacher (Ed.), *Topics in psychoendocrinology*. New York: Grune and Stratton, 1975.

Mastrovito, R.C. Acute psychiatric problems and the use of psychotropic medications in the treatment of the cancer patient. *Annals of the New York Academy of Sciences*, 1966, *125*, 1006–10.

May, Rollo. *Love and Will*. New York: Dell, 1974.

Meerloo, J. Psychological implications of malignant growth: survey of hypotheses. *British Journal of Medical Psychology*, 1954, *27*, 210–15.

Miller, F.R., and Jones, H.W. The possibility of precipitating the leukemic state by emotional factors. *Blood*, 1948, *8*, 880–84.

Miller, H. Emotions and malignancy. Paper presented at the American Society of Clinical Hypnosis Convention, San Francisco, November 1969.

Miller, S., Remen, N., Barbour, A., Nakles, M.A., and Garell, D. *Dimensions of humanistic medicine*. San Francisco: Institute for the Study of Humanistic Medicine, 1975.

Minuchin, S. *Families and Family Therapy*. Cambridge: Harvard University Press, 1974.

Minuchin, S., Baker, L., Rosman, B., Liebman, R., Milman, L., and Todd, T. A conceptual model of psychosomatic illness in children. *Archives of General Psychiatry*, 1975, *32*, 1031–38.

Minuchin, S., Rosman, B., and Baker, L. *Psychosomatic Families*. Cambridge: Harvard University Press, 1978.

Minuchin, S., Rosman, B.L., and Baker, L. *Psychosomatic Families: Anorexia Nervosa in Context.* Cambridge: Harvard University Press, 1978.

Montagu, Ashley. *Touching: The Human Significance of the Skin.* New York: Columbia University Press, 1971.

Morris, Sarah. *Grief and How to Live with It.* New York: Grosset and Dunlap, 1972.

Moses, R., and Cividali, N. Differential levels of awareness of illness: Their relation to some salient features in cancer patients. *Annals of the New York Academy of Sciences,* 1966, *125,* 984–94.

Muslin, H.L.; Gyarfas, K.; and Pieper, W.J. Separation experience and cancer of the breast. *Annals of the New York Academy of Sciences,* 1966, *125,* 802–06.

Nakagawa, S., and Ikemi, Y. A psychosomatic study of spontaneous regression of cancer. *Medicin Psicosomatica,* 1975, *20*(4), 378.

Napier, A.Y. and Whitaker, C.A. *The Family Crucible.* New York: Harper and Row, 1978.

Nelson, D.H. Spontaneous regression of cancer. *Clinical Radiology,* 1962, *13,* 138.

Nervous factor in the production of cancer. *British Medical Journal,* 1925, *20,* 1139.

Orbach, C.E., Sutherland, A.M., and Bozeman, M.F. Psychological impact of cancer and its treatment. *Cancer,* 1955, *8,* 20.

Paloucek, F.P., and Graham, J.B. The influence of psycho-social factors on the prognosis in cancer of the cervix. *Annals of the New York Academy of Sciences,* 1966, *125,* 814–16.

Parkes, C.M., Benjamin, B., and Fitzgerald, R.G. Broken heart: A statistical study of increased mortality among widowers. *British Medical Journal,* 1969, *1,* 740–43.

Pelletier, Kenneth R. *Mind as Healer, Mind as Slayer.* New York: Delacorte 1977.

Pelletier, K.R. *Toward a Science of Consciousness.* New York: Delacorte Press, 1978.

Pendergrass, E. Host resistance and other intangibles in the treatment of cancer. *American Journal of Roentgenology,* 1961, *85,* 891–96.

Pendergrass, E. Presidential address to the American Cancer Society. Meeting, 1959.

Peper, E., and Pelletier, K.R. Spontaneous remission of cancer: A bibliography. Mimeograph, 1969.

Pincus, Lily. Death and the Family. New York: Pantheon, 1974.

Progoff, Ira. At a Journal Workshop: The Basic Text and Guide for Using the Intensive Journal. Dialogue House, 1975.

Psychophysiological aspects of cancer. In E.M. Weyer (Ed.), Annals of the New York Academy of Sciences, 1966, 125 (3), 773–1055.

Rahe, R.H., Meyer, M., Smith, M., Kjaer, G., and Holmes, T.H. Social Stress and Illness Onset. Journal of Psychosomatic Research, 1964, 8, 35–44.

Rapaport, F.T., and Lawrence, H.S. A possible role for cross-reacting antigens in conditioning immunological surveillance mechanisms in cancer and transplantation: II. Prospective studies of altered cellular immune reactivity in cancer patients. Transplantation Proceedings, June 1975, 7(2), 281–85.

Rasmussen, A.F., Jr. Emotions and Immunity. Annals of the New York Academy of Sciences, 1966, 125, 1028–55.

Remen, N. The masculine principle, the feminine principle, and humanistic medicine. San Francisco: Institute for the Study of Humanistic Medicine, 1975.

Reznikoff, M. Psychological factors in breast cancer: A preliminary study of some personality trends in patients with cancer of the breast. Psychosomatic Medicine, 1955, 18, 2.

Reznikoff, M., and Martin, P.E. The influence of stress on mammary cancer in mice. Journal of Psychosomatic Research, 1957, 2, 56–60.

Riley, V. Mouse mammary tumors: Alteration of incidence as apparent function of stress. Science, 1975, 189, 465–67.

Rollin, Betty. First You Cry. New York: New American Library, 1977.

Sacerdote, P. The uses of hypnosis in cancer patients. Annals of the New York Academy of Sciences, 1966, 125, 1011–19.

Samudzhan, E.M. Effect of functionally weakened cerebral cortex on growth of inoculated tumors in mice. Med Zhurn., An Ukrainian SSSR, 1954, 24(3), 10–14.

Samuels, Mike, Hal Bennett. *The Well Body Book*. New York : Random House/Bookworks, 1973.

Samuels, M., and Samuels, N. *Seeing With the Mind's Eye*. New York: Random House, 1975.

Satir, V. *Conjoint Family Therapy*. Palo Alto: Science and Behavior Books, 1964.

Scheflen, A.E. *Communicational Structure: Analysis of a Psychotherapy Transaction*. Bloomington: Indiana University Press, 1973.

Scheflen, A.E. Malignant tumors in the institutionalized psychotic population. *Arch. Neurol. Psychiat.*, 1951, 64, 145–155.

Schmale, A.H. Giving up as a final common pathway to changes in health. In: Z.J. Lipowski, Ed., *Psychosocial aspects of physical illness*, Vol. 8. Basel: S. Karger, 1972, 20–40.

Schmale, A.H. Hopelessness as a predictor of cervical cancer. *Social Science and Medicine*, 1971, 5, 95–100.

Schmale, A.H., and Iker, H. The psychological setting of uterine cervical cancer. *Annals of the New York Academy of Sciences*, 1966, 125, 807–13.

Schonfield, J. Psychological and life-experience differences between Israeli women with benign and cancerous breast lesions. *Journal of Psychosomatic Research*, 1975, 19, 229–34.

Schonfield, J. Psychological factors related to delayed return to an earlier life-style in successfully treated cancer patients. *Journal of Psychosomatic Research*, 1972, 16, 41–46.

Second conference on psychophysiological aspects of cancer. In M. Krauss (Ed.), *Annals of the New York Academy of Sciences*, 1969, 164 (2), 306–634.

Sehnert, Keith, H., and Eisenberg, Howard. *How to be Your Own Best Doctor— Sometimes*. New York: Grosset and Dunlap, 1976.

Seligman, A.M. *Helplessness*. San Francisco: W.H. Freeman and Company, 1975.

Seligman, M.E.P. *Helplessness: On depression, development, and death*. San Francisco: W.H. Freeman and Company, 1975.

Selye, H. *The Stress of Life*. New York: McGraw-Hill, 1956.

Selye, H. *Stress without Distress*. New York: Dutton, 1974.

Shands, H.C. The informational impact of cancer on the structure of the human personality. *Annals of the New York Academy of Sciences*, 1966, *125*, 883–89.

Shook, Robert L. *Survivors: Living with Cancer.* New York: Harper & Row, 1983.

Simonton, O.C., Matthews-Simonton, S., and Creighton, James. *Getting Well Again.* Los Angeles: J.P. Tarcher, Inc., 1978.

Simonton, O.C., and Simonton, S. Belief systems and management of the emotional aspects of malignancy. *Journal of Transpersonal Psychology*, 1975, *7*(1), 29–47.

Smith, W.R., and Sebastian, H. Emotional history and pathogenesis of cancer. *Journal of Clinical Psychology*, 1976, *32*(4), 863–66.

Solomon, G.F. "Emotions, stress, the central nervous system, and immunity." *Annals of the New York Academy of Science*, 1969, *164*(2), 335–43.

Solomon, G.F., and Amkraut, A.A. Emotions, stress, and immunity. *Frontiers of Radiation Therapy and Oncology*, 1972, *7*, 84–96.

Solomon, G.F.; Amkraut, A.A.; and Kasper, P. Immunity, emotions and stress. *Annals of Clinical Research*, 1974, *6*, 313–22.

Solomon, G.F., and Moos, R.H. Emotions, immunity and disease. *Archives of General Psychiatry*, 1964, *11*, 657.

Stein, M., Schiavi, R.C., and Camerino, M. Influence of brain and behavior on the immune system. *Science*, February 6, 1976, *191*, 435–39.

Steiner, C. *Scripts People Live.* New York: Bantam, 1974.

Stephenson, I.H., and Grace, W. Life stress and cancer of the cervix. *Psychosomatic Medicine*, 1954, *16*, 287.

Stern, K. The reticuloendothelial system and neoplasia. In J.H. Heller (Ed.), *Reticuloendothelial structure and function.* New York: The Ronald Press Company, 1960, 233–58.

Surawicz, F.G., Brightwell, D.R., Weitzel, W.D., and Othmer, E. Cancer, emotions, and mental illness: The present state of understanding. *American Journal of Psychiatry*, 1976, *133*(11), 1306–1309.

Thomas, C.B. What becomes of medical students, the dark side. *Johns Hopkins Medical Journal*, 1976, *138*(5), 185–89.

Thomas, C.B., and Duszynski, D.R. Closeness to parents and the family constellation in a prospective study of five disease states: Suicide, mental illness, malignant tumor, hypertension, and coronary heart disease. *The Johns Hopkins Medical Journal*, 1974, *134*, 251–70.

Ulene, A. *Feeling Fine*. Los Angeles: J.P. Tarcher, Inc., 1977.

Wallace, R.K., Benson, H., and Wilson, A.F. A wakeful hypometabolic physiologic state. *American Journal of Physiology*, September 1971, 795.

Waxenberg, S.E. The importance of the communications of feelings about cancer. *Annals of the New York Academy of Sciences*, 1966, *125*, 1000–05.

Weinstock, C. Psychodynamics of cancer regression. *Journal of the American Academy of Psychoanalysis*, 1977, *5*(2), 285–86.

Weisman, Avery D. *On Dying and Denying*. New York: Human Sciences Press, 1972.

West, P.M. Origin and development of the psychological approach to the cancer problem. In J.A. Gengerelli, and F.J. Kirkner (Eds.), *The psychological variables in human cancer*. Berkeley and Los Angeles: University of California Press, 1954, 17–26.

West, P.M., Blumberg, E.M., and Ellis, F.W. An observed correlation between psychological factors and growth rate of cancer in man. *Cancer Research*, 1952, *12*, 306–07.

Weyer, E.M., and Hutchins, H., (Eds.), *Psychophysiological aspects of cancer*. New York: New York Academy of Sciences, 1966.

Wheeler, J.I., Jr., and Caldwell, B.M. Psychological evaluation of women with cancer of the breast and of the cervix. *Psychosomatic Medicine*, 1955, *17*(4), 256–68.

Wolf, S. Effects of suggestion and conditioning on the action of chemical agents in human subjects: The pharmacology of placebos. *Journal of Clinical Investigation*, 1950, *29*, 100–09.

Index

Autonomy: *(continued)*
    children, 199–203, 209
    choice of death, 227–28
    as side benefit of cancer, 194
Ayoob, Joe, 59, 69

Backache, stress and, 127
Balance of power, family, 115
Bartrop, R. W., 169–70
Beavers, W. R., 117
Belief as factor in cure, 8–9
Benefits, *see* Side benefits of cancer
Benson, Herbert, 129
Big Brothers of America, 184
Big Sisters of America, 184
Biofeedback, 10–12, 15
Biopsies, 23, 24
Blood markers, 15
Bone cancer (osteogenic sarcoma),
    24–25, 43, 73–75, 91
Bone-marrow cancer (multiple
    myeloma), 23
Breast cancer, 48–49
Bresler, David, 217

California, University of:
    at Los Angeles, Medical School
        Pain Clinic, 217
    at San Francisco, study on heart
        disease and pets, 68, 178
Cancer:
    definition of, 5
    See also specific types
Cancer centers, depersonalization of
    patients by, 81–84
Cancer Counseling and Research
    Center, 17, 20, 49, 52, 110,
    126, 128, 130, 221–22
    founding of, 1, 15
Cancer hotlines, 141
Carcinogens, 2
Change, 234–35
    emotional, in patient, 109–16
    family game plan and, 41–44
    family health and, 126
    in family's balance of power, 115
    and stress, 41–42, 127–28
"Cheerleading" attitude, 56, 92–96,
    98, 154, 174, 224, 233–34
    See also Rescuing vs. helping
Chemotherapy, 11, 24, 40, 62, 79
    for children, and peer pressures,
    208–9

conversion factor in side effects of,
    214–15
fears about, 142–43
handling side effects of, 213–14
imagery and, 145, 216
mental pain management with,
    219
Child abuse in life history of
    cancer patients, 17, 19
Children:
    adult leadership in family and, 45,
    119
    diagnosis of cancer in other family
        member and, 34
    and family teamwork, 51–53
    first-born, cancer-proneness of,
    89
    how to share information with,
    96–97
    as patients, 24–25, 28, 35–36,
    40, 58, 198–209, 219
    expression of feelings by,
    94–96
    honesty about diagnosis,
    200–202
    need for autonomy, 199–203,
    209
    overprotectiveness of parents,
    94–96, 101–2
    overreaction by family, 205–6
    peer pressures, 208–9
    relations with doctors,
    200–202, 209
    special outlook of, 203–4
    physical affection and, 184
    siblings of child patients, 206–7
    talent for imagery of, 204
Communication, 84–85
    with doctor, 76–81
    family therapy and, 66
    of feelings, *see* Feelings, expression
        of
    improved, as side benefit of cancer,
    188, 192–96
Community resources, *see* Self-help
    groups
Concentration camps, 107–8
Conflict resolution, family health
    and, 122–23
Conversing with Pain (Bresler), 217
Conversion pain, 214–15
Counseling, 35, 110, 177, 193
    for family members, 49

Relaxation techniques, 38, 50–51,
144
biofeedback, 11
for family members, 42–43, 50–51
family support for, 130–31
in pain management, 217
in stress management, 42, 50,
128–31
Religion:
and acceptance of diagnosis,
29–32
and death, 230
and fear, 145–46
Religious organizations, outside
support from, 63
REM (rapid eye movement) sleep, 139
Rescuing vs. helping, 158–68
in depression, 174
by doctors and hospitals, 162–64
how to avoid, 164–68
reasons for, 159–62
Resentment, 159
at newly assertive patient, 114
as reaction to diagnosis, 26–27,
29–30
Responsibility, individual, and
health of family, 118
Retirement, stress of, 127, 128
Right hemisphere of brain, 11, 217
Rockefeller, Happy, 138
Roosevelt, Franklin D., 144

Sadness-happiness split, 156
St. Luke's Hospital (Chicago),
study on depression and
cancer, 18
Sanford, Carol, 58
Second and third opinions, 22,
36–38, 71–73
Secondary gains, see Side benefits
of cancer
"Secret wish," 103–5
Self-esteem, low, 17–19, 114
Self-help groups, 35, 63–65, 141–42
"Selfishness," desirability of,
18–19, 110, 132
Sexual relations, 14, 184–86
lack of interest in, as symptom of
depression, 172
Shock:
after diagnosis of recurrence,
223, 225–26
initial reaction of, 22–24

Sick-healthy split, 155–56
Side benefits of cancer, 187–97
affection and attention, 187–89
fear of loss of, 196
how to maintain, 194–96
improved family communication,
188, 192–96
quality of life, 189–92
recurrence and, 226
Silversten (researcher), 131
Simonton, O. Carl, 1, 6–15
Simonton approach, 20
development of, 6–15, 17
Single cancer patients, 67–69
physical affection and, 183–84
side benefits of cancer to, 193
Sleep:
depression and, 172
fear and, 128, 139–40
family members' need for, 42
Split ambivalence, 150–57
definition of, 150–51
detection of, 156–57
rescuing behavior and, 160
varieties of, 153–56
Spontaneous remissions, 7, 9–10,
16
Stanford Hospital, patient-staff
relations at, 84
Stress, 2–3, 17, 19, 169
awareness of, as side benefit of
cancer, 194
change and, 41–42, 127–28
denial of feelings and, 89
in doctors treating cancer, 77–78
on family members, game plan
and, 41–44
hormones and, 129–31, 133,
139
management of, 3, 127–35
expression of feelings, 133–34
exercise, 131–32
recreation, 132
relaxation techniques, 42, 50,
128–31
precancer, 8
recognition of, 134–35
Support systems, outside, 179–80
availability of, 57–59
for depressed patients, 177
as extended family, 55–56, 69–70
friends, 56–62
groups and organizations, 63–65

ABOUT THE AUTHOR

Stephanie Matthews Simonton is a psychotherapist who has specialized in counseling cancer patients. She pioneered the development of a model for emotional intervention in the treatment of cancer which considers a patient's emotional health a significant factor in combating the disease. That program, which has become known as the Simonton approach, was approved by the Surgeon General's Office in 1973 and has gained both national and international attention. She designed a professional training program to teach medical and psychological professionals the treatment program.

She founded the Cancer Counseling and Research Center of Dallas, Texas, a non-profit treatment, training, and research facility.

In recent years, she has developed corporate prevention programs, applying the principles used to treat cancer to healthy individuals who wish to improve and maintain their health. She is a frequent lecturer at medical, psychological, and various industry meetings on the subject of the psychological aspect of health.

She currently resides in Little Rock, Arkansas.